CHRISTIAN APPROACHES TO LEARNING THEORY

A Symposium

Edited by Norman De Jong

Major Papers Delivered
at the
First Annual Conference

Trinity Christian College
Palos Heights, Illinois

November 11-12, 1983

UNIVERSITY
PRESS OF
AMERICA

LANHAM • NEW YORK • LONDON

Trinity
Christian
College

ISBN (Perfect): 0-8191-4320-0
ISBN   (Cloth): 0-8191-4319-7

FOREWORD

We who profess the name of Christ in the academy face a continuing challenge arising from our faith. We strive, of course, for mastery in our disciplines, but we also assume an obligation to work out within and among our several academic pursuits an integration of the faith profession with the academic profession. We take it as a necessity that faith and learning are not only compatible, but of a piece.

Although this kind of enterprise is most effectively done in community, Christians in higher education often find themselves isolated in their work, either as one of very few department members in the typically small, Christian liberal arts college or one of very few Christians in a large secular university. This isolation, together with the great sense of need to be about the task of approaching our investigation with the mind of Christ, provided the impetus for Trinity Christian College to undertake a series of conferences. The first of them has produced this volume.

We took up learning theory as a topic because it seemed as needful as any for such a discussion. Many Christians are working in this area, and secular theories, at least, abound. Is there a Christian theory of learning? Could there be one, or many? We asked other Christians from throughout North America to tackle some questions which we had posed and then invited them to share through this conference some of their own propositions and questions. Their interchange at Trinity was invigorating, enlightening, and fruitful. We now share the products with a larger audience, in the hope that even more of these isolated Christian scholars can be brought into this significant undertaking.

Although acknowledgments are made elsewhere, I would like to place here a personal note of appreciation to Dr. Norman De Jong, Professor of Education at Trinity, for his attention to all sorts of details in addition to providing the guiding light without which neither the conference nor this publication would have materialized. As editor of this volume, he trimmed and shaped the major conference papers to their present form in the hope that they might serve college communities as fresh insights into Christian approaches to learning theory.

Burton J. Rozema
Vice President for Academic Affairs

iii

Acknowledgements

No publication or conference can be successful without the efforts of many persons. People of vision and courage, organizers, administrators, typists, envelope stuffers, critics, and respondents are all essential. So it was with the First Annual Conference on Christian Approaches to Learning Theory held on the Trinity Campus on Nov. 11 and 12, 1983. To recognize appropriately every individual who contributed to that success and to the process of publication which resulted from that conference would be difficult and almost impossible. Some effort at acknowledging the work of key persons, however, is necessary and appropriate.

Of the highest significance are the twelve persons who contributed major papers to the conference and whose names are linked to the twelve chapters in this publication. All of them prepared their manuscripts a full two months prior to the meetings and willingly subjected them to the critical eyes of selected responders. Once the conference was finished and their bruised egos restored, each presenter took his or her paper back to the drawing board and reworked it for publication. In many instances whole sections were deleted and others were modified almost beyond recognition. To each of them, for all their efforts, a hearty thanks.

Also contributing immeasurably to the entire process were those persons who served as designated responders or referees. Chief among them were Nicholas Wolterstorff of Calvin College and Jack Fennema of Trinity Christian College. Painstakingly reading through every paper and listening to at least half of the presentations, they skillfully and fruitfully served to critique the conference as a whole and to point the direction for future efforts.

Responders to individual papers were also important, giving each presenter a sounding board against which to bounce his initial theoretical formulations. Serving ably in that capacity were Eleanor Syler (Evangel College), Donovan Graham (Covenant College), Robert Mulder (Wittenberg University), Henry Beversluis (Calvin College, emeritus), Elizabeth Rudenga (Trinity Christian), Clifford Schimmels (Wheaton), Mike De Vries (Trinity Christian), John Roose (Trinity Christian), Dick Cole (Trinity Christian), Kaye Cook (Gordon College), and

v

Harry Van Belle (Redeemer Reformed College). Although
space would not permit the printing of their critiques
in this publication, their work was much appreciated
and most helpful in refereeing the editing of these
papers.
Enlivening the conference in an unusual format
were Larry Reynolds (Dordt College), Wally Cox (C. B.
N. University), and Michael Boivin (Spring Arbor
College), who independently responded to three
propositions, each answering from his own religious-
philosophical perspective and thereby engendering a
lively interchange of ideas. To each of them a
bouquet.
Amongst the host institution's faculty and staff
are a number of others who deserve recognition.
Assisting the editor as a planning committee were
Burton Rozema, Jack Fennema, Edward Vander Weele,
Maarten Vrieze, and Henk Sliekers. Each devoted hours
of their time to plan, organize, and run the
conference, attending to a myriad of details before,
during, and after the sessions.
Never getting enough credit for all of their work
were the editor's very able office assistants. To Ann
Boerema, faithful secretary, and to Alisa Mennenga and
Linda Van Kampen, student helpers, goes a special word
of appreciation for their performance on tasks that
were sometimes tedious, boring, tiring, and yet always
important. Thanks, and Godspeed, as you tackle the
next assignments which lurk just ahead.
Finally, to all those who attended, the First
Annual Conference owes much of its success to you.
Your positive Christian attitudes, your willingness to
listen and to dialogue, and your enthusiastic response
did much to convince all of us that the work on which
we had so tenuously embarked could go forward with
faith and confidence. Reinforced in our communal
undertaking to develop and articulate a Christian
perspective on learning theory, you have given to all
of us the assurance that such must and can be
accomplished.

The Editor

CHRISTIAN APPROACHES
TO
LEARNING THEORY:
A Symposium

Table of Contents

Page

Foreword.............Burton Rozema..............iii
Acknowledgements......................................v
Introduction...........Norman De Jong..............ix

PART I PERSPECTIVES ON LEARNING
Chap. 1   A Christian Approach to Learning Theory....3
          Ruth M. Armstrong
Chap. 2   Creation, Redemption, and Doing Your
          Best: Gaebelein's Approach to Learning...13
          Robert J. Eells
Chap. 3   Toward a Theory of Learning Deviance......31
          Corrine E. Kass
Chap. 4   Biblical Knowing and Classroom Method-
          ology......................................47
          Donald Oppewal
Chap. 5   Kinds and Contexts of Knowing.............69
          Maarten Vrieze
Chap. 6   Living and Learning: A Matter of
          Perspective...............................83
          John H. Kok
Chap. 7   Learning vs. Revelation: A Paradigm
          Clash.....................................95
          James E. Martin

PART II PRESCRIPTIONS FOR THEORY BUILDING
Chap. 8   Toward a Responsibility Theory: Becoming
          Who We Are...............................119
          Peter P. De Boer
Chap. 9   Cybernetic Learning: A Christian Inter-
          pretation................................137
          Gerald D. Bouma
Chap. 10 Motivation for Learning Faith-Knowledge..153
          Marion Snapper
Chap. 11 Learning as Incarnation: A Contextualist
          Approach to Learning About Learning......171
          Bert Hodges
Chap. 12 Past, Present, and Future Directions in
          Learning Research........................195
          Paul Moes

CONCLUSION
The Challenges That Confront Us...................211
          Norman De Jong

Introduction

A pluralistic and heterogeneous culture such as that which characterizes democratic societies in the late twentieth century poses significant questions for the serious scholar. Is there one uniform philosophy of education which should suffice for all students? Is there one approach to learning theory which can truthfully guide all those responsible for teaching youth, whether at the elementary, secondary, college, or university levels? Is the pursuit of knowledge and insight a neutral endeavor, in which secular, agnostic, existentialist, Marxist, Catholic, and Protestant can all join hands? Can Darwinian evolutionists and committed Christians, in spite of all their antithetical assumptions and presuppositions, be jointly enlightened as to the true nature of learning through their mutual usage of textbooks which adhere wholly and exclusively to the presuppositions of the evolutionists?

Such questions nag at the soul of the Christian. Rejecting the whole pretense of neutrality as ill-disguised myth, the Christian scholar has been forced to reassert cultural-philosophical pluralism and heterogeneity, all the while clamoring for a public hearing in the conflict of theories and the competition for allegiance.

Long disturbed by the absence of textbooks espousing a Christian, Biblical perspective in the field of educational psychology, approximately 150 Christian educators representing various disciplines gathered at Trinity Christian College in an effort to develop Biblical perspectives on learning theory. Specifically they came to address such questions as:

1. Is it Biblically and/or philosophically defensible to claim that God only informs our "religious life" while claiming intellectual growth and educational progress for ourselves?

2. Is all knowledge a seamless whole and organically unified, or are there creationally established categories of information, i.e., separate and distinct disciplines?

3. Is there a Biblically defensible rationale for the recent gulf between epistemology and educational psychology, or should philosophers, learning theorists, and

educators be working collectively for a common purpose?

4. Is God the Holy Spirit intimately involved in a child's learning to read, or is His work limited to categories of Grace?

5. Are learning to spell "cat," to sing a song, to obey one's teacher, to trust God's promises, to discern between truth and false-hood, and to marvel at the majesty of the universe all essentially the same, or is each learning uniquely and qualitatively different?

6. If "faith," "belief," and "knowledge" are distinct and separate, as we are traditionally led to believe, how would we define each and justify their separateness? If they are not separate and distinct, what are the implications for the classroom?

7. Is there one generic form of learning, or are there varieties of learning style, affected by mental ability, ethnic or racial origin, and cultural patterns? Do blacks and whites, brilliant and retarded, Oriental and Occidental, all learn in the same way?

8. Should one theory suffice, or must there be multiple theories?

9. What are the benefits, if any, of Christian students searching and studying the scientific empiricists' theories for a true explanation of learning, if it is known in advance that the assumptions and presuppos-itions are in diametrical opposition?

10. Is focus on learning theory of significant consequence to warrant the efforts necessary to articulate a Christian alternative?

The answer to the last question above became obvious when more than 150 scholars from colleges and universities encamped at Trinity for 16 hours of formal, intense dialogue on the above issues. Almost all bore their own expenses of transportation, meals, registration, and accomodations, thus signifying their level of commitment to the project at hand.

The conference was an unqualified success, even though all would agree that the work had only begun. Questions sometimes went unanswered, and issues were left unresolved, not because avoidance was practiced, but because new ways of thinking were suggested and routes were opened where none of us had ever been.

It soon became apparent, when the conference papers were assembled, that each of the above questions would not be definitively answered through the efforts of a single conference. What did become evident, however, was that a variety of Christian scholars, representing various intellectual and religious traditions, could come together and collectively shed light on a topic that was bigger and richer than any of us had imagined. Unafraid to admit that all of us had much to learn about that marvelous, multi-dimensioned phenomenon called learning, each shared, questioned, and compromised in order that new insights and understanding might be gained.

This publication is a culmination of that conference. It is not the last word on learning theory. Rather, it is an edited version of the best insights currently available to Christian scholars who seek a public hearing for Christian approaches to something which is at the heart of the whole educational process. Although readily admitting that a formally articulated learning theory is not prerequisite to effective teaching, each would assert that truly Christian instruction will more likely occur if the learning process is correctly and truly understood. What we offer, then, is a primer, a direction-finder, that will suggest to both scholars and college students some of the essential ingredients that will make both teaching and learning a more harmonious and God-glorifying enterprise. Each of the authors in this text makes a unique contribution to that process. In some chapters there is overlap and even redundancy, while in others there is new, divergent insight and occasional clash of opinion. Collectively, they open new vistas and new panoramas which suggest new ways to teach and to learn.

Chapter 1 opens with a clear, unambiguous discussion of the interrelation between knowledge and faith. In it Ruth Armstrong outlines in general terms the differences between a Christian approach and that of the empirical, evolutionary psychologists who have dominated the discussion for the last century. Continuing that very clear, practical, and

distinctively Christian emphasis, Robert Eells
demonstrates the difference that Christianity makes in
the life and work of a well-known, evangelical
educator. Focusing on the life and thought of Frank
Gaebelein, he explains in the language of the layman,
not only how we learn, but what we ought to learn.
For the college student in particular this popularly
written and very practical chapter will prove a
refreshing change of diet from the heavily abstract and
highly theoretical pieces which of necessity follow.
    In Chapter 3 Corrine Kass raises the whole
question of learning deviance, which ought to be of
particular interest to those in special education. Do
children with learning disabilities or unique handicaps
learn in essentially the same ways as do "normal"
children, or must separate theories be formulated for
each? Relying on her wealth of experience, this
nationally known authority offers a highly readable and
practical explanation of both stages of development and
learning deviance.
    Donald Oppewal argues persuasively that learning
theorists must assert a wholistic view of man, who
functions in all learning experiences, not just
intellectually, but socially, emotionally, physically,
and spiritually. Seeking to extend the Biblical
anthropology, he searches the Scriptures for a truly
Biblical epistemology and sensitively probes the
relationship between God and man as a dynamic
interaction, suggesting the significance of divine
revelation as the ultimate model or paradigm of human
knowing. The student will find this to be a very
helpful bridge to cover the gap between revelation and
learning.
    Where Oppewal sought to narrow the perspective,
Maarten Vrieze seeks to expand and enlarge it. While
exploring the multi-faceted nature of knowing and the
multiple meanings of the word, Vrieze focuses most
poignantly on the "antithesis." Asserting that the
competition of ideas is particularly relevant to the
schools, he describes the conflict for control of the
minds of youth as a necessary dimension of any learning
theory. What Oppewal expressed as the need for
"choosing" and "commitment" as phases in the learning
process, Vrieze describes in more general terms as the
idealogical battle for men's minds.
    In Chapter 6, John Kok grapples with the questions
posed to the conference and attempts to put learning
into perspective as one significant dimension of
living. Continuing the wholistic emphasis set earlier
by Armstrong, Eells, and Oppewal, his contribution is

in paraphrasing and clarifying the questions that still must be answered.

Chapter 7 cannot be digested adequately in one reading, unless one has a mind and vocabulary as brilliant and conceptually far reaching as that of James Martin. Abreast of the most recent literature, he concerns himself with demonstrating the inadequacy of the computer simulated human intelligence model or paradigm. What the typical theorist calls "learning" Martin labels as the "development of competent judgment," implying by his very choice of terms that the essence of learning involves choice-making, putting him into the same theoretical framework as Oppewal, Vrieze, and Kok. But Martin does not stop there. Analyzing and arguing for what he calls "value realization," he introduces the significant and essential matter of axiology into the discussion of epistemology.

Martin also suggests that the process of learning may ultimately be a mystery to the finite human mind, beyond our comprehension in this sin-darkened world. If that is true, as I think it is, then we must be patient enough to await the day (in eternity) of our full illumination, but also be very wary of the partial and God-denying "answers" of the secularists, who seem forever bent on knowing the unknowable. What we need, says Martin, is "a long overdue...epistemology and associated psychology which makes room for persons... for self-revelation and love." What we have been getting from the secular psychologists is "a series of increasingly barbaric...theses that man is a piece of meat."

Martin's argument is both brilliant and highly abstract. Because it is both at once, it bears reading and re-reading.

The chapters which make up Part II are much more prescriptive than are those in Part I, where the emphasis was primarily on developing an overall perspective. Peter De Boer opens this section with what he labels as a "Responsibility Theory." Rather than putting the focus on the assimilation of knowledge, or the development of competent judgment, he places the spotlight of attention on human response to divine revelation and God's sovereignty. True to his action-oriented theory, he focuses attention on such practical concerns as curriculum organization and classroom methodology. Learning theory, he insists, is not an impractical abstraction, but a necessary basis for responsible teaching.

What James Martin insists is "incomprehensible in
traditional scientific terms" Gerald Bouma attempts in
Chapter 9. Relying primarily on a model of man
analagous to an advanced computer system, Bouma seeks
to explain how the unique mind of man may possibly
function. By relying on the computer model, he runs
the risk of either baptizing a machine or ascribing to
technological hardware spiritual and humane qualities.
In light of all the perspectives outlined in Part I,
the reader will have to judge which, if any, of these
prescriptive approaches contains the greatest promise
for a meaningful, effective theory of learning.
     Writing out of a context of church education,
Marion Snapper develops and explains in Chapter 10 the
theory of "cognitive dissonance," originally
articulated by Leon Festinger. Showing this to be the
obverse side of "shalom" or peace, he posits that the
human's most powerful drive or motivation is in seeking
a return to the wholeness and peace which was lost in
Adam and Eve's fall into sin. There is much in
Snapper's thesis to commend it to us. Not only have
all of us experienced the conflict, dissonance, and
peace that he describes, but the theory comports well
with the perspectives articulated earlier by Oppewal,
Martin, and De Boer. Intrinisic to all learning is the
element of judgment or discernment amongst competing
beliefs or ideas, a dimension which Snapper elucidates
in language that the classroom teacher understands.
What he suggests is that at the heart of every
significant learning experience is decision-making and
potential conflict. What makes this theory
particularly appealing is the central place he gives to
the antithesis, that on-going battle between God and
Satan for the allegiance of men (and children).
     Bert Hodges in "Learning as Incarnation: A
Contextualist Approach" argues clearly and effectively
that learning cannot be understood by itself, in
isolation, but must always be understood in the context
of who the learner is, what is to be learned, how
learning is to be accomplished, and the means by
which learning can be measured. Borrowing an analogy
from the discipline of ecology, he argues that learning
can only be understood correctly if viewed as part of
an ecosystem. In developing this ecological or
contextualist approach, Hodges also substantiates a
point made earlier by Oppewal, Martin, and Snapper;
namely, that all learning always involves decision-
making, or discrimination. As Hodges develops his
thesis of learning as incarnation, he opens for us new
possibilities, new ways of thinking about ourselves in

the world.

Paul Moes in Chapter 12 not only assumes the wholeness or organic unity of man, which Oppewal and others had asserted, but adds the significant declaration that God is actively and intimately involved in the learning process. Building from a base of Biblical assumptions and presuppositions, Moes goes on to analyze and critique 20th century empirical psychology, demonstrating with varieties of evidence that the secular theories should no longer have credence with educators. By weaving his way quickly through a maze of both connectionist and cognitive theories, he concludes that Christians should arrive "at a totally different view of learning." Regrettably, he leaves the reader wondering what that "totally different view" of learning is. He points us in a direction, and suggests that it is "out there" somewhere among the Biblical givens, but leaves it for others to develop the theory.

The conclusion reached by Moes is reflective of that reached by Nicholas Wolterstorff in the closing session of the conference. Their conclusion, however, cannot negate the strong bonds of agreement and common perspective which bound the conference participants together and which holds high promise for future efforts. As educators and students identify those essential elements on which agreement has already been reached, the outlines of a Christian approach to learning will be readily apparent and immediately serviceable to all who read.

PART I

PERSPECTIVES

ON

LEARNING

Chapter 1

A Christian Approach to Learning Theory

by
Ruth M. Armstrong
Associate Professor of Psychology
North Park College

A Christian approach to a theory of human learning
differs from a secular one on both the two main issues:
the nature of the learner and the learning process.
The difference can be explained by just one statement;
according to the Christian, these are both God-given.
The interrelation between knowledge and faith
seems natural and reasonable. Both faith and learning
are based upon the ability to lay hold upon, to
apprehend and internalize an idea, truth, or value.
Both assume a belief or system of beliefs. Both
demonstrate confidence in certain principles. Both
affect the way a person acts. Therefore, it not only
is indefensible to claim that God informs only our
religious life as separate from cognitive growth; it is
impossible, for they are two dimensions of the same
practice. A Christian learning theory assumes that God
is the author not only of our faith but also of our
intellect. "The fear of the Lord is the beginning of
Wisdom, and knowledge of the Holy One is understanding"
(Prov. 9:10).
    It follows then that a Christian approach to
learning must operate on a premise of faith.
Confidence that the world can be made comprehensible
comes from basic trust. Even apart from a religious
context, psychoanalyst Erik Erikson (1963) saw the
importance of this and built his entire structure of
healthy psychosocial development upon that foundation.
Once trust is established, it is exciting and
intriguing, but no longer threatening, to initiate, to
do, to be, and to seek answers to the mystery of good
and evil and why existence rather than non-existence.
    The goal of Christian learning theory, then, is
the productive application of faith-power to learning.
Knowledge is illuminated by faith. It permits the
confident exploration of ideas. Faith engenders energy
(Matt. 17:2); it changes aspiration into actuality and
transforms the possible into the real (Allport, 1950).
When we are defined as children of God, and affirmed as

His highest creation and heirs to His kingdom (Rom. 8:16,17), we have a perspective that is both unique and magnificently challenging. Learning without this divine assurance becomes merely a set of competitive intellectual exercises culminating in a vacuum or in the pervasive nihilistic question: What's it all about? By contrast, a Christian theory of learning is purposive; it assumes that life has direction. The mind is not simply a warehouse of ideas, but is rather the mainspring of an individual's striving and achieving. "A man will continue to research," wrote Teilhard de Chardin (1959), "only so long as he is prompted by some passionate interest, and this interest will be dependent on the conviction, strictly undemonstrable to science, that the universe has a direction." Learning lacks meaning until organized into some overall design.

Against this backdrop, what is the doctrinal purpose of learning? As Kieran Egan has stated in his insightful book, Educational Development (1979), it is to demonstrate a Christlike sympathy and sensitivity, that the learner might have life and have it more abundantly. That is a statement at once too simple and too profound, but it must serve as the Christian educator's guiding ethic.

Faith and information which have spiritual relevance enable the learner to make sense of his or her world and experience. This is an intention which perceives a religious center to one's knowing. It determines the validity of purpose, so that the end becomes bound with the act. In the words of Morris Bigge (1982, p.4), "Any sharp distinction between theoretical, imaginative knowledge and the action that stems from such knowlege is faulty. Action...is either linked with theory or it is blind and purposeless. Consequently, any purposeful action is governed by theory." It is the combination of purpose and striving that we call faith.

The thesis of this paper, therefore, is that faith, trust, belief, knowledge and learning are all parts of the same process, and that the Holy Spirit not only infuses but also fuses all these into one integrated effort. The end result is commitment to truth as revealed according to God's will and instrumentation.

With this in mind, we make bold to say that each learner is endowed so as to be potentially God's chosen instrument, for we are assured in the Holy Scriptures that--as author of our being--God has created us in His own image (Gen. 1:26,27; Ps.8:5), and moreover that God

4.

s spirit (John 4:24). This precludes for Christians the acceptance of the machine model of man, or of learning as a faculty operating only on some predictable, controllable level of physiology. Learning has been researched extensively by experimental psychologists, but such knowledge as derived depends largely upon powers of anthropomorphic indwelling, a generalization from the experimenters' own experiences. As pointed out by philosopher Michael Polanyi (1958), the lower level of life is unspecifiable in terms of the higher because man has a whole universe of "mental passions" in contrast to the physical passions which he shares with the animals. Mental passions are a desire for truth, works of art, and noble acts which enrich the mind of all humanity, and it is this desire that determines the spiritual dimension of the human mind.

This is not to negate the laboratory demonstrations of the "laws of learning," but to contend that the human mind is not restricted to them. In their conscientious effort to be objectively scientific, experimental psychologists have reduced the image of man (and woman too, for that matter) to molecules and mechanisms, or to what Perry London (1958) has wryly referred to as an "elegant pile of junk." It must be remembered that no matter how objective or scientific, the principles of learning emanate from the human mind. In other words, we come to know more about the mind itself than about the rat's behavior. In our study of learning, we commit ourselves to knowledge of intellectual choices and interpretations. And as soon as we do that, we admit to possibilities and to moral meaning as opposed to the dictum of simple determinism.

Nor is the human mind restricted to Freud's primacy of the irrational; for while we do not discount the reality of the unconscious, we rest in the belief that God oversees the unconscious as well as the conscious and may even speak through it (e.g., Dan. 1:17). Indeed, Jung believed unconscious forces to be necessary for intellectual wholeness, and that if repressed from conscious thought, they will seek expression in the form of dreams and symbols, or in extreme cases as delusions and hallucinations. There needs to be a proper balance of conscious and unconscious factors affecting our intellectual understanding. With this outlook, psychoanalysts today have expanded their studies to include such ego processes as perception, attention, memory, and thinking (Kagan and Havemann, 1980).

5.

The role of epistemology is to investigate the origin and nature of knowledge, while the business of education is to provide and disseminate that knowledge. The two go hand-in-hand. If the divine is to be accepted as an active element in human understanding, the issue ultimately concerns how learning, as an attribute given and approved by God, can best function to influence behavior.

This leads to a central characteristic of Christian learning, which is that it necessarily acknowledges and incorporates values. The presence or absence of pure ideals and moral implications (whether recognized or not) affects learning and establishes educational guidelines. For example, it is the contention of educator Jerome Bruner (1966) that the aims of education are essentially to assist the development of human beings to use their potential to achieve good, to make an effective contribution to society, and that when we lose sight of that objective, the pursuit of learning becomes sterile. Since Educational Psychology is an important branch of this endeavor, it follows that it can function productively only to the degree that it facilitates these positive aims under the rubric of applied learning theory.

To this end Christian learning theory should clearly align itself with ethical standards. As we have noted, an important distinction of a Christian approach is a view of the learner as a special creation of God. Without this, the study of learning becomes an end in itself, and the value of the learner is diminished. This is the way to depersonalization; procedure takes precedence over persons.

The outcome of acknowledging a divine source is determined by how religious affirmation influences thought. Thought cannot be disengaged from experience, nor experience from its results. Whatever is perceived as truth will guide a person's behavior and is consequently of critical importance. To cite Egan (1979) again, values, ideologies, and metaphysical beliefs constitute the central focus of learning, and these therefore are theological as well as educational issues.

Support for such a proposition is not hard to find. As this nation has increasingly lost its moral compass, the quality of learning has progressively declined. The byword today is to be open to all manner of programs and projects. As a result, we are in danger of losing thereby the ability to discriminate excellence from that which is merely novel or momentarily diverting, or forfeiting the ability to

"discern righteousness and justice" (Prov. 2:9).
The qualities of good character, personal
accountability and respect for the legitimate rights of
others are still the task of basic education, which
cannot be separated from its religious roots.
A corresponding characteristic of Christian
learning theory is its emphasis on affect as well as
cognition. Concepts that have an emotional component
form attitudes and transform lives. A person learns to
reject wrong-doing not simply as a conditioned response
but because he or she hates it (Ps. 97:10, Prov. 8:13).
Likewise, a person chooses good because he or she
delights in it (Ps. 1:2; Gal. 5:22, 23). That is to
say, wrong-doing may be positively reinforcing and
still be rejected; the effects of doing good may well
be aversive, yet still be chosen. Any theory of
learning which does not emphasize affective as well as
cognitive factors fails to inculcate these dispositions
or belief systems which Allport (1950) categorized as
"sentiment," which in turn prepares a person for
adaptive behavior. Learning deprived of this unit of
mental life is empty of real substance because it lacks
opinion, excitement, or zeal. We do not merely obtain
new information; we evaluate it. We do not simply
acquire new responses; we test them. As Albert Bandura
observed in his APA presidential address (1974), human
learning is "actively judgmental."
That is also why the computer analogy is
inadequate. Knowledge is not simply storage and
retrieval of sensory input. It is selecting and
understanding and feeling and applying. Interpretation
naturally varies with experience and cultural milieu,
but regardless of ethnic and racial origin, or (normal)
levels of intelligence, the human mind seeks to derive
meaning. An individual's perceptions are subjective;
they depend upon the beliefs (or lack of beliefs) which
underlie his/her unifying philosophy of life. (See L.
Postman, B. Bruner, and E. McGinnis' classic study,
1948). Thus, knowledge can be seen to accrue through
the same transcendent processes as those required for
faith. Unlike the computer, the human mind does not
primarily encode facts, it seeks rather to know why,
and that is a quality that lends it a theological
dimension.
In accepting such a dimension, a Christian
learning theory postulates that the desire to learn or
the need to know is innate (i.e., that the motive to
learn is God-given). As Kagan and Havemann acknowledge
in their book Psychology, an Introduction (1980, p.
326), "There are obviously some forces within the human

personality that initiate, energize, direct, and organize behavior." (It is noteworthy that many psychologists appear to accept such "forces" as given, but without venturing to say by whom!) Learning traits such as curiosity, the will to competence, the urge to solve problems, to seek certainty and to live up to standards can reasonably be regarded in Christian learning theory as inborn.

According to theologian Wolfhart Pannenberg (1982), there is a longstanding use of the term spirit in relation to intellect, which may be called a field of spiritual awareness. The Biblical concept is of the divine spirit as origin of mind. Only this, claims Pannenberg, can explain how the human mind can grasp reality and the nature of things, being active in every moment of experience, starting with sense perception. It represents the power of spiritual dynamics in the natural processes.

Do we have psychological data which lend credence to these observations concerning innate natural processes and active experience of the mind? Actually, any inherent hierarchical or stage theory is based upon such assumptions. Humanistic psychologists have long supported the case for intrinsic motivation, although they, too, stop short of crediting any source. In Maslow's hierarchy of needs, for example, the need to know and understand represents a goal of self-actualization toward which all human beings bytheirverynature (emphasis mine) are motivated. Christian learning theory would go a step beyond self-actualization to self-transcendence as the ultimate goal, that humans by their very nature are motivated to seek Wisdom beyond their own.

Consider also the cognitive psychologist Jean Piaget (1952) who assumed an established developmental progression of natural processes in which the human mind is actively aware and relating from the very beginning. Experience can virtually be explained as pre-ordained actions of the subject. Similarly, consider psycholinguist Naom Chomsky (1968) who postulates an innate language acquisition device, ready to function under normal conditions of stimulation at the appointed time. Or Kohlberg's sequence of moral development in which persons differ in rate but not in levels of progress from premoral to postconventional stages of understanding. According to such theorists, all these seem innately programmed (or, to the Christian, divinely ordered).

Moreover, inborn learning ability has been seen in the mind's immediate preference, (even in fancy) for

8.

organization, configuration, and wholeness, demonstrating an awareness of elements essential to a
particular Gestalt (Fantz, 1961; Haaf and Bell, 1967).
Indeed, it has been suggested that there is a
particular Gestalt which leads to perception of
transcendence beyond life and death. The spirit is
related to form and wholeness. In the words of
Pannenberg, quoted by Elvee (1982, p. 148), "The human
mind longs for full participation in the spirit that
would satisfy his hunger for wholeness and disclose to
him the nature of every creature. But the unambiguous
satisfaction of such yearning is given to the mind, not
in the form of definitive and exclusive possession that
the mind would inevitably surpass again, but only in
the ecstasy of faith, and its hope, and in the creative
love born from such faith." This aptly summarizes the
Christian position on learning.

In his classic work, The Individual and
His Religion, Gordan Allport (1950) speaks for
many in observing that ultimately religion is a search
for complete knowledge, for "unfissioned truth." This
is also the function of learning. The degree to which
theory supports this search is the degree to which it
demonstrates its usefulness in clarifying the necessary
integration of faith and learning.

9.

References

Gordan Allport, The Individual and His Religion, New York: MacMillan Co., 1950.

A. Bandura, Behavior Theory and the Models of Man, presidential address of the APA, New Orleans, August, 1974, as quoted from J. Kagan and E. Havemann, Psychology: an Introduction (4th ed.), Chicago: Harcourt, Brace, Jovanovich, Inc., 1980, p. 123.

Morris Bigge, Learning Theories for Teachers, New York: Harper and Row, 1982.

N. Chomsky, Language and Mind, New York: Harcourt, Brace, Jovanovich, 1968.

Richard Elvee (ed.), Mind in Nature (Nobel Conference XVII), San Fransisco: Harper and Row, 1982.

Erik Erikson, Childhood and Society, New York: Norton, 1963.

R. L. Fantz, "The Origin of Form Perception," Scientific American, May, 1961.

F. A. Haaf and R. Q. Bell, "A Facial Dimension in Visual Discrimination by Human Infants," Child Development, 1967.

J. Kagan and E. Havemann, Psychology: an Introduction, Chicago: Harcourt, Brace, Jovanovich, 1980.

Perry London, Behavior Control, New York: Harper and Row, 1971.

Jean Piaget, The Origins of Intelligence in Children, New York: International Universities Press, 1952.

Michael Polanyi, The Study of Man, Chicago: The University of Chicago Press, 1958.

L. Postman, B. Bruner, and E. McGinnis, "Personal Values as Selective Factors In Perception," Journal of Abnormal Psychology, 43, 1948, pp. 142-154.

Pierre Teilhard de Chardin, The Phenomenon of Man, New York: Harper and Row, 1959.

Chapter 2

Creation, Redemption, and Doing Your Best:
Gaebelein's Approach to Learning

by
Robert J. Eells
Associate Professor of History
Trinity Christian College

Many educators consider Frank R. Gaebelein the
leading example of an evangelical educational
reformer.[1] And rightly so, for few individuals have
had so great an impact on Christian education as the
late Dr. Gaebelein. Note especially two examples of
his hegemony: First, his authorship of such seminal
works on Christian education as Christian Education in
a Democracy (1951)[2] and The Pattern of God's Truth
(1954).[3] Second, his vanguard leadership of the
Stony Brook School--a Christian preparatory school on
Long Island which he helped found and where he served
as headmaster for over forty years. Dr. Gaebelein's
recent death (January 19, 1983) enables us to pause and
begin to evaluate some of his impressive contributions
to Christian education.

Unfortunately, little has been written about his
educational philosophy perse, perhaps due in part to
his stance as an "unashamed generalist" (to use his own
words). Generalists are, admittedly, sometimes
difficult to pin down; in Gaebelein's case, scrut-
inizing his philosophy is well worth the effort.

We need first to focus on Dr. Gaebelein's
understanding of the overall learning process in
children. How and what do children learn in the
context of Christian education? The answer-
-constructed from his numerous published works--is
multifaceted.

1. By Being "Children"...

Children are, first of all, children of God,
according to Gaebelein, and thus in a very real sense
they have been programmed to learn by their creator.
They have a built-in longing to know who they are, to
solve the mystery of personal identity. Further, they
are eager to learn, impatiently seeking a challenging
reality.

For Gaebelein, it is also important to recognize
that God has structured learning so that it "lawfully"
unfolds developmentally, i.e., following certain

stages of mental and spiritual growth. When it comes
to identifying these stages, however, Gaebelein is
vague. He mentions none of his own devising, referring
only to the "thought-provoking" work of humanist
philosopher Alfred North Whitehead.[4]
     Gaebelein's reliance on a non-Christian like
Whitehead isn't surprising; the headmaster stresses the
theological concept of "common grace" in developing his
educational philosophy and approach to the learning
process.[5] Common grace, he believes, provides a
solid foundation from which to appreciate the many
contributions of non-believers to education. Common
grace is important, moreover, because it implies the
existence and centrality of its counterpart--"special"
or redemptive grace.
     Gaebelein, the lay-theologian, assigns top
priority to special grace. This is his way of
acknowledging the undeniable reality of sin in the
world. Such a recognition allows him to disclose a
fuller meaning to the originally good "programming" by
God of the learning process. It is insufficient to
exhibit so much faith in the foundation--as some
optimistic humanists do--when it has been seriously
undermined: Sin has fractured the foundation in such a
way that children are no longer merely eager to learn,
nor are they blissfully traversing from one development
stage to another.
     That fractured foundation has produced a "bent"
creation, and the bentness is manifested both
personally (rebellious and selfish children) and
socially (a rebellious and selfish culture affecting
children).[6] Gaebelein's solution to this distortion
is twofold, internal and external. The first and more
external is to focus on the need of all children for
educational discipline: "In many ways, the acid test
of a Christian school is its handling of
discipline."[7] This acid test receives a passing
grade only when discipline is administered "in love."
Through loving discipline, children will learn that
their own eagerness has boundaries and that mental and
spiritual growth--despite God's patterns--is not easy.
     Alas, external discipline alone ignores the
internal solution, what might be called the "heart" of
the matter. Only when this aspect is considered,
according to Gaebelein, will the fullest meaning be
unfolded and the beginnings laid for a new foundation.

2. By Being Born Again...
     The cornerstone for the new foundation is the
conversion of individual students. Conversion, for

Gaebelein, is understood in the traditional evangelical sense: being "born again" by the grace of God through faith and being adopted into the Body of Christ. It is an absolute prerequisite for true biblical knowledge. Leading youth to Christ is thus the first principle and goal of Christian education.

Conversion alone can function as the chief cornerstone because it is the most radical of all human experiences; through it "all things" are new, "including the intellect and the whole outlook upon life....the scales have fallen from the eyes of the heart (and) henceforth everything is seen with the clear sight of the newly created in Christ Jesus."[8]

Naturally, Christian teachers are the agents of evangelism in the schools. Gaebelein doesn't see this as hindering their calling as professional educators; rather, he sees evangelism as a fulfillment of their divinely-ordained office. Only Christian teachers can fully understand what is going on in the lives of children and teens as they grow and mature, and as they experience the mystery of conversion.

How does conversion affect the learning process? According to Gaebelein, in three interrelated ways: Firstly, children learn how to become more mature emotionally.[9] This is especially important now, when western civilization is plagued by emotional illness. Secondly, children learn that life is coherent and has a meaningful direction:

> the Christian youth (through conversion)
> can be identified by his sense of direction.
> He knows where he is going and why he is
> going there....While he by no means has
> 'all the answers,' he has made a commit-
> ment that colors his outlook, and his
> purpose is in everything to do the will
> of God.[10]

Thirdly, children learn that they have been transferred from the "natural" to the "spiritual" room of creation, and this enables them to exercise the precious gift of spiritual discernment: "The natural man comprehends natural, i.e., worldly, things. His spiritual faculties are undeveloped and he has no contact with the eternal. Not until he is 'born from above' can he truly understand the spiritual values which comprise 'the deep things of God'....[11] Although Gaebelein realizes that the ability to exercise spiritual discernment--led by the Holy Spirit--is gradual for children, it is nonetheless real.

3. By Being Raised in a Christian Home...

Crucial as is the school to the learning process for children, it is superceded by the home as the "greatest educational force" in the lives of children. What traits in particular set the home apart from other necessary institutions and relationships? In Gaebelein's writings the answer is readily apparent. First, he draws upon an insight from sociology: The home establishes the proper "feeling tones" for children, i.e., a loving environmnent. As a result, children quickly learn to give respectful obedience to parents, and by implication to all adults. Without such behavior future growth would be "blighted." Further, since learning begins in the home, children there initiate the process of habit-formation, so crucial for wholesome lives:

> The fact is that a good home provides for young children the most perfect of educational structures. It is here that the child has his earliest opportunity to learn....the ideas and habits a child gains from his earliest youth set the pattern for his subsequent behavior.12

Finally, Gaebelein suggests that the family is indispensible because parents serve as the first and most lasting role models for children. Teachers, as we shall see, are also significant models, but parents are the most important models of all--the greatest of all teachers. All the more reason, then, for them to be dedicated and consistent Christians with balanced personalities of their own.

4. By Attending to the Means of Grace, the Church...

The Christian home does not stand alone as a complement to the Christian school in the educational endeavor; in Gaebelein's view, the (visible) church, too, has a role to play. Christian education is a task of the local church, a task led by the pastor as the "chief teacher." Happily, the pastor is aided by a host of church and para-church organizations: Sunday School, Daily Vacation Bible School, and the Bible Conference Movement. Through the church, et al., children learn that grace is available to repentant sinners, that a covenant relationship exists between God and themselves, and that experiencing individuality

16.

within the Christian community is at the core of the
Gospel.13
        In sum, powerful and lasting contributions are
made by the Christian home and church to the on-going
learning process of children. Yet, the most important
contribution of home and church, in Gaebelein's eyes,
has yet to be mentioned.

5. By Being Rooted in Scripture...

        For children raised in a Christian environment-
-even those who have not yet experienced conversion--
home and church combine to point beyond themselves to
God's self-revelation in Scripture. Apart from
Scripture, even the nurturing received in these
primary institutions will bear little fruit. If
conversion is the spark that gives new life, then daily
immersion in the Bible, according to Gaebelein, is the
engine that powers the Christian learning process.
Commitment to Scripture is a theme which appears
throughout Gaebelein's works, regardless of subject.
        Preeminently a man of "the book," he begins and
ends with Scripture, describing it as authoritive,
infallible, ever-relevant, our ultimate standard, our
only "superlative" in this broken world. In
Gaebelein's own home and church, his parents and others
"lived in and by the Bible";14 subsequent events have
only confirmed his personal history. Like Luther, he
"takes his stand" on Scripture.
        What does a confessional approach mean, though,
for the learning process in children? Instrumentally,
it would seem, they learn by being "bathed" daily in
Scripture. But what central biblical themes emerge
which shape the on-going development of children?
        The Bible is our starting and ending point, says
Gaebelein, because it <u>refers us to Christ</u>, our Savior
and King. Thus, through the Bible, children learn that
the living Christ, the greatest model of all, is the
author of Scripture and the center of the biblical
message. Union with Christ, they come to realize, is
true life indeed; separation from Him brings loneliness
and eventual death.
        The Bible itself is also a <u>framework for all
truth</u>, setting forth the moral and spiritual
absolutes, the eternal checks and balances needed for a
daily walk and even survival in this world.15 For
Gaebelein, such a framework gives Christian children
"perspective" in a rapidly changing and often hostile
environment. Perspective, combined with spiritual
discernment from conversion, means that these children

have tremendous potential for serving God. Unleashing
this potential is even more the task of the school.

Finally, while children are becoming firmly
planted in the Word, they discover the hard way that
they must submit to it. Submission is more than
intellectual assent. Observing the life of Christ-
-who perfectly submitted to Scripture--and the lives of
biblical "saints" brings home this lesson to them.

6. By Experiencing a Wholistic, Integrated, Biblical
Education...

Christian educators, too, must submit to
Scripture. In Gaebelein's view, obedience to the Word
in recent decades has opened the eyes of educators to
the expansive implications of God's sovereignty over
His creation: All creation belongs to Him, including
human knowledge and understanding--especially that
which flows from a structured education (i.e.,
schools). Gaebelein was an early leader in this
educational renaissance, being perhaps the first
evangelical educator to use the phrase "all truth is
God's truth" in reference to Christian education.[16]

Commitment to "all truth is God's truth" has
always led Gaebelein in his search for, and
construction of, a "thoroughgoing Christian philosophy
of education." Such a proposition compels him to
define Christian education broadly, and he is quick to
acknowledge that within schools both formal and
informal education takes place. By "informal" the
headmaster has in mind what traditionally is referred
to as extracurricular activities--clubs, societies,
drama, athletics, etc. "They also have their place
within God's truth and, no less than mathematics or
science, history or literature, must be united with
it," he fondly states.[17] When properly understood
and utilized, extracurricular activities add flesh to
the educational skeleton, according to Gaebelein.

In his published works, however, Gaebelein directs
more of his attention to the "formal" side of
schooling, the curriculum itself. It is here that his
commitment to Scripture shines brightest. In the
context of a liberal arts curriculum--what he prefers
to call "general education"--the Bible is the very
center. For him this means

the study of the Bible in vital union
with the essential general studies and
indeed all learning. The centrality of
the Bible in Christian education is

organic. It not only provides a unifying
frame of reference for every other
subject; it also gives life and power
to the whole curriculum....in its
dynamic influence it might better be
termed 'a heart-curriculum' than a
core curriculum.[18]

Sola Scriptura! remains his clarion call. The
entire curriculum must draw its energy from the
biblical motor!
In lesser hands this could lead to the worst kind
of reductionism and biblicism, where so-called
"secular" subjects are but window-dressing added to a
self-sufficient foundation of "sacred" topics covered
by Theology and Biblical Studies. Nothing of the kind
occurs with Gaebelein. "All truth is God's truth" means
an outright denial of the radical separation of the
curriculum (and life) into unrelated compartments:

...Christian education must renounce
once and for all the dichotomy between
sacred and secular. Truth in science
and history, art and music, philosophy
and literature belongs just as much to
God as truth in religion....Christian
education...acknowledges that all
truth,wherever it is found is of God. For
Christian education there can be no
discontinuity in truth, because every
aspect of truth must find its unity
in the God of truth.[19]

In short, the fabric of Christian education is
seamless. It is the task, the joy, of educators to
implement this biblical truth as fully as posssible.
Gaebelein's own program for implementation,
notably presented in The Pattern of God's Truth,
revolves around the principle of integration--a
deliberate synthesis within the curriculum of the
sacred and the secular. Only when the sacred and
secular are seen as intimately complementary will
Christian education meet the need of the hour.
While his concept of integration is worthy of
special consideration not possible within this essay,
the most radical proposal for integrating biblical and
nonbiblical subjects ought to be mentioned: Gaebelein
suggests that Christian schools abandon their separate
Bible departments! Separate departments exacerbate the
traditional suspicions about theologians among the

19.

liberal arts faculty as well as isolate Biblical
Studies from the main body of the curriculum.
Christians schools need a faculty of "lay-theologians"
who are "able and willing to take a class in Bible
conjointly with their other work. A single such
teacher in each department of the major departments is
a goal at which to aim."20 Integration, Gaebelein
believes, will inevitably follow from such cross-
pollination.
    The implications of all this for the learning
process of children should be obvious: Children learn
best in a school setting which honors the Bible and
which attempts to integrate all nonbiblical conceptual
knowledge with the basic biblical doctrines and themes
Learning is further aided when schools undertake
practical changes in methodology and pedagogy, and when
the whole range of extracurricular activities is
brought under the school umbrella. While intentions
like these may strike the reader as overly idealistic,
they have been the raison d'etre of The Stony Brook
School since its founding over sixty years ago.

7.   By Doing the Truth...

    Theoretical knowledge is fine, but not enough.
Students at Gabelein's Stony Brook always have been
encouraged to do the truth. Works must complement
faith. Why? Because works are an essential "outcome"
of the Gospel, and because "It is a valid principle in
education that students learn by doing."21
    In varying degrees evangelicals long have
recognized this principle. Christian schools, for
example, consistently encourage children to put their
faith into practice in the familiar "spiritual" areas-
-chapel programs, Bible studies, personal witnessing,
etc. These are important activities, not overlooked by
Gaebelein. As a vanguard reformer, however, he has
always gone further, much further.
    Students must be actively committed to "social
concern." The proof of the pudding, for Gaebelein, is
in the natural realm. "Self-sacrificing action in
behalf of others," he emphasizes, "the contribution of
time and effort to the needs of the underprivileged,
training in the consecrated use of money, understanding
companions of different...backgrounds--these are some
directions that voluntary expression of a student's
faith should be encouraged to take."22 Through such
involvement students learn the fullest implications of
the Good News. If students still hesitate to roll up
their sleeves, he simply refers them to the models of

Christ or the Apostle Paul.

Moreover, the whole school community has a mandate to "do the truth," administrators and teachers as well as students. Gaebelein carefully notes these examples of Christian administrative action: an ethical financial policy, stewardship of resources, fair salaries, and truth in public relations (not over-selling the school to its constituency).[23]

Everywhere students need to be confronted by the fact that faith <u>plus</u> works is the pattern of God's truth. Gaebelein has always held that the most effective way to get this message across is for adults to be role models for youth. Students carefully watch the overall behavior of headmasters as well as other administrators. However, the greatest burden for modeling falls in the laps of the teachers.

8. By Following the Example of Teachers...

Listen to the headmaster: "(The) evangelical forces of America must be awakened to the glory and dignity of Christian teaching. Regardless of the climate of opinion surrounding them, Christian parents must by word and deed uphold before their children the essential worth and significance of teaching...."[24] His admiration for teachers is so high that <u>in loco parentis</u> seems to be the school's guiding principle.

Small wonder, thus, that his list of character traits is so inclusive--emotional balance, humor, patience, firmness, endurance, openness, self-control, and common sense. (Who among us?) Then, he adds, teachers must see their profession as a "calling from God," and they must manifest a basic love of youth. The latter is especially important for young children, who "only know whether a teacher loves them, understands them, and, enlisting their active interest, is able to lead them."[25] The personal touch is important for the mere survival of impressionable young children, and it plants other seeds as well.

As they mature, children respond to the loving touch with ever more substance. Gaebelein sees them modeling their teachers intellectually (through critical self-awareness) and practically (through acts of social concern). Thus, integration is a problem which can be most adequately addressed through the lives of individual teachers. Those teachers who live by integrating faith and works are the most effective "evangelists" for children and youth in general.

It is evident that Gaebelein wants only the best

teachers from the evangelical community. Nothing but the best will suffice, for Christian education is serious business. Few things are as shocking to him as mediocrity; mediocre teachers can do "lasting damage by implying that Christianity stands for the second best."[26] God requires Christians' best effort, in the natural realm as well as the spiritual--for children as well as adults.

9. By Doing Their Best...

Students, therefore, not only learn by doing the truth, they maximize their learning by "going the hard way," by "striving for excellence" in all their pursuits.[27] Gaebelein universally condemns the second- and third-rate. Children, as well as teachers, must be their best and do their best. Since sound learning is the main business of the Christian school, Gaebelein applies this principle first to the academic realm:

> (Academic) preparation itself is work,
> and the student who to the glory of
> God does first-rate work in English or
> mathematics serves the Lord just as much
> as the student who indulges so fully in
> outside Christian activities that he
> lacks time to do his work in physics,
> or even in Bible. To speak bluntly, too
> many evangelicals manifest a contentment
> with intellectual mediocrity, and this
> attitude is reflected in the young
> people who come to the Christian
> schools....[28]

Nurturing of first-rate minds among children in Christian schools is essential, because "One of our great needs is to learn how to think Christianly about every aspect of life."[29] Children experience great joy when they begin to make sense, conceptually, out of the complex world around them.

Striving for excellence also has a significant affect upon the personal character of children. According to Gaebelein, when children at Stony Brook strive for excellence, they tend to improve themselves emotionally and morally. Traits such as diligence, moral virtue, self-control, godliness, and brotherly kindness are all associated with, among other things, doing one's best as a Christian.

Striving for excellence in sports is important,

22.

too. For Gaebelein, "Softness of body is not compatible with the injunction to 'endure hardness as a good soldier of Jesus Christ'."[30] Children can learn-
-as did the Apostle Paul--that by-products of strenuous athletic competition often are wisdom and a sharpening of the inner man. Here, lasting character traits are learned--esprit de corps, endurance, unselfishness, giving honor to others, etc. In fact, Gaebelein acknowledges that in the real world of children and youth, "The tone and character of a student body is often determined more in the gymnasium and on the playing field than in the classroom."[31]

Further, pursuit of the best in the arts rounds out the educational process for children and builds character in children as it does in adults. Above all, Gaebelein urges youth to adopt habits of "good taste"[32] as they experience the arts, i.e., music, painting, literature, and entertainment. If the arts are the "signature of the humanity of man,"[32] that is all the more reason for youth to shun the trite, the sentimental, and the vulgar. "For young people," he says, "to live day by day with shoddy literature and vulgar entertainment may tear down what they have heard in church and learned in (school)."[34] Not tearing down, but elevation is the need of the hour.

When children flee from the aesthetically mediocre toward the excellent, important truths unfold. They learn that the best music can enhance worship, elevating the soul; that superior art can express biblical truth through beauty; and that the great literature of western civilization is based upon a Judeo-Christian vision of morality and ethics. Such a role for art, Gaebelein concludes, "cannot be brushed aside as mere luxury."[35] It is an integral part of a wholistic philosophy of Christian education.

Finally, striving to be and do the best has one other didactic function: to confront children with their own broken humanity, their sinfulness. At this point, I would suggest we have come full circle in our examination of Christian education. We are back to levels one and two--a common humanity and a universal bentness. Perhaps this is Gaebelein's major point: The more Christian children strive for excellence, the more they realize their own inadequacy. They learn that in and of themselves it is not possible even to be good, to say nothing of being "the best." They are thus driven to a transcendent source, to Christ who is "the ultimate meaning of excellence!"

23.

10. By Being Raised in Political Freedom...

No portrait of Gaebelein would be complete without
examining his political philosophy. He wrote his
seminal works in the early and mid-1950s, a time when
anticommunist hysteria peaked within conservative
Christian circles. To expect him to be unaffected by
such turmoil or the fear accompanying the later Bay of
Pigs fiasco and Cuban missle crisis would be naive. A
consistent thread of anticommunism is woven into the
fabric of Gaebelein's social and political perspective.
No doubt his father's influence can be seen here, 36
but even more determinative has been his experience at
Stony Brook. From this vantage point he concludes that
Christian education must not only interact with but
dutifully support American democracy.
Civil religion is not the reason for this
conclusion. Gaebelein is well aware of the dangers of
"super-patriotism," of seeing democracy as a religion.
America, alas, is not a Christian nation in any vital
sense of the term. Yet, democracy still must be
supported, according to Gaebelein, because it remains
the best political system the world has to offer. In
this broken world we should be thankful for a political
system that "is responsive to human needs, growing,
changing,...yet continuing free."37 In short, we
must support democracy for a most practical reason: It
responds to the spiritual longing in the human heart
for religious freedom. Without such freedom, there
would be no Christian schools like Stony Brook, which
are important expressions of religious faith. In his
eyes, the Gospel itself would suffer terribly.
Only a democratic political order, Gaebelein
believes, will tolerate a separate educational system
as we have come to know it in the West. Thus, the very
possibility of learning, in the full-blown sense of
American Christian education, presupposes political
democracy. Internally, children must learn to cherish
this fundamental truth about democracy, and to protect
this fragile system against its enemies.
Protection of democracy is most effective through
an educational system that enhances "Christian
citizenship." Here, as elsewhere, students learn
through involvement, by doing the truth through the
training ground of student council and similar
organizations. Students must go well beyond mere
involvement, however: "I am convinced that the school
that insists on excellence to the glory of God, that
demands hard work of its pupils--and of its teachers-
-is well on the way to effective citizenship

education."38 Nothing else, I suggest, would be consistent with the philosophy of Frank R. Gaebelein.

CONCLUSION

As evangelicals, we can be thankful for the public life and ministry of Dr. Gaebelein. More often than not he points us in the right direction when we focus our attention on the structural conditions underlying Christian education. His ministry reminds us of the dynamic way in which human nature, God's redemptive grace, consecrated human effort, and the political environment all interact to produce growth in children.

Are there weaknesses in Gaebelein's approach to learning? Note the following possible examples:

1. At times, his perspective seems almost too "personal," overly shaped by his own family and educational experience. Perhaps he tried to re-create his own childhood experiences as he went about the task of educational reform at Stony Brook. I wonder if that leads to an unfortunate bias--the imposition of an elitist "renaissance ideal" upon Christianity. He was sensitive to this charge and denied it, but I remain unconvinced.

2. Emphasis on self-discipline and good works is appropriate when discussing the moral aspect of Christian education; but I wonder if Gaebelein's emphasis was excessive. Does his Christian child resemble too closely the central character in a nineteenth-century Horatio Alger story?

3. Gaebelein's bibliology was colored with strokes of biblicism. Biblicism was present in his contention that Christian principles of child training will inevitably result from a "thorough study of every reference in the Bible to children...."39 Biblicism is also evident when he spoke of the relationship of the Bible to science. On the one hand, he correctly observed that the Bible is not a "textbook" of science; on the other, he stated--without sensing any contradiction or ambiguity--that "Scripture statements having to do with scientific matters are invariably correct."40 Gaebelein recognized that the Bible can be misused by sincere Christians; and he wouldn't exclude himself.

4. His view of Scripture also affected his ontology. While denying a radical separation of sacred and secular realms, he still presupposed their existence and built his world view upon them. And he accepted the traditional way of assigning priority to the "higher" realm: "Above the mental (and creaturely)

25.

is the spiritual. A man's spiritual nature is of far greater value than anything else."[41] Gaebelein derived this conclusion from his absolute commitment to the priority of Scripture. Nothing on the level of the "mundane" can equal the Bible.

It did not occur to him that the Bible can have priority without implying the existence of an hierarchical arrangement of two distinct realms of being. Gaebelein's ontology, at times, was closer to Aquinas than to Calvin and other theologian/ philosophers in the Reformed tradition.

5. Finally, bibliology and dualism left their imprint on the human thought process itself. Gaebelein, as previously noted, wanted youth to be both critically-minded and committed to bringing all thoughts captive to Christ. These are laudable goals; but what did this mean for him? Is it really possible for youth to think Christianly? According to the headmaster: "It is not that the product of Christian education thinks differently from secular youth, nor that he necessarily thinks more ably....some of the ablest minds have been blind to the Gospel....But once Christ has been received, subsequent thought is lifted to a higher level as new vistas open up for the mind."[42] What could these new vistas mean for the conceptualizing process, if they do not imply that Christian youth—at least to some extent—think differently and/or more ably?

At one point, Gaebelein stated that Scripture must be used in accordance with its own "inherent laws." We need to learn more from his life about the normative nature of thought life per se and the normativity associated with discipline other then theology. In other words, is a distinctly Christian, internal reformation of non-biblical thought really possible? Hopefully, further study of Dr. Gaebelein will lead to an affirmative answer.

ENDNOTES

[1]See recent tributes in the form of interviews in J.D. Douglas, "Frank Gaebelein: Striving for Excellence," Christianity Today, 23 (April 20, 1979), pp. 10-13, and William Petersen, "A Gentleman and a Scholar," Eternity, 30 (April 1979), pp. 32-34 & 42f.

[2]Christian Education in a Democracy (New York: Oxford Univ. Press, 1951).

[3]The Pattern of God's Truth (New York: Oxford Univ. Press, 1954).

[4]Christian Education in a Democracy, pp. 122-23. He states, though, that we must accept Whitehead's insights only in so far as they are true.

[5]For Gaebelein's understanding of common grace see A Varied Harvest (Grand Rapids: Eerdmans, 1967), pp. 108 & 118.

[6]See "What are We Doing to Our Youth?" A Varied Harvest, pp. 49f.

[7]The Pattern of God's Truth, p. 91.

[8]Christian Education in a Democracy, p. 192.

[9]Ibid., pp. 253-54. Gaebelein says, "The therapeutic effect of genuine conversion cannot be over-estimated...."

[10]Ibid., p.263.

[11]Exploring the Bible (New York: Harper and Brothers, 1929), p. 132.

[12]Christian Education in a Democracy, pp. 242-43.

[13]For Gaebelein's perspective on the relationship between children and the church see "Youth and the Church," A Varied Harvest, pp. 53f.

[14]"Reflections in Retrospect," Christianity Today, 14 (July 31, 1970), p. 10.

15See "What is Truth?" A Varied Harvest, p. 177.

16This phrase abounds in The Pattern of God's Truth.

17The Pattern of God's Truth, p. 86.

18Christian Education in a Democracy, pp. 119-20.

19Quoted in "The Bible College in American Education Today," School and Society, 87 (May 9, 1959), p. 224.

20The Pattern of God's Truth, p. 49.

21Christian Education in a Democracy, p. 59.

22Ibid., p. 60.

23Ibid., pp. 61-62.

24Ibid., p. 207.

25Ibid., p. 195.

26Ibid., p. 186.

27See "The Idea of Excellence and our Obligation to It," A Varied Harvest, pp. 97f.

28The Pattern of God's Truth, p. 103-04.

29Quoted in Douglas, "Frank Gaebelein: Striving for Excellence," p. 11.

30Christian Education in a Democracy, p. 268.

31Ibid., p. 267. Gaebelein, quoting another source.

32For his approach to art and "good taste" see "Toward a Biblical View of Aesthetics." Christianity Today, 12 (Aug. 30, 1968), pp. 4-6.

33Gaebelein quoting Chesterton in Douglas, "Frank Gaebelein: Striving for Excellence," p. 11.

[34]A Varied Harvest, p. 110.

[35]Ibid., p. 106.

[36]See David Rausch, "Arno C. Gaeblelein: A Fundamentalist View of Communism," a 1982 paper available from the Conference of Faith and History.

[37]Christian Education in a Democracy, p. 12.

[38]A Varied Harvest, p. 19.

[39]The Pattern of God's Truth, p. 5.

[40]Exploring the Bible, p. 139. I take him to mean "scientifically" correct.

[41]Ibid., p. 2.

[42]Christian Education in a Democracy, p. 275.

Chapter 3

Toward a Theory of Learning Deviance

by

Corrine E. Kass
Professor of Education
Calvin College

Madeleine L'Engle, in her Walking on Water,
quotes a French priest who was conducting a retreat:

> To love anyone is to hope in him always.
> From the moment at which we begin to judge
> anyone, to limit our confidence in him, from
> the moment at which we identify (pigeon-
> hole) him, and so reduce him to that, we
> cease to love him, and he ceases to be
> able to become better. We must dare
> to love in a world that does not know
> how to love.

It is risky business to label and categorize human
beings. However, as Christian teachers and leaders, we
must take such risks for the purpose of providing
service to those who by virtue of being different may
be discarded or segregated.
   In this paper I should like to consider teaching
and learning from the perspective of a Christian
developmentalist with a special interest in a
particular form of developmental deviance (learning
disability or dyssymbolia).

Teaching

Any teaching begins with a view of the human
being. If the teacher starts from the blank page
notion, the original sin notion, the Deweyian notion of
learning through experience, the Skinnerian view of
behavioral conditioning, or the Piagetian developmental
stage notion, that view will influence how one teaches.
   My preference is the developmental stage view,
with a critical-age feature. The critical-age feature
refers to a belief that certain learnings must occur
within certain age ranges, or the quality of learning

will thereafter be negatively affected.

The first rule for teaching is that there be an interpersonal relationship between the teacher and the learner. On the part of the teacher, that relationship involves authority and empathy. By understanding the age-related task requirements the teacher presents appropriate tasks with authority (the adult knows something the child does not know); by understanding the mind of the child (deviations included), the teacher can guide the learner with empathy. Following is a consideration of the impact of "authority" and "empathy" on learning.

Authority means that the learning is acquired first of all from outside oneself. Dr. Clarence Vos, in a paper entitles "Biblical Perspectives on Authority in the Home," points out that since we (adults) are made in God's image, we are his representatives. Genesis 1 says that man is to "have dominion over...all the earth." Vos explains the statement in Genesis 2 that God put man in the garden of Eden "to till it" could better be translated "to serve it." Dominion is not properly exercised unless it is performed in the spirit of service. Vos says that "authority is constituted of these two elements: dominion and service, and that the only kind of dominion that is legitimate is a dominion exercised on behalf of those over whom it is exercised."

To carry out the authority which we must practice "on behalf of" children, with and without learning problems, we must not only understand the developmental stages, but we must understand the relationship between those stages and instruction. While the critical-age notion suggests that there is within the human being a "program" which unfolds, our authority must be practiced in such a way that the child's capabilities can be used to the upper limits of age-related characteristics. Instruction must be provided.

There is a complex relationship between development and instruction. A child must be "ready" to learn the three R's, but we do not wait for such readiness to magically appear. Jerome Bruner, in The Relevance of Education, says that pedagogy takes on increasing significance with capacity for symbolic activity: "The first point to be born in mind about human development is the extent to which it is from the inside out."

Of course, teaching does not mean keeping the learner dependent on outside instruction. There must be maturation, there must be mastery, there must be independence, there must be responsible action (see

Wolterstorff's Educating for Responsible Action).
The teacher must understand how to match instruction to
the needs of children at different ages. This requires
not only knowledge about what to teach (authority) but,
just as importantly, requires intuition and empathy for
all learners, strong and weak alike.

Empathy means understanding the mind of the
child. Perhaps something of this meaning is given us in
the scriptural emphasis on the importance of childlike
qualities for entering the Kingdom of God. We adults
think we know what these qualities are since we were
once children ourselves. Actually, our understanding
of the characteristics of children (trust, humility,
unconditional love, respect for authority, and
obedience) is colored by the experiences, intellect,
will and power of the adult. In the process of
development, old ways are put away and new ways take
over. Reality and truth are judged differently as we
grow older. At adulthood only remnants remain of the
ways we interpreted the world when we were young.

Since children are imitators by nature, children
reflect the image of God to the extent that caring
adults in their world show them the image of God. It is
my contention that any caring adult, any caring
teacher, any caring parent can provide instruction for
learners, even for learners who deviate. What is
needed is awareness of stages of development and of
problems within each stage. It's not that anyone and
everyone has enough knowledge or a license to practice,
but not having enough knowledge or a license does not
excuse us from daring to interact, tell, model, show,
give reasons, and serve. Charles Curran, from Loyola
University, writes:

> Much of modern education is based
> on the premise that the knower is
> to communicate only on an impersonal and
> intellectual level. Moreover, the same
> impersonal, intellectualistic kind of
> response is expected from the students.
> In this way we are all unconscious
> victims of a factualized, mathematicized
> mode of relating: that is, we solve
> problems rather than communicate with
> each other because it is far safer to
> solve problems. Problem-solving
> contains none of the uncertainty and
> ambivalence and risk that is inherent
> in an open human communication.

A term which is useful to describe this interpersonal relationship is one used by Charles Williams in <u>Descent into Hell</u>: "coinherence." By this is meant the opposite of self-sufficiency, a constant interaction with other people, giving and receiving help in the power of Christ. Teaching, then, is not power manipulation of the child, but consists of a wish to communicate. In order to communicate with the learner who is having trouble, one must understand the learner. Child-nurturing in home, school, and church is fraught with moral responsibility for personal interaction. No one may be shunted off because of deviation from a so-called standard of excellence.

What we are as persons is critical for teaching. Craig Dykstra, in <u>Vision and Character</u>, gives a Christian educator's alternative to Kohlberg. He criticizes Kohlberg for following a juridical point of view which focuses on making judgments about rightness or wrongness of acts. Dykstra recommends, instead, a visional approach to life, which treats all of life as a mystery. The way in which one sees reality is in light of one's vision regarding that reality. In order to make mature moral judgments, Kohlberg would suggest that one must be a moral philosopher. Dykstra, on the other hand, says that

> people who have a sufficient cognitive capacity for empathizing with the needs of others, the capacity to sustain a sense of the continuous identity of other persons, a capacity for imaginatively interpreting the nature and meaning of situations, and a sufficiently rich, imaginal repertoire by means of which to carry out such interpretations may be able to make extremely perceptive and fully moral judgments.

In <u>Between Man and Man</u>, Martin Buber says about the role of the teacher:

> There is only one access to the pupil: his confidence. For the adolescent who is frightened and disappointed by an unreliable world, confidence means the liberating insight that there is human truth, the truth of human existence. When the pupil's confidence has been won, his resistance against being educated gives way to a singular

34.

happening: he accepts the educator
as a person. He feels he may trust
this man, that this man is not making
a business out of him, but is taking
part in his life, accepting him before
desiring to influence him.

The younger the child, the more influence the
teacher's personality has on the human being. That is
especially true for negative effects. A negative
self-concept results from not being acceptable to
teachers who are not sure of their own authority and
who do not have empathy. Poor school achievement may
be a precipitating factor. A negative self-concept, or
lack of trust in authority may be irreversible by sixth
grade.

What I am suggesting is that learning occurs on
the basis of internalization of social interaction.
Vygotsky wrote, "The function which is today divided
between two persons will be interiorized and become the
independent mental function of the child himself."

Learning

Understanding deviance begins with understanding
the norm. By norm, I mean what the human being is by
nature, not the statistical norm. As adult Christians,
we know that we are a complex combination of God's
creation and man's fall. We are on a continual journey
through life striving to serve with faith, hope, and
love (with Christ's love as our example). The norm for
children, however, is different than the norm for
adults by virtue of the characteristics peculiar to
children. If we are to train children in the fear of
the Lord, to train them in wisdom, to bring them as
close to the norm for their age as possible, we must
understand the developing child.

Our understanding of children begins with a
philosophy about the nature of children. Traditionally,
the world has thought of children as "little adults,"
as blank pages, or as animal-like, to be conditioned
with appropriate reinforcements. None of these ideas
is correct. From a Christian perspective, the child is
none other than a young son or daughter of the first
parents, born in sin and in need of salvation. Within
the child is the human tendency toward sin and the
human propensity toward religion. Understanding of,
and responsibility for dealing with these tendencies,
however, cannot be expected until the child has

35.

developed a certain degree of reason (usually around ages 11 to 14).

The path to adulthood is not simply a matter of continuous growth and an accumulation of knowledge and reason. In children, there are periods of time when they are building the foundation for action by observing and imitating adults, and there are periods when action occurs. These periods alternate until maturity is attained. As children progress toward adulthood, they approximate mature concepts which are partially correct and partially incorrect, partially learned and partially innate. For example, children develop religious concepts partly through religious instruction and partly due to their developmental (God-given) propensity toward religion.

David Elkind conducted a study of children's concepts about institutional religion. He interviewed Jewish, Catholic, and Congregational Protestant children regarding their religious group membership and their ideas on prayer. Between ages five and seven, the children had global, undifferentiated concepts of their religious identity (thinking in racial, national, and geographic terms) and they had vague and indistinct notions of prayer (knowing that these had to do with God, but depending almost entirely on learned prayers). From ages seven through nine, children began to think of denominations as places where some action occurred, and to think of prayer in a similar fashion, relating to particular activities. From ages ten through twelve, children show more reflection about producing evidence of innermost beliefs and convictions stemming from their religious group membership and to think of prayer as "private conversation with God." Increasingly, prayer becomes both more objective and more subjective with age.

William A. Koppe reports another interesting study of children in the Lutheran denomination. Age-level differences were noted on three questions: (1) What is the child's concept of participation in the church? (2) What are the child's concepts of God, Jesus, and the Holy Spirit? and (3) On what basis does the child guide his behavior? Koppe found that children recognize the importance of God very early in life, but start with a simple awareness. Gradually, children shift to a subordinate role of seeking God's will for one's life. Up to about 12 years of age, children are closely tied to what one does in church, and after 12, what one is to do in grown-up life. The children in Koppe's study understood from early years that God loves us and that Jesus is a friend, but the concept of

36.

the Holy Spirit did not appear until between the ages nine and 12. As to guides for behavior, Koppe suggested that approval and disapproval guide children to preliminary concepts of right and wrong by the time they are five or six years, but it takes until about 11 years of age for actions to be guided by intention to serve good purposes.

Recent scientific evidence based on observations of children's physical and intellectual characteristics follow much the same developmental progression. Jean Piaget, the famous Swiss child developmentalist, suggested that the stages involve structural changes in the human being, not just physiological, but changes in reasoning as well.

New evidence about brain growth has been suggested by Herman Epstein, who has demonstrated some evidence that there are brain growth spurts that occur for about two years, with a two year plateau between each spurt. These spurts of growth appear between the ages of three and ten months, two and four years, six and eight years, ten and twelve years, and finally between 14 and 16 years.

Learning Deviance

Most handicaps are visible, particularly the severe ones such as blindness, deafness, severe mental retardation, and physical limitations. Some, however, are not as identifiable and the individuals with invisible handicaps are likely to be misunderstood. Learning disability is one such handicap. It is a severe handicap in the acquisition and use of symbols (letters and numbers) which is due not to lack of intelligence, but to developmental dysfunctions in the central nervous system. Rote skills in reading, spelling, writing, and calculating are the most difficult to acquire. Facility in comprehension seems to help somewhat (the human system has a marvelous capacity for compensation), but this ability breaks down with complex thinking tasks. What most of us take for granted-- the automatization of the acts of reading, writing, spelling, number facts, social perception--are lacking in the learning disabled, making them feel that they are less intelligent than others, when in fact they are not.

Learning Disability is a condition for which it is not easy to feel compassion. There is the appearance of normalcy, but a perverse sort of behavior which stems from a probable brain damage. What is most frustrating is that from appearance and intellectual

capability one would expect normal behavior. When
normal behavior does not occur, we must take the risk
of labeling in order to successfully treat the child.
This is also the time that, rather than limiting our
confidence in the child, we begin earnestly to "hope in
him always." The learning disabled may understand
words, but have difficulty understanding nuances
underlying the words. Vygotsky, a Russian psychologist
in the 1920's, wrote: "To understand another's speech,
it is not sufficient to understand his words--we must
understand his thought. But even that is not
enough--we must also know its
motivation. No psychological analysis of an utterance
is complete until that plane is reached." That
psychological analysis is so natural, even intuitive,
to most human beings that it has been a surprise to
find it defective in the learning disabled.
     The professional must understand the physical,
intellectual, emotional, and moral needs of all human
beings, including those with this subtle handicap.
Often, when mothers are concerned about children who
seem to be learning differently and mention it to their
physician, the doctor may be inclined to say, "Don't
worry, the child will grow out of it." Teachers, too,
often say in effect, "I don't have time to do anything
about this problem if I find out the child can't help
it." No one is excused from following the ultimate
rule for living (the Ten Commandments), including those
who deviate from the norm. Change is required for all
(i.e., put off the old man, put on the new), but change
is necessary all the more for those who are different,
who are weak, who are handicapped. We must be at the
ready to teach those who appear to be unteachable, to
make it possible for them to lead productive lives as
close to the norm as their corrected handicap will
allow.
     We find a reference in Exodus 4 where God tells
Moses that he must lead the Israelites in spite of his
speech impediment:

          The Lord said to him, "Who gave man his
          mouth? Who makes him deaf or dumb? Who
          lives him sight or makes him blind? Is
          it not I, the Lord? Now go; I will help
          you speak and will teach you what to say."
          But Moses said, "O Lord, please send some-
          one else to do it." Then the Lord's anger
          burned against Moses and he said, "What
          about your brother, Aaron the Levite? I

know he can speak well. He is already
on his way to meet you, and his heart
will be glad when he sees you. You
shall speak to him and put words in
his mouth; I will help both of you
speak and will teach you what to do.
He will speak to the people for you,
and it will be as if he were your
mouth and as if you were God to him.

Age-related Characteristics of Learning Disability

In order to understand learning deviance, it is
necessary to summarize critical age-related
characteristics of those who require extraordinary
teaching so as to become responsible, self-supporting
adults who can be successful in life despite severe
difficulties in acquiring and using the symbol systems
for reading, writing, calculating, and the most
advanced forms of thinking. These are, by each age-
range, or stage:

Stage 1: Sensory Orientation
At birth there is a physiological readiness to
respond to the environment. Infants learn with their
entire bodies, but mainly through seeing, hearing, and
physical touching. Some deficits shown by the learning
disabled are the following:
1. Visual Pursuit, the ability to follow
stimuli with the eyes. Related to this is the
discrimination of the familiar from the unfamiliar.
Right from birth, it appears that infants with learning
disability, while not blind, do not use their eyes as
do normal infants. The learning disabled either look
at everything without really discriminating or they do
not look. It has been noted that they do not show the
normal fear of strangers. Remediation involves much
physical contact. This is important for all babies,
but more so for the handicapped.
2. Auditory Discrimination, the ability to
react differentially to sound, including speech. While
these children are not deaf, they seem to have
disturbances in attention, revealed in either
supersensitivity or passivity. The learning disabled
do pick up enough so that they are able to score within
the normal range on a verbal intelligence test, but the
affective aspect may be deficient during the early
months when the parent-child relationship is the most
important. Irritability, distractibility, and
restlessness are typical symptoms. Remediation

involves a great deal more repetitive verbalizing than for the normal.

Stage 2: Memory

Young children from 18 months to seven years are good imitators. They can memorize letters, numbers, Bible verses, more than one language, repetitive stories. They are not self-conscious about saying what they think they heard (e.g., "Gladly, my cross-eyed bear"). The trust that children have naturally for parents and other care-giving adults is the reason they are willing to imitate as accurately as possible. This is a sensitive period for learning the symbol systems. The learning disabled display the following deficits:

1. Hyperexcitability, the ability to control one's own reactions to stimuli, both external and internal. The hyperexcitability of the learning disabled appears to be internal noise--what triggers it is not obvious from the external situation. While normal children can "work off steam" by running around a bit, the learning disabled seem to become more "revved up." Because of this deficit, the learning disabled often cannot pay attention. Their behavior seems irrelevant. Remediation requires that the external stimulation must compete with the internal noise and must be of such intensity as to capture their attention. Nurturing adults must provide constant repetition and verbal instructions.

2. Rehearsal, the ability to practice input for later recall. It is the means by which incoming information reaches the long-term memory store. The learning disabled appear not to practice material for later recall--they have been called "passive learners." Remediation should provide opportunities for a great deal of verbal rehearsal and imaginal rehearsal. Exercises in naming, imitating, and imaginative play are useful.

Stage 3: Re-Cognition

From ages eight to 12, children begin to recognize that life is more complex than they earlier were able to comprehend. Now they find out that there are meanings behind actions, and they begin to explore these meanings. Words may have multiple meanings, words may be substituted for other words, prefixes and suffixes change words meanings, and context may change meaning. They begin to note how others feel about them, which is the beginning of empathy. They begin to note how their actions affect others, which is the beginning of conscience. Earlier, they did things to please important adults and God; now, they can begin to understand that obedience to authority is a

40.

responsibility. The qualities of obedience and respect are added to trust. The learning disabled display the following deficits:

1. Visualization, the ability to recognize wholes from sensation of parts. It is the internal representation of overlearned symbol sequences, the ability to note likenesses and differences in things and words, to relate ideas, to note absurdities in what is seen and heard, to understand structural aids such as prefixes, suffixes and root words, and to understand words with multiple meanings, similar meanings, and opposite meanings.

Visualization requires a foundation during the Memory Stage of accurate perception of all parts within the whole. A common problem shared by bright children and learning disabled is that of skipping the rote learning aspects of the Memory Stage and operating almost exclusively from context clues. Visualization means that both parts and context help to determine meaning--not just context. Remediation requires a careful distinction between understanding from context and accurately perceiving parts. The child must become aware of the tools for determining meaning. These tools include all previous learning which should have occured during the preceding stages: attention which is appropriately and sequentially paid to language symbols, rehearsal of symbols, and the ability to return to accurate (rote) examination of symbols whenever necessary for determining meaning.

2. Haptic Discrimination, the ability to note differences in the sense of touch and muscle sensations. The kinesthetic and tactile senses help to build-in recognition of meaning through body movements. As the individual develops, more senses become involved in meaning--while the auditory and visual are important during Stages 1 and 2, by age nine or ten, arm muscle movements in writing and spelling, and eye muscle movements in reading must help carry the stimulus load.

The remedial method most suitable for training kinesthetic discrimination is the Fernald method (Fernald, 1943). This method has the child look at a word or phrase, attempt to hold it in mind without saying the letters, and then write it from memory while saying the word or phrase slowly. It is important that the child pay attention to the muscle sensation while writing. The remedial method most suitable for training tactile discrimination is to train the child to write words in a flowing manner rather than "drawing." Release of tension can sometimes be accomplished through writing without looking.

41.

3. Figure-Ground Discrimination, the ability to sift the relevant from the irrelevant. The learning disabled appear to be distractible and need remedial help to focus on important features of a task. Direct connections must be made between learning a task in isolation and transferring it to new situations. For example, these children must be required to spell words correctly in text which they have learned in isolation. Verbalizing tasks while doing them forces a connection between auditory feedback and action, thus closing out interfering stimuli. This produces the internalization of learning which is so important for this age range.
Stage 4: Synthesis

After 12, earlier learning becomes habitual; the attention is now turned toward work for its own sake and toward helping others because of a wish to be responsible rather than just to please the adult. This is what we call coming to the "age of discretion." What it means to be a Christian can now be explored in depth. The need for confidence in one's self is very strong during the teens-- they desire respect and the feeling that they are needed. The characteristic most desired in others is empathy, and we find the beginnings of empathy during the early teens. Identification with adult models is now complete-- rather than just imitating their parents and teachers, youth take on the religious and intellectual values of their parents and teachers. The characteristic added to trust, obedience, and respect is responsibility with support from authority. The deficits noted in the learning disabled are the following:

1. Monitoring, the ability to note and correct errors when these occur. During this Stage, we ought to be able to take correct responses for granted, but errors should arouse a feeling in the system that something is not right. Habitual accuracy and the ability to detect errors is deficient in the learning disabled. Remediation requires the undoing of bad habits which the child has acquired earlier. The focus is on errors, detecting them, analyzing them, and correcting them.

2. Visual-Auditory-Haptic Coordination, the ability to associate information from all sensory modalities. Since all senses are integrated by this age, it is not reasonable to assess individual senses for strength or weakness. Remediation requires tasks which force all the senses to work together. Writing from dictation is just such an activity. Sounds must be blended into wholes, symbols must be in correct

42.

sequence, and movement must be fluid. Material for
dictation should come from the student's textbooks if
at all feasible.
Stage 5: Communication
    The last Stage, which begins around age 14, is
defined as the process by which learned concepts and
automatized modes of response are used in the service
of expressing ideas to others and receiving ideas from
others, both consciously and unconsciously. The
synthesized skills of speaking, writing, gestures, and
reading take on a personalized style, and personal
responsibility is taken for the consequences of what is
communicated. The characteristic of <u>responsibility</u>
is added to <u>trust</u>, <u>obedience</u>, <u>respect</u>, and
<u>responsibility with support from authority</u>. The
learning disabled have difficulty in comprehending what
is communicated to them through print, through speech,
through body language, and possibly through music and
art. They also have problems expressing their own
ideas in writing and mathematics. Remediation requires
dealing with strategies for learning as well as
content. Content is best taken from the student's
courses at school. Educators must constantly improve
their knowledge about the human being (not just the
discipline which they teach) in order to understand
that all difficulties of students are not necessarily
due to lack of intelligence or motivation--there just
might be a central nervous system dysfunction!

Conclusion

    In the learning process, both the teacher and the
learner have great responsibilities. As Wolterstorff
so pointedly states, "In its depth all human
responsibility is responsibility to God, and all
defection from responsibility is at its root letting
God down." Our responsibility as teachers and leaders
is no less great to the deviant individual than to the
average or above-average. We are "called to <u>serve</u>
all human beings everywhere, working and praying for
healing, liberation, and fulfillment in all of life...
willingly undergoing sacrifice and suffering when
necessary. (We) do not have the option of remaining
passive in the face of deprivation and oppression and
distortion."
    Teaching the deviant learner requires a deep
sensitivity to this responsibility. It is time that
Christian institutions have direct statements of
beliefs and attitudes concerning individual differences
in philosophies and theologies of education. It is not

enough to merely acknowledge a variety of gifts in the many parts of the body of Christ. It is not enough to provide separate institutional caring in places where those with mental, physical and emotional deviance may be sent when they do not meet criteria for "normalcy." This normalcy, as defined subvocally through a process of natural selection of the fittest, through a process of looking to standards of acceptable performance as being performance attained by the greatest number of individuals in a given setting, is not God's standard for dealing with our fellow image-bearers.

Teaching the deviant learner also means that we must guide and train from the earliest years. It means that, during the early years, we must not leave one iota of such training to anyone who does not have Christian values. It means that we must not look upon children as essentially "good" or "bad," but a reflection of the sin of our original parents and the image of God as shown them through their earthly parents. It means that the actions of children must be guided and corrected by those who have responsibility for those children--parents, teachers, extended family, and adult members of each child's church.

Finally, our responsibility as teachers is to have undying hope in each child. We must recognize their place in the kingdom and teach them the importance of that place. We must instill within each child, and especially the deviant child of any age, a sense of their immeasurable worth to God and to our society.

The deviant learner, too, must, recognize his great responsibility in light of his differences. Children vary in abilities to learn; however, all can learn. God has created each child uniquely, and then pronounced "It is good!"

References

Bronfenbrenner, U. "Contexts of child rearing: problems and prospects." American Psychologist, 1979, 844-850.

Bruner, J. The Relevance of Education. New York: W. W. Norton and Co., Inc., 1973.

Buber, M. Between man and man. Translated by R. G. Smith. Boston: Beacon Press, 1955.

Curran, C. Counseling-learning in second languages. Apple River, IL: Apple River Press, 1976.

Dykstra, C. Vision and character: A Christian educator's alternative to Kohlberg. Ramsey, NJ: Paulist Press, 1981.

Elkind, D. The child's reality: three develpmental themes. Hillsdale, NJ: Lawrence Erlbaum Associates, 1978.

Epstein, H. Growth spurts during brain development: implications for educational policy and practice. In J. S. Chall and A. F. Mirsky (Eds.), Education and the brain, (The Seventy-Seventh Yearbook of the National Society for the Study of Education, Part 2). Chicago, IL: The University of Chicago Press, 1978.

Koppe, W. How persons grow in Christian community. Yearbooks in Christian Education, Vol. 4. Philadelphia: Fortress Press, 1973.

L'Engle, M. Walking on water: reflections on faith and art. Wheaton, IL: H. Shaw, 1980.

Luria, A. The role of speech in the regulation of of normal and abnormal behaviors. New York: Liveright, 1961.

Vos, C. Biblical perspectives on authority in the home, a lecture to F. I. T. Instructor Training Group, 1974.

Vygotsky, L. <u>Thought and language</u>. Cambridge, MA:
    MIT Press, 1962.

Williams, C. <u>Descent into hell</u>. London: Faber and
    Faber, 1945.

Wolterstorff, N. <u>Educating for responsible action</u>.
    Grand Rapids, MI: Christian Schools
    International, 1980.

Chapter 4

BIBLICAL KNOWING
AND
CLASSROOM METHODOLOGY

by

Donald Oppewal
Professor of Education
Calvin College

Reformed literature on education, particularly in
the last decade, is replete with evidence that the
Bible exhibits an anthropology of holism, the view that
the human being is a unity, one who functions in
various relations but in organic unity.[1]   The
literature contains little that carries this
anthropology into the arena of epistemology and
knowing.   Even less attempt has been made to ground
classroom methodology in any theory of knowing, leaving
classroom pedagogy as independent of theoretical
underpinning in philosophy.

This essay provides one answer to the question:
How do persons, conceived as whole beings, come to know
anything, whether it be God, an idea, or an object?   It
presupposes that the case for holism in anthropology
has been sufficiently treated by others, and focuses on
the biblical evidence for holistic knowing as that
which should shape christian thinking about teaching
methodology.   Some attention will be given to the
implications for goals and for achieving an integrated
curriculum.

HOLISTIC KNOWING

Descriptions of how the human being comes to know
are as numerous as positions in anthropology,
metaphysics, and ethics.   The philosophical literature
abounds with disputes between schools of epistemology,
and new ones are always being formed and refined.   Thus
philosophy of education textbooks typically include
attention to epistemology, identifying the various
schools of philosophy, like idealism, realism, and
pragmatism, and showing their respective implications

for goals, curriculum and teaching method.

If the Reformed educational vision is to be comprehensive, educators must attempt to articulate classroom methodology which is congruent with its goals and curriculum, as well as its biblical anthropology. The case for a holistic theory of knowing must then be made, followed by its implication for a model method of classroom instruction.

Spectator or Participant?

Many models of knowing exhibit what may be called a spectator theory of knowing. In correspondence theory the knower is depicted as examining some evidence (whether with the senses or by the mind) and noting some degree of correspondence between such evidence and objective reality. The outcome is beliefs which are taken to be true reports of how things are. This view can be called a spectator view of knowing because the verification process is mental, a seeing with the mind, although assisted by the senses. The method does not require any further action upon such objective reality to confirm or repudiate beliefs.

Another variation on the spectator view is that of coherence as the test of truth. In this view knowledge is reliable in the degree to which a given belief is internally consistent with others, with all knowledge derived by rational deduction from self-evident truths.[2]

This deductive mode of knowing, best seen in the curriculum named geometry, when it is taken to be superior to other forms of knowing, is a claim that best fits the consistency theory of knowledge, a variation on what is here called a spectator theory of knowing.

What shall the educator wishing to think biblically do with such epistemological method? Is reasoning from self-evident truths to their deductive conclusions the paradigm method of knowing for a Christian? Is a Christian version of coherence theory compatible with the Bible? Or is a version of correspondence theory what the Bible reflects?

A number of Reformed philosophers and theologians have rather recently argued that both correspondence and consistency epistemologies are deficient.[3] Some have argued that they do not comport well with the biblcal perspective on knowing.[4] Others have focused on the defects of Catholic epistemology as it relates to natural theology arguments for the existence of God.[5] From these it is clear that thinking about epistemology is in ferment among Reformed thinkers.

It would seem that prominent in such new efforts
should be attempts to discover in Scripture itself
patterns which indicate that it does exhibit, but not
outline, a theory of knowing. Scripture is no more a
textbook on epistemology than a textbook of science.
It is a record of those who experienced God, and who
acted in obedience or disobedience to God. We shall
have to infer what theory of knowing such writers
reflected.

The Interactive Model

A promising approach, and one rich with
implications for teaching methodology, is one which we
call here variously a participant or interactive theory
of knowing. Briefly put, it is that knowing is a
process of thinking-doing, of mental-physical acts. To
know a rock is thus to engage in both mental acts about
its nature in the scheme of things, but also to push or
pull it to discover its nature or know the truth of it.
Similarly, to know God is to engage in constructing
mental acts about Him (rooted in revelation) but also
to know Him by responding to Him, by what Scripture
calls obedience or disobedience.

While the above seems to describe two separate
acts, separated in time and even place, such is not the
intent. It is rather that mental action is only one
aspect and the physical action the other, both
constituting together the act of knowing. Put in the
technical language of one Bible scholar,

> The perceiving subject exists in an
> active relationship with that which
> he perceives, not in the "tabula rasa"
> relationship of passive observer. Thus
> the perceiver and the perceived exist
> as poles of a dynamic continuum, rather
> than as dichotomized, static entities.[6]

Scriptural instances of the use of the term "know"
in this sense abound. When Abraham knew Sarah and she
conceived and bore a son, the word "know" is not merely
a euphemism for sexual intercourse, but a clue to the
Biblical paradigm of knowing. It captures the concept
of interaction as that which constitutes knowing, in
this case a person. It is in the give and take, mental
acts of classifying Sarah as female and wife and the
physical act of sex, that he knew her. Without the act
of intercourse (itself a term from Latin suggesting

49.

two-way action) the knowing is that of spectator, not participant.

When Job says, "I know that my Redeemer liveth" (Job 19:25), he is not uttering this, spectator-like, as a process of rational induction or deduction, but out of engagement with God, undergoing and responding, of perceiving God as having such and such qualities, and of living with poverty, illness, and despair. It is uttered as a conclusion to both his mental constructs and his doing.

Christ also spoke in this manner when referring to truth and knowledge. He spoke of "doing the truth", "living in the truth," "abiding in" and thus "being in the truth."7 Knowing the truth thus consists not simply of mental acts of accepting propositions about Christ, but of doing what Christ did, and thus knowing Him who said, "I am the way, the truth, and the life." More instances could be given to indicate that there is a pervasive use of this sense of knowledge in Scripture.

If the foregoing are not to be disposed of as merely poetic utterances or isolated word studies, they suggest that Scripture indeed speaks a special language when it comes to epistemology and a description of knowing. It excludes forms of thinking in which only propositions are regarded as instances of knowing, and belief is defined as a product of certain mental acts following accepted rules of logic. Scripture distinguishes between 'believe in' and 'believe that', where the latter refers to propositions or assertations, such as belief <u>that</u> Christ arose from the dead. Scripture instead says to believe <u>in</u> the Lord Jesus Christ, and you shall be saved, implying a different conception of knowing. As the book of James has it (James 2:14-20), belief <u>that</u> there is a God is what even devils possess. Belief <u>in</u> God includes the response of discipleship, not just intellectual perception that some such being exists. When James says that "faith without works is dead" (vs. 26), the epistemological significance is that head knowing is incomplete knowledge without deeds. James notes of Abraham: "You see that his faith and his actions were working together, and his faith was made complete by what he did" (vs. 22).

Philosophers may try to pull apart thinking and doing, allowing only thinking to produce knowledge, with deeds or doing being a separate act of applying such knowledge. Scripture does not talk that way. It talks instead, as the passage above indicates, of "working together" and that faith is "made complete" by

doing. James even notes a parallel between a holistic
view of man and such holistic view of knowing when he
concludes: "As the body without spirit is dead, so
faith without deeds is dead" (vs. 26).

The distinction between belief in and belief
that is one that is susceptible of many
interpretations in ordinary language.[8] The point
being made here is that the first is not merely a
linquistic oddity, and is not simply reducible to the
second.

The Apostle's Creed, that great ecumenical creed
of Christendom, uses believe in consistently, as in
"I believe in God, the Father"..."and in Jesus Christ,"
and continuing in Article VIII with "I believe in the
Holy Spirit." These all suggest the holistic view of
knowing in which there is commitment to a way of life
out of which these propositions arise. They are not
uttered as intellectual assent to these as the result
of reasoning from first principles to such conclusions.

Thus, both Scripture and creeds speak a different
language when it comes to a model way of knowing. Some
Reformed thinkers have caught this vision when faith
(knowing) is declared to be not mere assent to
propositions rationally derived. The Biblical
alternative is sharply stated in the following:

> How, then, ought we to think of faith?
> I suggest that the model we must have
> in mind is not that of believing
> propositions, but rather that of
> believing in a person. You all know,
> from your own experience, what it is to
> believe in a person. It is to trust him,
> to be loyal to him, to serve him, to
> give him one's allegiance, to be willing
> to work for him, to place one's confidence
> in him.[9]

The context of the above quote indicates that the
paradigm of knowing is knowing God in person; it can be
offered as a model of all knowing. Thus knowing an
idea or an object has the same components as knowing a
person. While it may seem strange to talk of being
'loyal' to a rock, it would be redolent of Scripture to
do so. Knowing God's creation does not follow an
utterly different model than knowing Him who created
it, and who exists in and is known through it. To know
a rock is then to have both mental and physical acts
relating to it. To know its nature is not simply to
preceive it in the mind as belonging to a given class

of objects, but also to act upon it: to break it,
stack it, sit on it, etc. In a word, it is to be in
interaction with it, in the best etymological sense of
that word. Knowing is an interaction, a process which
goes on between (which is what inter means in
Latin) the knower and the known. To pull the two
apart is to reduce knowing to a mental proposition-
making act. Also, to do physical action alone, without
the associated mental acts, is to reduce knowing to
doing as blind stimulus-response behavior. Neither is
the full Scriptural meaning of the act of knowing.
    The biblical model of knowing as an interaction
between the knower and the known is named by some
theologians as co-relation, in which the knower is in
the Truth, participating in it and walking in it.10
Others have called it a praxis theory of knowing,
interpreting the term as "reflective action, that is
practice that is informed by theoretical reflection, or
conversely, a theoretical reflection that is informed
by practice."11   Both of the above develop
extensively, more than is possible in this paper, the
scriptural and other kinds of documentation for the
position stated here.

Revelation and Knowing

    Revelation is a key term in theological talk
concerning epistemology. It refers to the whole area
of Christian concern about both nature and source of
truth or knowledge. Reformed thinkers have
distinguished between two means of revelation: general
and special. The latter refers to scripture and the
former refers to the physical creation and history.12
What has not been treated sufficiently is the question
of whether the two sources of knowledge call for
commitment to two methods. The thrust of this section
on holistic knowing is that a single generic method of
knowing is compatible with the biblical message and
will lead to a single generic classroom teaching method
that is most appropriate for teaching the young how to
know in an identifiably Christian way.
    All creation and not just Scripture are
potentially revelational, for, according to the
psalmist, the heavens declare the glory of God and the
firmament shows his handiwork (Psalm 19:1-6). In the
words of Romans 1:18-21 such revelation is available to
all men. Some, however, "suppress the truth by their
wickedness" even though "what may be known about God is
plain to them" (vs. 18 & 19). It should be noted in
the above that it is not lack of intellectual

capability which prevents some from knowing God, but
disobedience, i.e., an improper response. Thus
revelation occurs only in the coming together of
objective event and response. As one interpreter says
it:

> As we respond in unbelief...our
> discernment is clouded and our
> decision making is perverted. Only
> as we respond in faith...can we
> discern (know) clearly and decide
> rightly.14

Stated even more bluntly is the following:

> Because man is a religious being,
> all knowing necessarily involves
> obedience to the Word of God. Knowledge
> is not a matter of (cognitive) facts
> plus (attitudinal) values. All
> knowledge involves analytical
> distinction, but no more than it
> involves commitment to obedient action:
> we can only really speak of
> 'knowledge' when an integral
> subjection to the norms for
> human acting is involved.15

From none of the above is there any implication
that there is no place for propositional truth in
appropriating revelation. Intellectual insight is an
integral part of knowing but itself incomplete.
Propositions arise out of interaction, out of
encounter, rather than standing alone as knowledge.
They are derivative, not ultimate; they are a means and
not an end. When Job asserted, "I know that my
redeemer liveth", it was after the fact of encounter;
when Paul said, "And we know that in all things God
works for the good of those who love him...(Romans
8:28), it was not rational deduction but experienced
interaction. Neither is there an implication that
truth or revelation is not objective, existing
independently of the knower. The interactive,
encounter model set forth above holds that such
objective reality (the revelation) and the human
responder are two foci of a single process, with the
responder discovering or uncovering what is by what is
done to it. It is a rejection of the spectator view in
which the knower regards objective reality from afar
rather than out of encounter. It is also far from the

pragmatist's model of knowing in which the knower makes truth by testing its consequences. Noting of consequences is one element in the interactive model, but not the sole test of truth.

Steensma and Van Brummelen are instructive in noting how Scripture speaks in a language quite unlike that of Greek modes of knowing which have so pervasively affected Christian thinking on this matter:

> The understanding that present day Christians have of "know" and "knowing" is often unrelated to the meaning of these words as revealed in scripture... (it) has been influenced by philosophical inquiry, especially as it came from the Greeks. For them "to know" was to be involved in objective investigation apart from context,...apart from one's immediate experience. "Knowledge" for the Greeks was a fixed possession. It sought the essence of things, not the relationship of the person to that which could be known. This "knowledge" was outside the person; it contained no personal significance nor did it require personal commitment.16

In summary it has been argued that the method of knowing that is most compatible with the biblical revelation is one in which the usual dualisms of thinking and doing, cognition and action are rejected in favor of a single generic mode incorporating both. Knowing propositions, whether facts of history, theorems in geometry or knowing that a rock is hard and heavy are all partial or incomplete forms of knowing. They are subsumed under the interactive method of knowing, one in which the action on the known by the knower completes the act of knowing.

Assuming the validity of this interactive model, we can then seek to develop a generic classroom teaching method which can incorporate the various phases of knowing into one methodology.

HOLISTIC CLASSROOM METHODOLOGY

Classroom teaching methods are often portrayed as little more than sets of techniques for effecting learning, each having a different configuration of teacher and student behaviors. Thus there is the lecture method, the simulation method, the audiovisual method, the demonstration method, the inquiry method, the Socratic method, the activity method, just to name a few.

Some treatments of teaching method also assume that the nature of the subject dictates the method(s). Teacher training institutions and some state certification codes lend support to this impression by requiring methods courses in each of the several teaching areas or subjects.

At a higher level of generality teaching method is sometimes conceived of as containing elements which cut across all subjects in the curriculum. The terminology then suggests that all lessons should have such strategies as set induction, stimulus variation, planned repetition, and closure, for example. These are more generic teaching skills, and are presumably appropriate to any lesson, whatever the raw material or subject being taught. Whether the material is linguistic, mathematical, artistic, or literary the elements of the lesson are the same, with only minor variations in emphasis.

What all of the above lack is any generalized conception of knowing. While each have implicit assumptions about how learning best occurs, their defense is usually stated in terms of their respective motivational value or retention value. Psychology is taken to be the discipline which vindicates the methods, individually and severally. No attempt is generally made to find an epistemological grounding for selection from among them, or a framework into which to fit them.

Crucial to a search for a method of knowing which is generic enough to embrace all knowing is the distinction between methods and methodology. The former is plural, the latter singular; the former is a series of discrete teacher maneuvers which can be used in varying combinations as the situation demands; the latter is a single generic and normative flow which endorses some methods more than others. What is also crucial in such search is the distinction between mastery and the latter on the process governing valid thinking.

Secular philosophers of education have proposed a methodology, a series of classroom events, whose flow is peculiar to their philosophical commitment to a way of knowing. It typically contains phases or elements, in a succession or order that will culminate in knowledge, not just information or discrete learnings. Plato, for example, both conceived such a methodology and exhibited it in his various dialogues, the

55.

Republic and others. Called the Socratic method
after his teacher Socrates, it contains a flow of
question and dialogue that is not random discussion but
knowledge seeking. When the dialogue is ended the
pupil has knowledge, conceived Platonically.

Other philosophers of education have proposed
quite different methodologies as better ways of
knowledge getting, better ways of getting in touch with
reality, as their philosophical allegiances dictate.
Pragmatist John Dewey and realist Harry Broudy would be
examples.

What is a Christian educator, wishing to be true
to Scripture, to make of such options? One conclusion
surely is that a teaching methodology is no more
philosophically neutral than is an epistemology. Also,
individual strategies like the lecture method may find
their place within several methodologies, although even
these are accorded a different status. If individual
methods and strategies are not neutral, not value free,
surely even less so is a methodology, particularly if
such is the classroom equivalent of the preferred
epistemological method of knowing reality reliably.

The second thing Christian educators can learn
from the presence of competing methodologies is that
one can be adopted safely only if the epistemological
counterpart of the classroom methodology proposed by
others, whether it arises out of Platonic idealism,
Deweyan pragmatism, or Broudyan realism, is fraught
with the danger of inviting the Trojan horse into the
city of Jerusalem. That is not to say that such
philosophical parentage automatically discredits such
teaching methodologies. Because of common grace, all
have some vision of the created world and each has some
possibility of being congruent with the biblical view
of knowing and teaching.

What can be said with confidence, however, is that
acceptance or rejection of any overall classroom
strategy for teaching children how to think and know
Christianly must be congruent with the biblical view of
knowing. To do less than to construct our own is to
run the risk of behaving secularly. To adopt only
methods, without framework of methodology, is to reduce
teaching and learning to the level of psychological
devices for retaining bits and pieces of subject
matter. It is to ignore the potentiality in
methodology for deliberately inculcating in the youth a
process, a mode of thinking for lifelong acquiring of
knowledge in biblical perspective.

Stemming from the description of the biblical
model of knowing, classroom methodology is, I believe,

characterized by an interactive flow between the learner and some raw material, a give and take between the knower and the to-be-known.

The Three C Phases

Methodology can be divided into three phases, which will be called the consider, choose, and commit phases. While the sequence is not arbitrary, neither is it rigid and inflexible. Movements back and forth among them are not only permissible but desirable, and within each several specific methods can be used, whether it is lecture, discussion, field trip, or reading, not to mention simulation or audio-visual.

In the consider phase the learner is confronted with the new material. Exploratory definitions and distinctions are made, and attention is focused on the various dimensions of the material. Such initial exposure must be selected so as to be related to the learner's life experience or previous learnings, so that it can truly be encountered and not perceived, spectator-like, as from a distance and without chance of more than belief that some such entities exist. Whether the raw material is a mathematical concept, like place value, or a phenomenon like dew on the grass on some mornings, the consider phase begins the interaction by having the teacher relate it to the learner.

Such material may not even carry a science, art, or history label (except in the mind of the teacher) but will be labeled with an aspect of the life of the learner as the pupil has experienced it. This initial phase will more powerfully provoke the second phase if it carries with it some problematic, some unrevolved elements which do not by themselves make sense, but which call for resolution. If the biblical model of believing in such material is to prevail, then the initial phase must introduce each cycle of learning in a context which not only relates to present life, but stretches the learner beyond the now to the future. It must have the potential for differing responses, different value judgments about its worth, different ways to react to it, always assuming such different ways are not simply intellectual classification, such as that a horse is a four-footed animal without a split hoof. In brief, this initial phase must have an element of perplexity in it, where such perplexity is not merely intellectual incompleteness, but an unresolved tension that is felt.

57.

Without the careful selection of the curriculum
material to meet the above criteria, the movement to
the second phase is difficult if not impossible.
    The second phase is the choose phase. Here the
options for response are clarified and their
implications better understood. Here the moral
tensions are sharpened and the principles which govern
the options are studied in more detail. It is in this
phase that biblical data and directives are most
explicitly brought into play, again by any number of
specific techniques.
    If the first phase dramatizes what it is that
the learner faces, the second phase highlights whatever
oughts are involved, these often but not always being
biblical oughts. The movement from is to ought will
enhance the likelihood that the interactive model of
knowing will occur because now the biblical mandates
are part of the learning situation and they call for
obedient response. The biblical data function as
perspective giving, and not just as more facts or
pieces of information. Also in this phase not merely
narrowly moral considerations arise, but also
aesthetic, legal, scientific, and other principles
relevant to the subject matter. This phase of the
methodology may occupy the longest time of the three
phases, because deepening understanding, as well as
exposing alternative points of view, is time consuming.
It is here also that multiple methods of instruction
can be subsumed. The lecture method, the discussion
method, the explication of readings, the simulation
method, and even field trips take their place in the
flow of the three C phases. It is in this phase of the
total methodology that acceptance or rejection takes
place, and prepares for the final phase.
    The third phase is the commit phase. It moves
beyond intellectual understanding, beyond exposure of
the moral and other considerations, and toward
commitment to act on both the is and the ought. It
highlights the response part of the total methodology,
with response identified as both verbal and behavioral.
While not all school situations allow actual action,
the commitment to a form of action is the absolute
minimum. Without this phase the knowing consists of
knowing that many possibilities exist in the
abstract, of head knowledge which is the beginning but
not the end of knowing. This phase may be the briefest
of the three in terms of classroom time if the
preceding two phases have been thoroughly done. Should
the action response be possible within the classroom or
outside the school setting, then the time involvement

58.

may be a greater proportion of this cycle of learning.

A brief example of how this methodology would handle a given piece of curriculum content may be helpful to the classroom teacher. Although examples run the risk of being criticized or rejected on various grounds, the following is offered as that which reflects the spirit, if not the letter, of the proposed holistic method.

The raw material is the person of Abraham Lincoln as President, and it is imagined as part of a larger unit on "Authority: Its Power and Problems."

1. Consider phase

In this phase the student is confronted with the facts of Presidential action in the Civil war, with the focus on economic, political, and military aspects of that conflict. What is slowly brought to the fore for special scrutiny is the problem of slavery in such a conflict between North and South. It ends with the information and the reasons for issuing the Emancipation Proclamation. Lectures, readings, films, and pictures are used to bring to life whatever were the factors in the situation.

2. Choose phase

In this phase the discusssion method is used prominently to sharpen the choices such a President had, and the political and moral dimensions of each. Then a version of the simulation method is used to make the historical question a personal, moral question: Should he have freed the slaves? What norms for society does the biblical vision exhibit for both peace and justice in any society, then and now?

Here the new content added is whatever biblical episodes or passages are relevant to the racial question, and the debate method can be used to highlight the possible biblical positions.

3. Commit phase

In this phase each student is asked to apply the principles in the choose phase in his/her own position on social questions like equal opportunity among races, intermarriage among races, and racial integration in schools. Individual decisions on what action one would follow in each would end the lesson.

The lesson is by no means teachable as it is outlined, particularly because the crucial factor

of the age or grade level is not specified. It is
given only to show the flow of such a holistic
methodology. The flow is intended to reveal the
necessary interaction of thought and action,
thinking and doing.

Method and Goals

Each of these phases can be related to the goals
of Christian education as they have been articulated in
Reformed thinking about schooling. Christian Schools
International has identified three distinct but
interacting goals: intellectual, decisional, and
creative. Each is an identifiable dimension of a
single goal of preparing the student to live the
Christian life. They may in summary be distinguished
as follows:

1. **Intellectual** dimension, focusing on
   achieving a grasp of states of affairs, what
   is.

2. **Decisional** dimension, focusing on achieving
   decisions where choice can be made based on
   relevant norms or standards, what ought to be.

3. **Creative** dimension, focusing on achieving
   life responses to both what is and what ought
   to be.[17]

Sometimes these goals are perceived as achieved
separately, in different areas of the curriculum, with
math perhaps featuring the first in clearest form,
religion the second, and physical education the third.
Such perceptions wrench apart what should be kept
whole, if the holistic nature of the learner and of
knowing is to be honored. All subject matter, if
taught Christianly, should be taught to achieve all
three, if not simultaneously at least sequentially. It
is here that the proposed methodology of the three C's
makes its contribution.

The proposed holistic methodology, if followed,
would keep all three goals together, with each phase of
the methodology making its unique contribution. The
first phase, the consider phase, lends itself best to
the intellectual dimension, and the choose phase lends
itself to the decisional dimension, with the
culmination in the commit phase lending itself to the
creative dimension.

What holds together the various curricular
materials, then, are the three goals and the three

phases of the generic methodology, which unites
whatever raw materials are being presented. While
clarification of each of the three dimensions can and
should go on,18 the holistic methodology would
provide the practical expression of their relationship
to each other. It holds together the triad of goals,
curriculum, and method which is a prerequisite of any
well rounded conceptions of teaching.

What remains is to indicate briefly what the
holistic view of man, the holistic view of knowing, and
the holistic view of classroom method signal about
curriculum content and organization.

HOLISTIC CURRICULUM

Curriculum materials can and have been packaged in
various ways. From the trivium and quadrivium of the
Greeks and Romans to the seven liberal arts of the
Middle Ages, and down to the proliferation of
disciplines and subjects of today's curriculum,
revisionists have all tried to take the encyclopedia of
possible knowledge and to divide it into a given number
of packages for learning in schools.

The curriculum of today's school is by now a
curious mixture of the old and the new, with new
contenders always jostling for a place in the school
day. Those who seek "basic education" want to reduce
the multiplicity of possibilities to a limited number
of generative subjects. Those who seek "relevant
education" seek to add to or alter these basics.

What is a Christian educator, who wishes to think
Christianly, to make of such a discordant symphony? In
the search for a curriculum that is distinctly
Christian, the educator runs the risk again of being
merely imitative, and in so doing inviting into the
walled city of Jerusalem the Trojan horses of the enemy
of secularism, idealism, or pragmatism. None of these
will do.

What many attempts at making curriculum distinctly
Christian suggest is that the Christian view of life is
to be integrated into the curriculum. Both publicity
brochures and serious essays speak of giving a
Christian perspective on life and learning. All agree
that some sort of fusion between Christian values and
subject matter is to take place, and that in some sense
the Bible is the center of integrated curriculum.

61.

Meanings of Integration

In one meaning of integration the academic disciplines are left in place and the teacher, with the assistance of Christian textbooks and other resources, adds a Christian interpretation or assessment to such subjects. Locating in God the order and beauty of mathematics, and the intricacy and design of the physical world in science are given as ways that the integration takes place. So too in history and social studies, Christian assessment of cultural practices or forms of government can occur in teacher resource or textbook talk.[19]

Thus the same academic subjects as in secular education are baptized by sprinkling (a very Reformed concept) with evaluations or interpretations, thus effecting an integration of Christian faith and subject matter. A committee of Christian scholars has indicated at least seven "ways in which the biblical revelation may give structure and direction to our work in the discipline."[20] All seven ways they describe indicate both the extent and complexity of this interpretation of integrating faith and learning, but they all assume the disciplines to be individually the framework within which such integration takes place.

A quite different view of integration is one in which the subject matter is chosen because it cuts across the academic disciplines.[21] Integration of the various disciplines into a new curriculum topic or subject is achieved by selecting some organizing rubric which by its nature calls for interdisciplinary content. For example the subject would be ecology or environment, but its content would not be limited to biology or botany; it would include political, social, and economic matters, each selected for its relevance to the problem of man and environment. The integration of the Christian perspective would operate at two levels: one in the choice of the organizing topic, and the other in the inclusion of biblical principles as part of the content.

Both of the above meanings given to the integration principle have their proponents and are well-intentioned attempts to honor the principle that the Christian faith should be operative in curriculum building.

While the above brief description of the two views of integration does not do full justice to either of them, our purpose here is to assess their major thrust in the light of the holistic theory of man, knowing, and classroom method outlined earlier.

To review briefly, such holistic conception would seek a curriculum content and organization that would most likely engage not just the intellect of the learner, but the will and the body as well. Such content and organization should also make it likely that the knowledge gained is the kind where action and doing are a constant and necessary ingredient., Finally, to honor the holistic methodology, the curriculum content should be the kind in which the full range of the phases of consider, choose, and commit can be incorporated again and again in each cycle of learning.

A Curriculum of Concerns

The second meaning of integration, in which the focus of units or courses is a perennial human problem and which cuts across the disciplines, seems a more likely candidate for fulfilling the demands of the preceding holistic epistemology and methodology of instruction. When the organizing rubric under which content is organized is a perennial human concern, adjusted to age level, then by its very nature it is value laden, and filled with ambiguities and alternative resolutions. Resolution of conflict points always toward action and life style, even when the school situation does not allow actual lifestyle follow up. It points toward discipleship and obedience because the curriculum is so organized that the topic cannot be confronted only intellectually, and the learnings cannot be just beliefs that such and such are the facts or theories of the matter. Moreover the Christian perspective is a central and not a tangential concern, or footnote addition to an otherwise self-contained discipline. The material is not baptized by sprinkling but by immersion in a Christian concern.

A full description and defense, both pedagogically and psychologically, cannot be given here. The case being made is that it comports best with a philosophical perspective, a Christian one. Psychological evidence would point toward its greater motivation and retention possibilities, towards a more likely adoption of a Christian perspective on life by the learner. Such evidence would also point to the power of teacher modelling Christian concern as well as modelling how Christians come to know.

This essay has provided a case for a holistic view of knowing as seen in biblical perspective. The curriculum and classroom method counterparts have been included to show that all aspects of schooling are affected by such a theory. It is given to encourage

Christian educators to making their teaching even more distinctly and consistently Christian.

End Notes

1. The following reflect a holistic view, with
    variations. Geraldine Steensma, "The First
    Key," in To Those Who Teach (Terre Haute,
    Indiana: Signal Publishing Co., 1971);
    Norman De Jong, "The Organic Unity of Man,"
    in Education in the Truth. (Nutley, New
    Jersey: Presbyterian and Reformed Publishing
    Co., 1969); G. C. Berkouwer. Man, The Image
    of God (Grand Rapids, Mich.: Eerdmans
    Publishing Co., 1962) pp. 194-207. Such a
    view is also evident in Paul Ramsey, Basic
    Christian Ethics (New York: Charles
    Scribners, 1952) pp. 249-259. See also
    Human Development, Learning and Teaching
    (Grand Rapids, Michigan: Eerdmans Publishing
    Co., 1961), p. 43ff; Arnold De Graff and James
    Olthuis (eds.) Toward a Biblical View of Man.
    (Toronto, Ontario: Institute for Christian
    Studies, 1978), p. 1.

2. See John Brubacher, Modern Philosophies of
    Education New York: McGraw-Hill Book Company,
    1962), pp. 74-86 and 89-95 for a discussion of
    disputes between coherence and correspondence
    theories.

3. See Philip Holtrop, "Toward a Biblical Conception
    of Truth and a New Mood for Doing Reformed
    Theology," Theological Forum (of the Reformed
    Ecumenical Synod) Vol. V, No. 2 (June, 1977).

4. Nicholas Wolterstorff. Reason Within the Bounds
    of Religion (Grand Rapids, Michigan: Eerdmans
    Publishing Company, 1976). In this work
    foundationalism is the view described in the paper
    as a spectator theory.

5. For a general critique of foundationalism and its
    inadequacies from a Reformed perspective see Alvin
    Plantinga, "On Reformed Epistemology," in The
    Reformed Journal, January, 1982, pp. 13-16; see
    also his "The Reformed Objection to Natural
    Theology," in Christian Scholar's Review, Vol.
    XI, No. 3 (1982).

6. Jerry Gill. The Possibility of Religious
    Knowledge (Grand Rapids, Michigan: Eerdmans

Publishing Company, 1971), p. 121. See also his
On Knowing God (Philadelphia, Penn.: The
Westminister Press, 1981), p. 95.

7.   See, for elaboration of this point Philip
     Holtrop, "A Strange Language: Toward a
     Biblical Conception of Truth," The
     Reformed Journal, February, 1977, pp. 9-13.

8.   H. H. Price, "Belief 'In' and Belief 'That'",
     Religious Studies, October, 1965, pp. 5-27.

9.   Nicholas Wolterstorff. Curriculum By What
     Standard? (Grand Rapids, Michigan: National
     Union of Christian Schools, 1966) p. 10.

10. See, for the best treatment of such a theologian,
     Steve Prediger, Truth and Knowledge in G. C.
     Berkouwer: The Contours of His Epistemology
     (Toronto, Ontario: Institute for Christian
     Studies, 1982).

11. Thomas H. Groome, Christian Religious Education
     (San Francisco, CA: Harper and Row, 1980),
     p. XVII. See also Chapter Seven, "In Search of a
     'way of knowing' for Christian Religious
     Education" for his elaboration of Praxis theory.

12. For a simplified summary of this doctrine see
     Louis Berkhof, Manual of Reformed Doctrine
     (Grand Rapids, Michigan: Eerdmans Publishing
     Company, 1933), pp. 23-26. For a more elaborate
     treatment of general revelation see G. C.
     Berkouwer, General Revelation (Grand Rapids,
     Michigan: Eerdmans Publishing Company, 1955).

13. Nature, Man, and God, p. 314.

14. Stuart Fowler in No Icing on the Cake, edited by
     Jack Mechielsen (Melbourne, Australia: Brookes-
     Hall Publishing Foundation, 1980) p. 29.

15. Douglas Blomberg, Ibid, p. 51.

16. G. Steensma and H. Van Brummelen (eds.) Shaping
     School Curriculum: A Biblical View (Terre
     Haute, Indiana: Signal Publishing Co., 1977)
     p. 5.

17. _Principles to Practice_ (Grand Rapids, Michigan: Christian Schools International, 1979) p. 1.

18. See Henry Triezenberg, "Up with Decisional Learning," _Christian Educators Journal_, November, 1976, pp. 23 ff. For further proposed clarification and revision of the taxonomy see Nicholas Wolterstorff, _Educating for Responsible Action_ (Grand Rapids, Michigan: Eerdmans Publishing Company, 1982).

19. For concrete application of this meaning of integration see the Christian Perspective on History series, published by Christian Schools International from 1973-76. For its application to the subject of civics see William Hendricks _Under God_ (Grand Rapids, Michigan: CSI Publications, Fourth edition, 1981). In this latter text there is persistence assessment of social policy from a Christian perspective, usually in the form of raising questions.

20. Calvin College Curriculum Study Committee, _Christian Liberal Arts Education_ (Grand Rapids, Michigan: Calvin College, Eerdmans Publishing Company, 1970) p. 59-60.

21. G. Steensma and H. Van Brummelen, _Shaping School Curriculum: A Biblical View_ (Terre Haute, Indiana: Signal Publishing Company, 1977). See especially chapter 6, "A Design for Elementary and Secondary Curriculum." See also Norman DeJong, _Education in the Truth_ (Nutley, New Jersey: Presbyterian and Reformed Publishing Company, 1969), Chapter II.

Chapter 5

KINDS AND CONTEXTS OF KNOWING

by

Maarten Vrieze
Professor of Philosophy
Trinity Christian College

At a conference of educators, every self-respecting presentation comments on the nature of education. This presentation is no exception. My remarks form a chain: one comment leads to another. The final link concerns the plurality of human knowing. Authentic education is possible in our society, but only on the condition that a) human knowing has the central place in it, and b) the plurality of that knowing is consistently respected.

Reflection on education is never done in a vacuum. It involves the reflecting in conflict and controversy. Education as it actually takes place in the many different schools is the scene of a fierce battle for power in and over society. There is a realization that whoever is in control of education is in control of the youth, and that he who controls a society's youth controls that society's future. One does not right away have to think of a Hitler or a Mao, for there are strategies different from the ones they employed. Ideological control of a society's education is often much more subtle, and much less spectacular, than what happened in Mao's China or Hitler's Germany. Critical reflection, however, presents a very serious threat to ideology. Critical is: to reach for foundations, to penetrate to roots in order to expose them, to unmask what hides behind the slogans, the practices, the convictions and beliefs. Our reflecting on education ought to be critical, aware of ideology, and out to break its hold.

First a remark about the nature of education. There is a close connection between what the western world believes that human knowing is and the way it educates its younger generation. Way back in our Greek past a contrast was created between what was to count as true knowing and what was to count as merely pseudo-knowing. That what approached the ideal of theoria, that curious seeing-with-your-eyes-closed of what was "real" and "actual" and "indestructible," was to count

69.

as true knowing, while one's experiencing-with-your-eyes-wide-open of what was constantly changing was to count, at best, as belief. That old contrast never totally disappeared from western thought; it still serves to value the scientist in his irrefutable and conclusive knowing over everyday's man in everyday's street. Still, it has had to yield to the modern contrast between the know-how of praxis and action, a knowing directed at mastery and control, and the many forms of knowing that lack that direction. Logical identification in the service of, and with a view to, technical grasp and comprehension, is the kind of knowledge that we moderns seek and cherish. Its progress excited us. Possessing it we feel secure, lacking it we feel threatened. With it we dare to face our individual and collective futures. For it we educate.

There are those in the world of education who, indeed, view education as a matter of control. The pupils who have gone through the kind of education that they practice are the ones who in the end know how to use and how to be used. Secular usage speaks of pupils who use their "natural abilities" to realize themselves and so to become "useful" citizens. A more biblical usage speaks of "talents" that need to be developed. The theme, however, is the same: both educator and pupil search for know-how, for knowing as mastery. Distinctive is the presupposition that <u>one is what one is</u>, and that <u>one can become only that what one already was</u> from the beginning. The educator who is good at what he does has the know-how that is needed to have pupils develop into what they already were: the multi-talented ones maturing into useful users of their many talents, the single-talented ones evolving as productive users of their one talent. The norm that directs this kind of education is derived from what suggestively is called the given. Educational research has "discovered" certain more or less stable patterns in the lives of children, and these must now serve as guidelines for the educator: what is the case = what should be the case. One could speak here of an organismic model; what the educator does is what one does in the nurturing of any organism.[1]

There are others who, even though they too view education as a matter of control, have different ideas about education. The organismic model, they feel, seriously underestimates the possibilities open to human mastery. Children do not "naturally" possess talents or abilities. In fact, they do not have any talents unless education provides them. Education is

the art of making people talented, or better: the
technique of constructing people with abilities and
possibilities. It is the construction of the useful
citizen, of the morally right Christian, or of whatever
else it is that we may choose as our educational
objective. A mechanistic model?

It is not my intention to elaborate on the various
movements or ideas in education with the help of these
models or metaphors. Instead, I ask what it is about
education that lends itself to the use of these models
and metaphors. Apparently, education has dimensions
that make it possible to absolutize as in organicism or
mechanicism. In other words, notions as growth,
maturing, evolving, developing, formation,
construction, and so on, are really more than
metaphors: they are legitimate analogies of the biotic
and technical dimensions of life in the act of
education.2 One nurtures a plant and one forms a
piece of pottery. In education, one does not nurture
that way and one does not form that way, but there are
aspects of education that make it possible to speak of
education as nurturing, and of education as forming.
The notions of nurturing and forming now receive a
distinctive modification, a characteristic twist. The
question is: what is that distinctive character of
education?

To clarify why I answer that question the way I
answer it, I first have to say something about the
perspective from within which I approach matters. By
perspective I do not mean that what I, standing in a
particular historic tradition, see, accept, expect,
understand, etc., but rather that what makes me see
what I see, understand what I understand, choose what I
choose. Perspective is that which discloses my
situation to me, that which directs me and makes me
take sides in my situation. In a way, perspective is
what the headlights of my car are when I drive through
a dark forest: they throw a beam of light on the road
ahead and thus enable me to distinguish what is there.
I stand within a perspective as within a light beam:
it illuminates my existence, my situation, my world,
and thus enables me to orient myself.

In the perspective within which I stand I
experience reality not only as a world created by a
living God, but very specifically as something of which
it would be totally insufficient to say that it is. I
have to add at least that what is, is in the manner of
meaning, in the manner of response. That is true of
all creation, including man. In his case we speak of
such meaning and responding as religion. It is impor-

71.

tant to recognize that: it implies that man is not just hanging around in his world, but is always engaged in meaning, in responding. It is his very nature, the very structure of his existence, to respond. Man is response creature.

It is not easy to give an adequate characteristic of the contents of the human response. We may speak of it as the human mandate, but one of its exciting dimensions is that even the charting of the mandate seems to belong to the mandate! Man is apparently called to take the initiatives and even to set the historic course! However that may be, it would seem obvious that the mandate claims all human beings everywhere, in all their many different communalities and solidarities. More than that, the mandate reaches across the generations to include them all. It is a mandate that can be completed only on the condition that every generation takes its place and does its share. I want to emphasize this here, for it implies that it is an essential dimension of the mandate that every generation has to engage in opening the door for the next one, receiving it, accepting it, incorporating it into the existing response communalities, and allowing it to situate itself in its historic place. A task has to be accomplished and an important part of what has to be done is to introduce a new generation to the task and to the situation in which it must be completed.

There is something entirely unique about human existence: new human beings enter into a historic situation that then becomes also their situation, into communalities that then become also their communalities, into a mandate that then also becomes their mandate, into responsibilites that then become also their responsibilites. Such an entry asks for ethical consideration.

Introduction is the appropriate term here. Every new generation needs to be (ethically) introduced so that it is able to orient itself, to assume its responsibilites, and to shoulder its task. This throws light on the distinctive character of education. If introduction of a new generation is an implication of the ethical dimension of the human mandate, then we may characterize that what we today call education as the ethically qualified accompanying, guiding, and leading of the members of a new generation when it enters into its historic task (the response), the human communalities of all different kinds (the response contexts), and the historic situation (what mankind's response so far has brought about).

Education understood in this manner has human knowing at its very center.3

The Bible often makes a unique use of the word knowing. When the author of Exodus describes what actually happened at the decisive moment at which God committed himself for good to a group of slaves, called Israelites, in ancient Egypt he says that God knew them. The curious use of the word knowing bends its way beyond what we usually mean when we use it. It opens a vista upon a God who gets himself involved in the blood and tears, grief and suffering that marks human life, a God who links his life to theirs. Knowing in the sense of getting irreversibly and integrally involved is not only used for what God does, but also for what people do, or fail to do.4 The author of Genesis, for example, when he tells the story of the first people and pictures how, in spite of everything that had happened, they remained deeply involved in each other's life, so that they even had their child, Cain, sums it all up in the simple remark that Adam knew his wife.5 When Jeremiah sees the astonishing corruption and exploitation in Judah and realizes that it is the way of life of people who do not want to link their lives to that of God, he characterizes what he sees by saying that the people refuse to know God.6 To know God, apparently, is to be caught up in God's commitment to his creation, in his concern with people, in his ideas of liberation and redemption, and to be radically "with Him." There is a theological expression one might use here: coram deo. The term implies that there is a Lebenslauf, a way of life and course of life, that one lives facing God and responding to Him.

I call attention to such uses of the word knowing because they bring out a dimension of human existence that makes it possible to say that human life in its broad and full sense of living before God and in the creational relationships that He established can be described as knowing. Man is not merely there. He is coram deo. His response is not inevitably chaotic, a confusion of unconnected moments. The pictures that Ecclesiastes draws of the brokenness of human life with a time for this and a time for that, so that human existence seems to be torn to pieces by a cruel incoherence, is revealing, but we should not ignore the point; namely, that man is simply unable to accept the disjuncture of life, the incoherence and disintegration of his existence, because God embedded the olaam in his heart.7 That means that God gives man the irresistible and irrepressible urge to seek the

wholeness of life, the integration of what otherwise
would seem discontinuous and unconnected. The
implication is: God picks up the pieces.8 There is
a knowing of God in coherence, as Lebenslauf. This
knowing coram deo is not strictly individual. Man
stands within a multiplicity of communalities and
solidarities in and with which he responds. We
could say that he exists coram deo cum hominibus, but
even that would not be saying enough. In his knowing
man is, both individually and communally, involved in
the unfolding of God's creation. The expression,
therefore, should be amended at least so that man's
knowing is characterized as a knowing coram deo,
cum hominibus, in mundo.9 Education is the
(ethical) introduction to this kind of knowing. It is
the kind of knowing the fulfillment of the human
mandate calls for. Only the education that aims at
this kind of knowing can be counted as authentic.
     In everyday life we seldom use the word knowing in
this fundamental sense. Its "everyday meanings" are
quite diverse: from having heard of to being familiar
with, from awareness to know-how, from erudition to
appreciation, from insight and comprehension to simple
experience. It is essential that one is clear about
this diversity of kinds of knowing. If education is
the introduction to life as knowing in a full and
encompassing sense, then it is extremely important to
include it among those diverse forms of knowing. Where
could we find a vantage point from where one has a
clear view of the many different kinds and forms of
knowing?
     What is sometimes called 'Calvinistic philosophy'
provides us with an effective tool - the so-called
modal analysis - that enables us to gain a sharp
picture of the diversity of knowing. It is here not
the place to offer a detailed account of this modal
analysis. It will be sufficient to note that it is
possible for abstracting reflection to distinguish a
number of entirely unique and mutually irreducible
fundamental modes in which any possible entity exists.
Some of these modes of being are such that in them man
confronts directives that force him to choose and to
decide. In the confrontation he 'translates' such
directives into norms and/or norm complexes that hold
in and for the concrete situation in which he finds
himself. It is the diversity of these response-
evoking modes of being that points the way in our
survey of kinds of knowing. It enables us to make a
number of critically important distinctions.

Awareness of the differentiation of modes of being
enables us to differentiate between various broad
categories of knowing, each characterized by the
peculiar position which a mode of being holds in the
structure of an act of knowing. Thus we can
distinguish between the following categories:
logical, or analytical, knowing, e.g. the scientist
    who grasps a theoretic connection or coherence;
technical knowing, e.g. the engineer who knows his
        material, the stress it can endure, the load it
        can carry, etc.;
lingual knowing, e.g. the interpreter who knows the
        color of an expression, the meaning of a gesture,
        etc.;
social knowing, e.g. the guest who knows his place,
        the visitor who knows his manners, etc.;
economic knowing, e.g. the business man who knows
        that a particular product is more valuable than
        another in a given transaction, and who knows
        that a particular deal is profitable, etc.;
aesthetic knowing, e.g. the art lover who knows his
        Picasso, the music lover who understands her
        Brahms;
jural knowing, e.g. a judge who knows that a
        particular act is unfair, or that a given
        sentence is just, etc.;
ethical knowing, e.g. the nurse who knows what a
        particular patient needs or a parent who knows
        how to comfort a frightened child, etc.;
pistical knowing, e.g. "I know that my Redeemer
        liveth..."10

A second distinction allows us to distinguish
further between various kinds of logical knowing.
There are in each mode of being moments that mirror the
other modes of being. In the logical mode of being we
distinguish, therefore, moments as logical quantity,
logical extension, logical acceleration, logical force,
logical development, logical awareness, logical
identification, logical exchange, logical accord,
logical order, logical consistency, logical certainty,
and the like.
A third distinction is now possible between
moments in the logical mode of being that have been
individualized in distinct, concrete acts of knowing
and moments as dimensions of concrete non-logical
acts of human knowing in which such dimensions are
subservient to the non-logical function that qualifies
the structure of such an act.

Other distinctions, of the same kind and along the same lines, are possible and systematic philosophy regards it its business to make those. That does not mean that the philosopher dreams them up. It merely means that he comes across an enormous diversity of kinds of knowing and recognizes the criteria of their differentiation. The three distinctions that I have mentioned are already sufficient for our discussion. They provide us with an awareness of the hundreds of structurally different kinds of knowing. I emphasize that the diversity of knowing is a structurally conditioned one. In other words, the differentiation of human knowing is due to the Creator's structuring of reality. That structuring guarantees each one of the hundreds of kinds and facets of knowing its indestructible identity.

When we take a close look at those different kinds and forms of knowing in its everyday sense, it strikes us that they are all taken up within the encompassing knowing that I discussed earlier. In a way, the encompassing knowing differentiates into the multiplicity of forms of everyday knowing.11 That has implications. One implication is that each kind of knowing is directed by, and seeks its place within, the encompassing knowing. Another, that knowing, in whatever form, or of whatever kind, is never static, never 'complete-and-therefore-at-a-standstill,' but always in tension, always 'on the move.' To know is not: to have access to a stockpile of data or bits of information as in what is mistakenly called the computer's memory: push the right key and the data appear on the screen. Knowing in every one of its forms and facets is dynamic, reaching out both to what lies in the ever-new past and to what lies ahead in the not-yet-there of tomorrow. Knowing Brahms, knowing the one you love, knowing a classical language, understanding the theoretical construct, grasping the reach of justice, realizing the scope of a creed, all that is not a matter of a static storing of data, but a matter of dynamically searching for greater depth, a further reach, the surprise and the responsibility of the new and unexplored. That's where the Lebenslauf comes to full expression.

There's more to be said about the plurality of knowing. Knowing is always the knowing of people, and people are, by the very structuring of their existence, always both individual and communal. In much sociological and pseudo-sociological reflection it is customary to focus attention upon a contrast between "the individual" and "the community" or "the society."

76.

The result is that the theorist gets caught in a
vicious circle: either the individual must be
identified in terms of the community, but that leaves
the community as something unidentifiable, or the
community must be identified in terms of the
individual, but that leaves the individual unidentified
and unidentifiable.[12] In either case, one is forced
to arbitrarily absolutize one side or the other of the
dilemma. Here the frustration of a closed world
picture really shows: within a closed world it is
simply unavoidable to be caught in such a
pseudo-dilemma and its vicious circle.[13] Only when,
so to speak, the roof caves in on the closed world is
there a possibility of escape from the dilemma. In a
biblical perspective it is not possible to contrast man
with society. Man's existence is structured so that he
is both personal and communal. He is response being
and his responding is directed from the heart of his
existence. Because of that, his being a person-with-a-
heart, he is unable to shift the responsibility for his
actions to someone else. And yet, his existence is so
structured that what he does, he always does in
communality, as a member of a multiplicity of societal
configurations. Each one of these communalities is a
context of some kind, a response community. Such
communalities are not merely logical, or even lingual,
constructs, the products of some sociologist's
admirable imagination. A communality is an entity, of
a unique kind, given with the structuration of created
reality. That structuration guarantees the communality
its identity and its distinctive structure. In the
approach to social philosophic and sociological
theorizing within the neo-calvinist tradition, an
attempt has been made to account for the plurality and
diversity of societal configurations and associations,
the multiplicity of structural principles and of
variable structurations that are the historical
consequences of the staging of societal differentiation
and of the phenomenon of intertwinement.[14] Important
here is the realization that the immense diversity of
societal configurations, precisely because each
communality is a response community and, therefore,
also a knowing community, increases and complicates
the plurality and diversity of human knowing almost
beyond comprehension.[15] Human knowing is a knowing
in, and with, the communalities in which we have
our place as a member. A communality knows in it
members: the company clerk in whose knowing of long
lists of amounts and figures, of profits and losses,
the company knows its financial state of affairs, or

77.

the church that believes in the believing, and
confesses in the confessing, of its members. Each
societal configuration gives its own distinctive color
and character to the knowing of its members. Each
societal configuration, thus, complicates the diversity
of knowing. That overwhelms.

The fact that any attempt to visualize the immense
diversity of human knowing frustrates theoretical
imagination is not a good reason to turn to a kind of
simplicity that according to popular American myth is a
mark of truth. On the contrary, the educator who
strives for authentic education has to derive
encouragement from the realization that the diversity
is structurally conditioned and that to recognize and
respect it is one of the best defenses against the
pressures of ideology.[16]

The question is whether in the face of such an
overwhelming diversity we should not concede that at
least in our time and in our society the task of
authentic education has gone beyond what the (average)
educator can handle. It would seem that if education
is as I sketched it, it calls for a society better
prepared than ours for the reception of a new
generation, one drastically different from ours in
orientation and organization. This is not the place to
offer a diagnosis of our time and society. It is
sufficiently obvious that the educator confronts a
society in which societal configurations are so
constituted and organized that they almost inevitably
swallow up, rather than ethically receive, the newcomer
and rob him or her from that exciting responsibility
that comes with authentic partnership and communality.
A society that has apparently yielded control to
(personified) impersonal pseudo-entities as "the market
mechanism," "the democratic process," "science," "the
media," "the system," and the like, and thus
illustrates how far it has gone along the road of
technicalization and the absolutizing of the economic
dimension of life, is hardly the place in which the
educator will be able truly to introduce the pupil:
any introducing in, and to, such a society looks more
like handing over people to the depersonalizing
forces of a no longer personal society.[17] The school
is now forced into the "as if" game: "Let's do as if
you were in the world of...What would you do in such
and such a case?" Such 'games' force children into the
role of uncommitted spectator and onlooker, a role that
once adopted is difficult to give up.[18] They compel
the educator to ignore the multifaceted character of
human knowing. Games lack the actual confrontation

with the matters that are really at stake in life. They lack the confrontation with true consequences, true choices, true obedience, as well as with the religious antithesis, actual evil, and actual ideology.

But what if the educator cannot even legitimately resort to such "as if" game-methods? It brings the conflict into the classroom. My question is whether it is not the time once again to focus upon - but this time in an end-of-the-20th-century-manner - the antithesis in education. It is no longer the "time of the fathers," with its questionless and self-evident set of "principles" and its unproblematic world and life view.[19] Still, there is the reality of a leveling of human knowing as never before and of ideology as instrument against any reformation of human life and human society. In education choosing sides can not be avoided any longer. There simply _is_ an antithesis. Who am I to impose my position upon the pupil whom I as educator introduce to the task, the situation, and the communality? Here is one of the most urgent issues in our day.[20] It requires again a particular kind of knowing to tackle it.

NOTES

1. Theodor Litt's well-known differentiation between fuhren and wachsen lassen which lies behind this differentiation between the models of organicism and mechanicism still deserves attention.

2. A systematic discussion of analogical moments in the theorizing on education, in P. G. Schoeman, <u>An Introduction to a Philosophy on Education</u> (Durban - Pretoria: Butterworth, 1980).

3. I prefer to approach education by focusing on knowing rather than on learning and teaching. Between teacher and learner in education there is the curious interaction that results in the teacher also learning and the learner also teaching.

4. Cf. e.g. Exodus 2:25, or Deuteronomy 9:24.

5. Genesis 4:1.

6. Jeremiah 9:6, and 22:16.

7. Ecclesiastes 3:11.

8. Ecclesiastes 3:15 "...und Gott sucht wieder auf was vergangen ist."

9. I use the word mundus here in the customary sense of <u>orbis terrarum</u> with perhaps even a suggestion towards its meaning in expressions as <u>mundus triplex</u> or <u>mundus triformis</u>.

10. I emphasize that I am speaking here of broad <u>categories</u> of knowing. It is obviously possible to differentiate further within each of these categories. In systematic philosophy one speaks of secundary, tertiary, etc. analogical moments.

11. I use the term differentiation with hesitation: when I add up the various kinds of everyday knowing I do not find the encompassing knowing. The latter rather encompasses, conditions, integrates, and thus stimulates the former.

12. I discussed this in some detail in my <u>Nadenken over de samenleving</u> (Amsterdam: Buijten en Schipperheijn, 1977), pp. 11 ff.

13. Closed world actually means: a world turned in upon itself, a world that has closed itself off from God.

14. By "the staging of societal differentiation" I mean that societal differentiation appears to go through various stages or phases. The term stage, or phase, should be used with some reserve, however. Cf. my <u>Nadenken over de samenleving</u>, pp. 167 ff.

15. A fascinating and extremely intriguing analysis offers George Gurvitch, <u>Les cadres sociaux de la connaissance</u> (Paris: Presses universitaire de France, 1966), esp. pp. 68 ff.

16. One ever-present feature of ideology is its pseudo-innocent ignoring of the (dynamic) structuring of created reality. The simplicity myth itself is an obvious example.

17. Structurally, a society is a patterned intertwinement of dynamically functioning societal configurations of all kinds. That does not mean that it is impersonal. On the contrary, the communities that intertwine in their diverse configurations are human communalities, existing in the personal and communal functioning of their members.

18. The spectator attitude is forced upon western man in his schools. The standardization that followed the peculiar marriage of technique and scientific attitude - techno-logy - and the mass phenomena that came with it at the same time - mass media, mass organization, etc. - are in their continued existence to a large extent dependent upon western man's willingness to stand aside as the spectator.

19. From the unproblematic world and life view we have now, it would seem, gone to the <u>absence</u> of "fathers" and the lack of a coherent view of life.

20. The educator stands <u>with</u> the pupil in the communality: to introduce is to <u>together</u> enter in, to <u>together</u> get caught up in; the school

as ethical communality of pupils and teachers
exists only in continuous interaction with
concrete historic society: both teacher and pupil
take sides in that interaction.

Chapter 6

LIVING & LEARNING:

A MATTER OF PERSPECTIVE

by

John H. Kok
Visiting Professor of Philosophy
Dordt College

"Live and learn!": not only the way you say it
makes a difference. Is it with a skeptical shrug of
the shoulders; or with the determination that learning
will (some day) open the door to life; or with the
confidence of one who knows he is cared for?
What one maintains life is all about has
consequences for what one says learning is all about.
So also for the Christian. That is why it makes good
sense also to take time to think and talk together
about the reciprocal relationship of living and
learning; about our being Christians and our
approach(es) to learning theory. Learning and learning
theory, of course, are two different but related
matters. In turning our attention to these matters it
will be good, first of all, not to forget that what we
hold to be the meaning of life is, just like what
others say living is all about, something we have
learned or come to know. Secondly, we come to know
what life is all about without ever thinking about
learning theory.
With that introduction the three points which I
would like to briefly discuss have been given: namely,
living, learning, and theory about learning. In doing
so I would, in addition to specifically addressing the
first two formulated questions of this conference, like
to suggest and give some support for the thesis that
learning is basically a matter of distinguishing what
is different in its context.
Before proceeding, however, just a word regarding
the term "theory about learning": I prefer it for its
clarity and certainty in comparison to others used.
Let me explain.
"Learning theory" is a term clear enough in its
generality, and yet in being so is also ambiguous.

83.

Learning after all is an activity, a human activity.
If we are then to talk about Christian approaches to
learning theory, what stops us from taking this to mean
our diverse ways of coming to know theory, be it a
particular theory or theory(ies) in general?

Convention or consensus, combined with intonation,
you may say: learning theory is a matter of the
theory of learning, like political theory is a matter
of the theory of (doing) politics. In other words,
what we are doing is discussing Christian approaches to
the theory of learning. Are we not all Christians and
are we not discussing our approaches to the theory of
learning? Or is it rather that we are discussing
Christian approaches (Christianity allowing for more
than one approach) to the theory of learning? These
are questions which deserve our attention.

But when, for the moment, we leave the predicate
"Christian" out of the picture, it must be the case
that what are at issue are our approaches to the theory
of learning.

But what is "the theory of learning" (or "learning
theory", if you prefer) that we are approaching? Is
there such a thing? I would say not, unless we want to
look for some lowest common denominator among all the
various theories and give it this name. From the
leading questions which this conference is to address
it is also obvious, in spite of their ambiguity, that
we are not here to simply discuss our approaches to
various and sundry theories of learning, be they
Peter's, Paul's or Mary's. No, if I see it correctly,
we are here to discuss our approaches to a Christian
theory of learning or at least our approaches to (the)
Christian theories of learning. We want to be busy
here, not just in a negative way: rejecting this and
that theory, in this part or that, with an eye to the
remainder after we are done subtracting. Nor is it a
matter of our wanting to be eclectic: picking and
choosing pleasingly palpable results from the labyrinth
of theories, with no eye to their compatability, but
yet trying to do so in light of what we believe as
Christians.

If it is then a matter of our approaches either to
a Christian theory of learning or to the Christian
theories of learning, that has our attention, there is
still quite a difference between these latter two.
"Approaches to a theory" does not imply that such a
theory necessarily exists as yet; "approaches to the
theories" implies that these do exist --"approaches"
therefore meaning something slightly different in each

84.

case. But be that as it may, it is obvious, among
other things from our being here, that these approaches
certainly do exist and, we can assume, also did exist
long, or sometimes not so long, before we came to know
about them.

These are the reasons why I prefer the term
"theory about..." to "theory of...." A theory dealing
with learning can never be without that process of
coming to know (i.e. learning) and its result (i.e.
knowing) which only then can be explored, questioned
and conceptualized in a theory. For we as Christians
certainly want to reject the reduction of reality, of
the richness of creation, to what we learn or can know
about it. Just like words so often fail us, knowing is
only a component of being. Nor are we of the opinion
that educators will have to hold their breath until
such a theory or theories have been formulated; that
instruction will bear no fruit until we get our theory
straight. That reciprocal relationship of teaching and
learning is going on, and has been going on for
centuries --uninhibited by the lack of theory. In
fact, too often they have been inhibited by bad theory.

To conclude this prefatory remark, I find that
"theory of..." all too easily continues to carry
undesirable overtones stemming from a perspective on
life in which "theoria" is held to be the door or road
to true reality. Practice on the other hand is held
to be little more than an inferior, tainted ectypal
copy of some transcendent archetype.

But now back to the matter at hand. First a few
comments about living, then about learning, so as to
turn in conclusion to some suggested guidelines for
discussing theories about learning.

LIVING

When we were younger, much younger than today, we
didn't know what life was all about. Our insight grew,
however, and hopefully is still growing. With the help
of parents, family, friends, teachers, preachers and
professors, we came to see that living, in that basic
and all-encompassing sense of religious life, that is
in (dis)obedience before the face of the living God, is
a matter of being both God's child and His servant. It
is a matter of being good and doing good in answer to
God's command to love Him above all and our neighbor as
ourself, in every area of life. We also came to know
how difficult that often is. Being obedient, living
obediently does not come easy; sin and struggle easily

surround us. Yet we carry on because we know (He
promised) that He is faithful; in fact, He was faithful
long before we came to an understanding of all these
things.

As we grew older we came to see that it was not
just a matter of those people's nurturing, teachings,
preachings and professing. Rather, we came to see the
importance of Scripture and how dependent mankind is on
His Word-revelation. We realized that without God's
word mankind would know little or nothing about Him and
about His covenanting relationship to that which He has
created; and that what someone who rejects the word of
God claims to know about Him turns out, upon closer
investigation, to be pure speculation --the result of
unbelief. Not that we have reason to boast. For we
also came to realize that both our holding for truth
all that God reveals in His word, and our firm
confidence that we too have been graciously granted
salvation by God through Christ, are not the result of
our own doing. It was He who spoke first to us and
turned our heart to Him, such that we, also believing,
accept Scripture as His word. And only then, our
hearts having been turned, did we come to attach great
significance to that word.

We came to see that it is also not just a matter
of "believing that...." The kind of responsive
adherence to God's revelation that I'm referring to is
expressed more fully in our believing in God, in the
Father and in the Son and the Holy Spirit. Taking Him
at His word, we came to proclaim His sovereignty over
all things, no matter in what it actually is: what
Scripture refers to as a "walking with God" and "a
holding and keeping of the covenant." It is on the
basis of Scripture that we can talk about the total
depravity of man, about death as punishment for sin,
and about the revelation of the grace of the sovereign
God in the Mediator. But not only talk. All these
things are real. God's word and comfort are just as
real as His creation. They are different and also make
a difference. They define for us what living is all
about. They inform, more specifically He informs,
our living, our religious life, that is our living here
and now always before His face. This is the essence
and what characterizes our living from day to day.
That's what life is all about.

God, of course, does not only inform our
religious life. He informs the lives of His children
throughout the world. Nor is He just active at
present. Proof abounds that He has also been busy
throughout the ages granting, inspiring and directing

the life of those who walk in His way. Together with
them we can say that all we know about God and His
relation to the cosmos, all we know about His will for
our salvation (and about what this salvation
presupposes) and hence all we know about the law God
posited for our believing rests directly or indirectly
on His word which we believe.

People who continually and seriously reckon with
Holy Scripture, relying on it and measuring their
daily life by it, do not want to withdraw anything from
the honor and service of God. Everything we do, in
other words, our whole life, we want to dedicate to
Him. Living before the face of God is therefore all-
inclusive: life is religion. Christian living is a
being-there which is informed by His word.

The knowing I have been referring to is implicit
to, but only part of, believing. It is a knowing about
things expressed and communicated in words. They are
personal and everyday words from His heart to ours.
They set the tone for our life and demand an
appropriate expressed response, including what we say
about these words. Yes, they inform our life. And
yet, woe betide lest we allow these personal words and
what they communicate (the "knowledge" they contain) to
be deformed into "information." In standing open to,
in giving an upright ear to those words, which also
really do say important things about the character of
our world --as created and upheld with hope now and
still coming-- I "know" right away that they are more
than merely "informative." To see Scripture only as
information amounts to its deformation. God's word
defines our horizon and determines our direction in
living.

A life informed by His word reckons with the fact
that He is God and that we and our world are His
creatures. It acknowledges that that which is created
is completely dependent on the Creator, subjected to
His sovereign law, word-revelation, and guidance.
Distinguishing between God and cosmos, it at the same
time does not forget that unique relationship which we
call the "covenant", a relationship in which mankind
occupies the most important place. In doing so, it
also sees that there is a difference between man and
that which is placed in subjection to him. Seeing
things in perspective, it distinguishes a manifold of
physical things as well as flora and fauna. Yet here,
too, for all their mutual differences, there are unity
and connection. Kingdoms and kinds and members of the
latter: individually different things, which in spite
of all their various ways of being-there are also one;

being more than a pile of functions, of those slices of
reality some study and know about in doing science.
When we look at man, the crown of creation, we also
witness a rich diversity, not only in the modes of his
existence --no one (person) is completely like an
other-- but in a myriad of differences. Yet these too
can be seen only in their context: a man or a woman is
not an individual, but an individual member of the
one human race. This connection, too, is
subordinated to that between mankind and God: the
covenantal context.

     Man is different than all the other earthly
creatures in that he has a heart (turned towards or
away from God). All the relationships on earth are
dependent on the relationship in which the human race
stands to God: fall and redemption of mankind are
correlate with blessing and curse for everything else
on earth.

     Salvation from this curse is attained through
Christ's love-filled obedience --He is still today
working out in the history of His people, in the
turning of hearts and the renewal of all of life.
Here, too, there is difference: being born again and
repentence do not coincide. But on the other hand,
here, too, there is no division: even the most broken
deed to the honor of God is in principle good. This is
the gift of life whereby we live and know that we are
cared for.

LEARNING

     Living involves and presupposes many things, among
which are learning (in the sense of coming to know) and
its result. Learning is an important, basic human
activity. As is true of everything else which is
human, learning is subjected to God's will and
dependent on His faithfulness and leading. Hence,
learning is never neutral. First of all, learning is
not neutral in the sense that it is done in obedience
or disobedience to the great commandment, God's law of
love. But like all human activity, we can say that
learning is individual; it is done here and now, by
you or me. And like political or economic activity,
learning is normed. Political activity ought to set
itself towards justice in our day and age and our
economic occupations towards stewardship, given the
means at our disposal. In like manner, our learning is
not neutral in that it should result in knowing and not
in erring.

Learning is as broad or extensive as living, but it is also as varied. We meet it everywhere. Learning involves getting to know --and knowing-- our parents, brothers, and sisters, the many people outside the family circle, those animals, plants and physical things with which we came into contact already when we were knee-high to a grasshopper. There is not respect for parents, no love for relatives, no friendship with a comrade without learning being implied. Of course there is more involved, but these ethical matters of friendship, love and respect, for example, all presuppose learning and knowing. The respect of a church-goer for his minister or priest, the love for our brothers and sister in Christ, the respect of citizens for those in governmental office, and a patriot's love of country --all are different and yet here too learning and knowing are presupposed. Just like the difference in the respect and love in each of these cases, we can also add that the learning and knowing implied in each also differ.

We did not always know that there was a difference between home and church and government. We learned that. That is why learning is so important. Through learning our eyes are opened to a diversity, a diversity which exists independent of our learning. While this diversity at times may seem chaotic, it is not when seen in perspective. Learning is pivotal in the unfolding of our abilities, of our activities at home, and later these outside the home (e.g. at school, where intellectual growth and educational progress are given their due focus, and eventually at a place of employment). Yet in all of these areas learning is presupposed.[1]

What is it that is presuppposed? In other words, what is this thing, this activity called "learning"? In thinking about this question I have found the following suggestion of the Dutch philosopher Dirk Vollenhoven to be very helpful: "learning is the activity of distinguishing that which is different in its context."[2] This suggestion, I find, evidences insight into what learning is all about and deserves further attention.

In bringing this generic definition of learning to your attention, I do not mean to imply that all learning is essentially the same. Learning, and the knowing which results, differs with respect to the something about which one learns.

For example, learning about God, discerning and noting so that we know His promises and trust them, differs in no small measure from learning about the

word "cat", discerning and noting its letters, their
irreversible order, and what they together denote, and
in knowing this word, being able to spell it. Learning
about the God of Holy Scripture can only be done
(correctly) when our discerning and noting is itself
done in trust and not, for example, by subjecting Him
whose promises they are to human inquisition. After
all, this learning and knowing is ultimately a matter
of accepting the trustworthiness of God as our final
ground. In contrast, the learning we do with respect
to that which he has created can most certainly be said
to be inquisitive and can be described also in terms of
our asking questions which are in keeping with the
nature of that which is being investigated.

The questions we ask of earthly things are not
only different given the nature of what we are learning
about. They also differ because the entirety of a
person's preceding experience, with its perception,
recollection and expectation --all serves as the
background or context for this questioning. Therefore,
differences on the side of that about which learning
occurs, as well as on the side of the person performing
this activity, prohibit us from saying that all
learning is essentially the same. Depending on the
context, there are different kinds of learning and
therefore also different kinds of knowing.
Nevertheless, there is a similarity to all instances of
learning which I find is grasped in saying that
learning is distinguishing that which is different in
its context.

Rather than giving a selection of examples, the
remainder of this section can best be spent by briefly
listing a number of important points implicit to this
definition. These points presuppose a situation of
knowing and not erring.

1) "That which is different" as well as "the
context of that which is different" exist independent
of the human activity we call learning. They are the
something about which we learn in the same way that
learning is the something about which we are
theorizing.

2) Whether one speaks of one or of an other
correlatum, in each case that which is talked about
differs from and is different than other contexts and
correlata. In each case that which is referred to is
identical with itself. Its distinctiveness is real.
Learning is not a matter of making distinctions, nor
of forming connections. Learning comes to right
results only when one discerns and notes what is the
case. To that extent we can also say that real
identity is the basis for all learning which results in

90.

knowing.

3) While what we learn about can be said to be
identical with itself, be it that which is different
and/or its context, such (except for the most inclusive
connection) do not exist void of a more encompassing
context. In fact, everything we can learn about exists
in an ordered variety of connections, some of which I
alluded to in my remarks on living. However, we do not
always learn about these more encompassing connections
at first, just as we do not begin living, knowing what
life is all about. No, we come to know about
connections and contexts, also the most encompassing
one --all of which were there before we began.
Learning something, and as a result also knowing
something, requires more than discerning and noting
that this something is this and not that, or thus and
not so, or right and not wrong. It requires
distinguishing that which is different in its
context, such that we can say it is, for example,
thus and not so in this respect or in that respect.
Learning, in other words, requires that we see that the
difference between that which is connected in this way
is inherent to the context.

THEORY ABOUT LEARNING

The learning I have been talking about above is
embedded in the cloak of human functions. It is one of
many distinguishable human activities. Diverse as
these may be, none is an island unto itself. Each must
be seen in connection with the human heart which
directs this functioning with respect to that all-
encompassing context we call the covenant. We come to
know the latter as existing long before we knew it.
After the fact we come to see that everything we learn
fits sooner or later within that context. The same
must be true of our theory about learning.

In learning about learning we will therefore do
well in keeping the following in mind:
1. Learning is a human activity with its own
character. It is an activity which cannot be reduced
to any other, certainly not to the sensitive acting/
reacting activity of animals. Man has a heart,
directed towards or away from his Creator. To forget
this is to live in a functionalistically reduced world.
2. The human activity we call learning is dependent on
what we, speaking relatively, can call "lower
functions." A person cannot learn without some
sensitive interest; organic functioning, especially of

the brain, is also a must. Malfunctioning organs, be
it a case of encephalitis or simply intestinal cramps,
stands in the way of learning. Learning also
presupposes the conversion of energy. These and other
matters (differences in age, periods of growth, and
activity) must receive the attention of any theory
about learning.
3. Learning takes time. It is impossible without
memory in the same way that it presupposes <u>present</u>
perception and an amount of expectation.
4. Learning is also always connected with one's
surroundings. Learning is learning about something,
and every result of this activity, be it knowledge or
error, is knowledge or error about such a "something."
This something by and large (as long as we do not
deliberately turn back upon ourselves) lies outside us.
5. Learning is also determined by so-called "higher"
or more complex human activity, activity which is more
complex/involved than distinguishing. Learning is
irrevokeably tied up with forming concepts, formulating
propositions, presenting demonstrations and avoiding
detours. If there are problems in these areas,
repercussions follow when it comes to learning.
6. Learning is always the learning of you or me, or in
other words that of an individual human being. This
human being is continually in contact with many other
human beings, with whose knowledge, in word and
writing, he becomes acquainted. Whether or not he
accepts or rejects the thoughts which come to him from
these inter-individual contacts, his own thoughts are
broadened, or sharpened and deepened by this contact.
7. Learning is nothing more than a human activity
which like all other human activity or functioning
works religiously in a specific direction and hence
never may be said to be neutral. It is always busy for
better or worse.

[1] These areas also all presuppose mankind's lingual mode of being. This, I think, can be tied to the fact that in each there is a difference to be noted between those placed in authority and those who must first listen with respect.

[2] Found in an article published in 1937, entitled "Schriftuurlijke wijsbegeerte en onderwijspraktijk" in Handelingen van het vierde nationaal christelijk schoolcongress, 29-31 October 1936. Education, he says there, is a matter of the pointing to differences with authority and the improvement of the learners' ability to distinguish.

Chapter 7

Learning vs. Revelation: A Paradigm Clash

by

James E. Martin
Professor of Psychology
Pennsylvania State University

Abstract

First, this paper contains a critique of a number
of current psychological theories of learning. These
theories are shown to be inadequate because they are
attempts to explicate abstract conditions for the
development of competent judgment. It is shown that
such conditions do not exist, and consequently, that
the process of making a novel and competent judgment
is, with respect to traditional scientific analysis,
free. Second, proceeding from epistemological
considerations, the ground is cleared for the
possibility of the kind of freedom required for an
autonomous judgmental process. Third, explication of
the axiological constraints on the judgmental process
points toward grounding that process in an autonomy
beyond that of the psychological ego--in an inner
access to the Divine.

"He that teaches man knowledge, shall he not know?"
(Psalm 94:10)

Learning vs. Revelation: A Paradigm Clash

Approximately twenty years ago psychological theorizing underwent a profound conceptual revolution. Responding to the insights of the linguist Noam Chomsky, the majority psychologists, concerned with language and cognition, shifted their theoretical orientation from the behaviorist-associationist view in fashion at the time to an essentially new, more mentalist paradigm. The Chomskian revolution resulted in part from the fact that it became clear that the associationist theories of thought were incapable of explaining the rule-governed creativity characteristic of natural language.

It is possible, however, that another revolution may be necessary. Again the question of creativity is central. Having been able to shed considerable light on the fact of rule-<u>governed</u> creativity it would be natural for us to turn our attention to the problem of rule-<u>changing</u> creativity. The argument presented here is that the current paradigm will fail at just this point. It will be shown that certain aspects of the problem of intellectual development cannot be handled within the received paradigm.

Subsequently, I attempt to develop epistemic foundations for an alternative to the presently received paradigm. In this new view the person is seen as autonomous in the sense that he prescribes his own rules, or law (auto=self, nomos=law). As this argument unfolds it becomes apparent that the process of development toward competence is under the control of axiological constraints mediated in the imagination.

Difficulties with the Received Paradigm

The first thesis is that virtually all presently proposed theories of the acquisition of knowledge and competent behavior must fail because they include explicit hypotheses about abstract structures of mind which are alleged to be responsible for the construction or recognition, and, by implication, the validation of knowledge. It is shown that the constraints responsible for the development of competence cannot be specified because they do not exist in abstract form. Moreover, their concrete character resides permanently and necessarily hidden from view.

As typically incorporated into psychological theories, the structures invoked to explain competence perform a dual function. First as part of a scientific

explanation, they tie the development of competence to
a causally integrated system of psychological events.
Second, as a part of an explantion of competence, they
relate psychological systems to the validity which
defines competence. We would hardly be interested in a
theory of development toward competence which accounted
for change, but not for change in the direction of
competence.

The argument is twofold. First, it is shown to be
impossible to fully elucidate such structures or
principles in advance of the development of human
understanding. The principles which are responsible
for the development of a competent apprehension of the
world only emerge in the context of that development.
The assumption behind explanatory developmental
theorizing is that it is possible to anticipate the
principles in question. Such principles can only be
reconstructed in retrospect, <u>after</u> human intelligence
has done its work.

Second, the core of what cognitive psychologists
want to explain, the act of judgment itself, is, in
principle, beyond the scope of the reconstructive
activity of the psychologist. To be able to reproduce
the result of an intellectual act, is not necessarily
to have described the nature of the act. The
psychologist's reconstruction is not merely incomplete
in the sense that all theories are incomplete, but it
is false in the sense that it involves a fundamental
and systematic distortion of the true nature of
intellectual activity. That is, it might be assumed
that a retrospective account, although not the ultimate
theory, would be something <u>like</u> that theory. All
such reconstructions are radically and inevitably
<u>unlike</u> anything approaching a true speech about
judgment.

The focus of attack will be the recent work of
cognitive scientists in the area of computer-
simulation of intelligence. The argument does not
depend on any consideration of the present state of the
art in information-processing or computer-simulation
research. It is important to understand that the claim
is not that the present strategy hasn't explained the
development of competent judgment--that would only be
to state an obvious fact. The claim is that the
strategy will never work because in principle it can't.

Moreover, despite their differences, the projects
of the computer simulators and their less rigorous
psychologist forebears are essentially identical with
respect to the criticism developed here. If,
therefore, the presented critique of the computer

simulation of intelligence is correct, that whole class
of psychological theories characterized by an attempt
to provide an explicit account of the abstract
principles which are responsible for the development of
competent thought (e.g. a learning theory) will have
been refuted.

The Problem of Context and Value

The impossibility of computer models of
intelligence resides in the fact that actual human
intelligence is grounded in a tacit access to the
reality about which human persons may be intelligent.
This access may be conceived to be knowledge of the
contexts, and/or values which define the domain or
domains that humans come to competently understand or
act in.
According to Kleindorfer and Martin (1983),

> This requirement that the computer be pro-
> vided with contextual information prior to
> the possibility of its intelligent response
> to a particular input, seems to us to sound
> the death knell of the project of computer
> simulated human intelligence. The reason
> for this is quite simple. In order to
> write an adequate program, the programmer
> must, at the very least, incorporate into
> the program an explicit and true knowledge
> of the various contexts within which the
> program will assign interpretations to, and
> derive implications of, input data. This
> is so because the possibility of giving
> a valid interpretation of, or reasoning
> about a stimulus depends on the validity
> of the knowledge of the context provided
> by the programmer.
>
> In this connection we turn to the
> phenomenon of value. It is our claim that
> Simon and his colleagues have misconstrued
> mind by seeing human intelligence as goal
> seeking. In our view, mind ought also to be
> conceived as value realizing. Value
> realization is distinguished from goal
> seeking in virtue of the fact that in
> goal seeking one searches for a well-
> defined end or goal--one knows what it
> is that one wants--as in a chess match.
> On the other hand, a process of value
> realization involves, in part, the
> bringing to consciousness of what it is

98.

that one is seeking in the process of
seeking it.

Value realization is distinguished from goal
seeking in that the project of value realization
includes criticism of ends, not merely the invention of
means. This follows from the fact that value
realization is grounded in a _tacit_ appreciation of a
valued good. Therefore, the character of the end
consciously sought becomes an essential question.
Accordingly, in cases of value realization, there
exists a dialectic which involves two subordinate
values. The first of these aims at providing adequate
means, and thus overcoming the distinction between the
value realizer and the valued good. The second aims at
elaborating that distinction. That is, precisely
because the good in question is tacitly appreciated,
the value realizer is required to take a critical
stance in relation to every attempt to realize or
achieve that good. It is because of this latter value
that there is no well defined goal in the process of
value realization. All fully explicit goals which we
may construct for ourselves are provisional at best,
and are subject to constant criticism. Therefore,
value realization is not achieved through attaining of
a well-defined end, but through the endless elaboration
of the antagonistic but complementary subvalues which
are constituted by tacit access to a good.
    In this context, the argument is as follows.
Human thinkers invoke tacit knowledge of context and
certain underlying values (logical and otherwise) when
engaged in competent thought. The characterization of
that knowledge and those values is an open-ended task
which is controversial, to say the least. Simulation
of intelligence will only be possible in those
relatively trivial and contrived situations where the
relevant context and values which inform human thought
can be explicitly laid out.[1]

The Necessarily Tacit Status of Value

The second proposal is more radical. It has been
shown that it is impossible to enunciate the structures
or principles which underly the development toward
competence. But it might be surmised that although
their full nature will always remain unknown to us,
some sort of natural laws or principles are
nevertheless finally responsible for that development.
In this case, the character of those criteria, like the
character of quarks, electrons and black holes, would

always remain in some degree, a mystery. It would be a mystery of the sort that is common in science. Scientists never pretend to give an ultimate account. What they might hope to do is give an imcomplete theory which is in some respects like the ultimate theory.

But, the incomplete explication of those criteria or principles in the framework of scientific theorizing will not result in a theory like the truth. That is, the truth would not consist in the full explication of those constraints represented as a natural and, therefore, as a formalizable system. Consider the following argument, which is found in George Spencer-Brown's remarkable treatise on the foundation of logic, Laws of Form. In an intriguing discussion, Spencer-Brown draws a distinction between mathematical proofs and demonstrations. A demonstration may be achieved by following a set of instructions, even though the demonstrator may be quite unfamiliar with the system in which the instructions are obeyed. Clearly, a computer program might be capable of carrying out, or following, a demonstration.

In contrast the procedures involved in a proof are not yet codified in a calculus. "In proving a theorem, if we have not already codified the structure of the proof in the form of a calculus, we must at least be familiar with, or experienced in, whatever it is we take to be the ground of the proof, otherwise we shall not see it as proof" (p. 94).

> A proof can never be justified in the same way as a demonstration. Whereas in a demonstration we can see that the instructions already recorded are properly obeyed, we cannot avail ourselves of this procedure in the case of a proof. In a proof we are dealing with terms which are outside of the calculus, and thus not amenable to its instructions. In any attempt to render such proofs themselves subject to instructions, we succeed only at the cost of making another calculus, inside of which the original calculus is cradled, and outside of which we shall again see forms which are amenable to proof but not demonstration" (p. 93)

We see immediately that the so-called "theorem proving" programs which have been developed do not prove theorems but merely demonstrate consequences. In order to prove a theorem about a domain one has to have (at least tacit) access to that domain. In order to demonstrate a consequence, one only has to follow a set of definite rules, or search through a set of rules until one finds a sequence which will result in the desired consequence.

But the ground of the valid conviction that a theorem is true of some system resides in the knower's relation to the tacitly apprehended ground and end of his thought. No matter how much of one's knowledge of a domain may be modeled along demonstrative lines, those demonstrations are embedded in the tacit context without which the issues of truth and validity would never arise. If one wishes to be convinced of what he has demonstrated, he must resort to proof and, thus, to his tacit access to the truth. Accordingly we see that the tacit realm which includes a real access to the truth which mind seeks can never be excluded from an account of intelliegence on the pretext that scientific theories are necessarily finite in scope. The fact is that if the tacit realm is not included in our account of mind, issues which are central to any reasonably adequate theory, such as what truth and validity are, and how the mind achieves them, cannot be addressed. But if the tacit realm is necessarily included in every account of judgment, then the presumption that the ultimate account would characterize thought as demonstration is false.

In this context, the inappropriateness of Turing's test is apparent. It might be possible for a computer program to demostrate a theorem which a human thinker had proven (i.e., not demonstrated). But it is manifest that the process by which the result had been achieved would be radically different in the two cases. The demonstration of a consequence does not model the process by which a person comes to validly believe it.

The attempt to model human thought as a kind of demonstrative process must fail because of the necessarily imcomplete nature of any demonstrative account. More important for our present purposes, it fails because it misrepresents the thought process and, in particular the developmental or learning process, as demonstrative. Human thinking does not, in general, follow a demonstrative (rule-governed or goal-seeking) procedure.

Accordingly, competent thought involves processes which are beyond explication in traditional scientific terms. No set of abstract, formalizable scientific laws of learning, programmed or otherwise, would provide first principles sufficient for a scientific

101.

account of intellectual development toward competence. This limitation does not result from the necessarily provisional character of scientific activity, but from the unique nature of thought itself. A natural system exclusively responsible for competent thought and representable by a Turing machine (however Utopian), simply does not exist. In this sense, thought is scientifically indeterminate. Thought is not subject to the categories of scientific psychological necessity. The values which direct the cognitive process are essentially beyond any explicit set of scientific first principles. They are constraints, but of a fundamentally different order than those of scientific analysis. In this respect thought is _free_ of the necessity of scientific psychological laws and principles because it is constrained by the inexplicable values of which we have been speaking.

It is clear that the _ought_ which grounds judgment lies forever beyond the categories of scientific description. This is true first because of the prescriptive character of the ought which may be opposed to the descriptive character of scientific language. It is also because the ought necessarily resides in the realm of the tacit and cannot be fully explicated even in prescriptive terms. It is our tacit access to the ends we seek. It lies outside what can be explicated in deterministic language. Inasmuch as the ought is _necessarily_ beyond the domain of explication in scientific terms, a theory of the development of competent judgment would not include such an explication. Therefore, insofar as the acts of willing and judging are constrained by what ought to be willed and judged, they are free of the constraints of scientific law (even psychological law). Willing, judging persons are _autonomous_ in the etymological sense of the word--they give rules to themselves. However, if these axiological constraints are beyond the categories of scientific thought, they nevertheless act upon and determine the world which describes _through_ the will and the judgment.

Toward an Epistemology of Revelation

The key that led to the following remarks was the recognition that the epistemic process is value-realizing, not goal-seeking. The onesideness of much epistemological discussion lies in the fact that it is usually unconsciously assumed that thought has a goal--truth, utility, etc. This assumption is false. Only

102.

when it is dropped can epistemology shed any light on the questions central to our discussion.

Realism and Idealism

In order to focus our discussion, I will begin by laying out an antinomy which has characterized the history of epistemology. In his book, Beyond Realism and Idealism, W. M. Urban argues that the history of epistemological inquiry has involved playing out a variety of conceivable positions vis-a-vis two fundamental presuppositions of the act of knowing. Although I will not attempt to trace his extensive argument here, I will support the same point briefly in the following discussion. The first presupposition is that the world is radically other. It is this presupposition which makes error intelligible and gives knowledge its value. The second presupposition, which is antinomous to the first, is that the world is not other than the knower. It is this presupposition which makes coming to know intelligible.

The clearest enunciation of the view that the world is not other in relation to the knower is found in naive realism. For naive realism the world is as it appears to be. Any inadequacy in appreciating the world stems not from a misrepresentation, misunderstanding, or misperception of reality, but simply in not yet having all the facts. A more adequate apprehension may be expected to emerge through the accumulation of more facts. But naive realism never lasts very long. It dissolves in the face of the fact of error.

The next moment in the development of epistemological consciousness is typically one form or another of representationalism (usually representational realism). At this point we have crossed over into a position which has as its primary goal to explicate the claim that reality is other than the knower. Representationalism in its various forms is an attempt to enunciate in a coherent way the fact that it is possible to be wrong. It affirms that we do not know the world directly but that what we know directly are constructions or theories which may or may not be correct. Traditionally some tie with the world about which theories are constructed has been affirmed by positivists and other representational empiricists. The key to their argument has been to claim that theory, in the final analysis, rests on the facts. The facts themselves are taken to be givens. They are said to be perceived directly.

However, this naive confidence in the facts (this vestige of naive realism) has been an object of the continual attack in the history of epistemolgical discussion. It has been repeatedly pointed out that the facts never emerge except in relation to conceptual frameworks within which they are interpreted. Accordingly, the facts may appear to be different for persons who hold different conceptual orientations toward the domain of inquiry. This point has been recently revived in philosophy of science by Thomas Kuhn and others. Kuhn has shown that attempts to settle scientific disputes by referring to empirical observations are limited by the degree to which investigators hold the same conceptual perspective.

Thus, representationalism which begins with the acknowledgement that we see the world through theories, ends in the facts having been swallowed up by the theories. At this point representationalism (as a version of realism) is not only making room for the possibility of error, it is moving toward a denial of the possibility of knowing.

Now, it is interesting to observe the complementary advantages and disadvantages of naive realism on the one hand, and representational realism on the other. The former is an attempt to explicate the presupposition that the world is "not other" in relation to the knower and that, therefore, knowledge is possible; the latter, that the world is "other" in relation to the knower and that, therefore, error is possible. Both views are somehow necessary. More accurately, the motivation behind naive realism--to explicate the possibility of error--must both be realized in any adequate epistemology.

Like both direct and naive realism, idealism conceives the knower to have access to the to-be-known. In the case of idealism, however, that access is conceived to be not only tacit but axiological as well. In recent versions of idealism (cf. Blanchard, 1939) reality is construed to be the manifestation or realization of certain values (e.g., rational coherence)--the same values which guide the critical process. It is the knowers' tacit access to the values that constrain reality which is said to make the development and criticism of knowledge a real possibility. Thus the relationship between the knower and the to-be-known is much more abstractly conceived in idealism than in direct realism. Because of this, idealism is compatible with the doctrine of the conceptual relativity of facts while avoiding the skepticism inherent in representationalism.

104.

On the view under discussion (Blanchard, 1939),
the truth is assumed to be that which would satisfy our
epistemic valuing. That is, what we seek when we seek
to know is simply the truth. We assume, therefore,
that the values which guide or direct our coming to
know, are satisfied by and realized in the object of
knowledge, the truth. In Blanchard's terms, the
imminent and transcendent ends of thought are one.
Accordingly, the relation between the idea and its
object is not assumed to be that of mere similarity.
Instead, it is relation defined in terms of the
epistemological values that constitute the learning
process. Ideas are said to be the partial realization
of those values which are fully realized in their
objects. Thus, error is conceived to be possible
because epistemic values are not fully realized in the
present idea of reality. On the other hand, because
truth is taken to be defined in terms of the same
epistemic values, criticism of putative ideas attains
to the possibility of validity.

Beyond Realism and Idealism

Elegant as the foregoing solution is, it has in my
view a fundamental defect. Its difficulty is that it
was thrown off balance by virtue of the fact that it
was a response to the epistemic nihilism entailed by
representationalism in its various forms. In that
context, the issue became, "how can I know, and know
that I know?". In this way, the awareness of ignorance
which was a product of criticism was seen only as kind
of privation. But this misconstrued the value
realizing (as opposed to the goal-seeking) character of
the development of thought. This historical
development of thoughts, taken as a whole, has <u>not</u>
resulted in our achieving a more coherent view of the
whole of reality than we or our ancestors possessed at
any previous time. While there is no doubt that with
respect to some particular problems, a kind of progress
has been made toward their solution, it is equally true
that this progress has itself resulted in the discovery
of much deeper obscurities than either we or our
ancestors had ever imagined. Blanchard began <u>The
Nature of Thought</u> with the claim that, "Thought is
the activity of mind which aims <u>directly</u> at the
truth" (my italics). Taken alone, this claim is false.
Because thought seeks truth, not as a goal, but as a
value, it seeks both a vision of reality as fully
coherent and intelligible, and also a vision of reality
as fully opaque and unintelligible. Thought has never

been, nor is it, nor will it be, satisfied with either
alone.

Urban's claim was that the foundational motive of
representational realism is to acknowledge the
otherness of reality. On the other hand, the
fundamental motive of idealism is to acknowledge that
reality is not other. Urban proposed that these
motives be held together as antagonistic and
complementary values in an ideal epistemology. It
should be claimed that the same motives direct the
epistemic process. In developing an epistemology which
is beyond realism and idealism, Urban saw these two
motives as being held in a complementary dialectical
opposition, as constraining our choice of an
epistemology. On the contrary, these same motives are
operative in the development of our ideas about
reality. In this context, what the knower seeks is a
vision of reality in which reality is seen to be
simultaneously imminent and transcendent, that is, at
once immediately, intelligible present and forever
absolutely other.

The realization of the former motive tends toward
an idealist--rationalist vision of the world as a
unity, the parts being internally related. The
realization of the latter tends toward the realist-
empiricist vision of the world as a diversity, the
parts being externally related. The limit points
defined by these motives would be, for the former,
simple unity determined for the knower, and for the
latter, the radical diversity of indeterminate things
in themselves. The actual development of experience
is under the constraint of both motives. Experience,
as we know, is neither an absolutely intelligible
unity, nor is it an absolutely unintelligible diversity
of individuals. Experience is the result of holding
together the partial realization of both of these
motives in one vision.

But how then, if at all, are these two ends
realized in one vision? The conception of a fully
intelligible determinate and full unintelligible
indeterminate reality which is at the same time
unambiguous is a manifest contradiction. By insisting
on the ambiguity one may avoid the contradiction. But
he can only do so at the cost of accepting two
realities. On the other hand, I propose that these
oppositions can be and are united in what I will call
the imagination resulting in one reality going in two
directions at once. In this way we come to see reality
as a mystery in the original sense of that term. In
its original sense, a mystery is a truth or reality

which, although hidden, may be revealed. What is both presupposed and sought in the activity of knowing is the absolute and free self-revelation of an absolute opacity. The autonomous self-revelation of the to be known constitutes the satisfaction of the two epistemic considered here. In the freedom of the act, the knower's desire for opacity is satisfied. In the revelation of that act, his desire for intelligibility is satisfied.

But in what imaginative form are these anti-thetical motives united? I suggest that it is in the notion of the person that this happens. For example, a reality might be apprehended as a personal and free self-revelation, in which it would be seen to be that which is simultaneously "other" (because free and "not other," because revealed), --unintelligible and intelligible. My suggestion is then that a full explication of the values which we seek to realize in knowing reveals that what we seek is a mystery which is in turn a self-revelation. Thus, the personal is a coincidentia-oppositorum held together, not through the concept, but through the power of the imagination.

The term imagination is used here with two allusions in mind. The first is mathematical. In mathematics the imaginary numbers were introduced to allow for the solution of certain equations (e.g., $X2 = -1$). As Spencer-Brown points out in Laws of Form, if we do not have recourse to the imaginary numbers, and if we assume that X is a function of unity, we must conclude that $+1=-1$. In Laws of Form, Spencer-Brown constructs a logical calculus which includes imaginary values. That is, the calculus contains values for X which allow us to both subvert and honor the distinction between X and not -X.

But it is clear that the two epistemic motives considered above are precisely these two, on which Spencer-Brown founds his calculus. The two epistemological motives - to honor and to subvert the distinction between ourselves and the world - constitute, as we have seen above, the motives to acknowledge the diversity and the unity of reality, respectively. At certain points it is inappropriate to decide to pursue one of these motives to the exclusion of the other. The symbol for this irreducible state of affairs is the person.

Urban (1949) argues that the values which ground realism and idealism may be understood as antagonistic and complementary without entailing contradiction. Antagonistic values may co-exist without logical contradiction. It is interesting to note that Weimer

(1982) has suggested that Spencer-Brown's calculus
might have relevance to the union of subjective and
objective aspects of the self. However, as Weimer
points out, in order to work this proposal out, we
would need to discover what "constitutes the necessary
analogue to imaginary numbers in the structural
analysis of the psychic domain," (p. 354). In the
present context I suggest that the imaginary values of
Spencer-Brown's calculus might be identified with the
person (or self) insofar as the person is a point of
union between pairs of antagonistic but complementary
values.2

The second allusion is poetical. I intend
something like the poetical creative imagination of
Coleridge (Barfield, 1971). Coleridge contrasted what
he termed the imagination to what he called fancy. For
Coleridge, fancy involves only the sorting through and
recombination of already constituted images and
meanings. Fancy is an expression of the mind's
capacity for symbol manipulation (roughly what I have
called rule-governed creativity). The imagination, on
the other hand, is involved when new symbols, meanings
and experiences are constituted (rule-changing
creativity). To the imagination Coleridge ascribes the
power to bring divergent experiences together in a
genuine and new unity. To the fancy is given only the
power to form a collection or aggregate of diverse,
already constituted structures. A self-revealing
person is in fact a genuine and always new unity, not
merely a collection of opposiong characteristics, and
is, in this sense, known in the imagination. This
coincidentia-oppositorum, held together in the
imagination, is a kind of metaphor. The person, then,
the primary constituent of the domain of psychological
inquiry is a metaphor - as is, we shall see, reality
taken as a whole.

The foregoing amounts to a hypothesis concerning
the epistemological basis for experiencing the
personal-communal world. Thus, it provides a
framework for our earlier remarks about the autonomy of
the person with respect to the categories of scientific
explanation. The person is _beyond_ rules. In the act
of judgment some aspects of mind come to be constituted
in terms of rules, but judgment cannot be understood as
resulting _from_ rules. The self-determining character
of the person in the act of judgment is not subject to
analysis in terms of rules. Neither the language of
empirical science (e.g., information science), nor of
idealist metaphysics is appropriate here. The ground
is cleared for the personal world, both free and

determined, which was pointed to above.

This personal-communal world is precisely beyond the realist-idealist dichotomy. The metaphorical character of the relation between the knower and the known is the coincidentia-oppositorum which constitutes knowledge. This coincidentia-oppositorum holds together the one and the many, the necessary and the free, the subjective and the objective, and the ideal and the real. In the imagination, and only there, do we find unity - a unity which does not annihilate the diversity which constitutes it.

Some Remarks on Development

An entirely new and intriguing set of questions emerges at this point. These questions concern the way in which mind develops under perpetually and necessarily unconscious constraints. We need a theory of intellectual growth which tells us how we are guided by such constraints.

It is proposed that the transition from the realm which must remain forever tacit is made through the imagination. In the imagination alone the oppositions that may be abstracted from our experience are both maintained and overcome. The process of guidance, in which the tacit reality constrains the development of thought, may be construed as being under the control of a self-revealing imaginatively apprehended reality. That is, the valued ends sought in the process of development are themselves to be viewed as autonomous and self-revealing (See Martin [1982] for more discussion).

The foregoing suggests an ancient mode of speaking about the creative developmental process. In this ancient tradition God, a god, or a genius, is spoken of as inspiring, and directing the creative process. Modern representatives of that tradition (e.g., Coleridge) have located the genius in the unconscious. But the term "unconscious" must, in this case, be understood in a pre-Freudian sense. In the context of Coleridge's idealism, the unconscious was not merely psychological, but was intimately connected to the constraints which constitute reality (Barfield, 1971).

To the members of this tradition, the source of the creative process is outside conscious control--beyond being governed by consciously manipulated rules. From the standpoint of the psychological ego, the creative act emerges as a kind of revelation or gift, for which it is not responsible. Once the creative act has occurred, the ego is responsible only to order

109.

the results of the original revelation for expression in a particular temporal context.

In the ancient view, the development of mind is neither a fully conscious (rule-governed) process, nor is it entirely without direction. The constraints on thought are unspecifiable, and assumed to possess an objective status which confers validity upon the developmental process. Moreover, these constraints are unseparable from the end sought. The self-revelation of the sought end requires, as we have seen above, both the unspecifiability (otherness) and valid determinability (not-otherness) of the object of thought.

Now it is impossible to predict or control the process of guidance owing to the freedom of the guide. We may begin, however, by sketching some of the steps on the path along which guidance leads. The moments of the development of epistemic reflection discussed in the previous section provide a map of this path. We have seen that two motives constrain the process. These in turn define stages of development toward the end outlined above. In the first stage, the problematic character of judgment is not yet brought to light. It is assumed that knowing is a kind of goal which is simply there to be taken -- no questions asked. The motive to honor the distinction between the self and the world has not yet become conscious. Thus, the freedom, the autonomy, the otherness of the epistemic end is not yet acknowledged. This stage is typified by the naive realist position described above. The second stage of thought, which culminates in the extreme and skeptical representationalist position, involves an acknowledgement of the otherness of the epistemic end, and a consequent denial of the immediacy of the to-be-known assumed by the naive realist. As argued above, a third stage of development is epistemic reflection results from the discovery of the self-revealing guide in which the two epistemic motives are held together in the imaginatively apprehended act of self-revelation.

These motives not only constrain the development of epistemology, but they also constrain the development of our vision of reality. Accordingly, stages parallel to the above characterize the emergence of every real discovery--simplicity, then knowledge of one's own ignorance, and finally appreciation of a revelation--the discovery of something new and whole and for which the discoverer is conscious of not being wholly responsible.[3]

The process by which we come to know is incomprehensible in traditional scientific terms, and it will always be so. The skeptical representationalists are correct. Both the truth, and the criteria of its recognition, are beyond our construction. We have no final grounds for securing truth, none at all, except the living, personal, self-authenticating truth. And that is not subject to our technical manipulation. Our responsibility is only to receive what is revealed.[4]

Biblical Relections

In conclusion, it is also worth noting that our discussion has direct relevance to theological questions. The ultimate ground of being, from the point of view developed here, could never be grasped with the concept. Thus philosophical versions of the Absolute, such as Hegel's, would be rejected. On the contrary, the goal which thought seeks and presupposes, the ground of the whole, is a mystery, hidden and revealed, free and determined, forever beyond the grasp of the concept.

And, of course, that is just what the Biblical revelation says about God. He is absolutely free and he has freely chosen to reveal Himself in Jesus Christ. "No man has seen God at any time, the only begotten God which dwelleth in the bosom of the Father, He has declared Him,"(Jn 1:18). In the confrontation with Moses at the burning bush(Ex. 3:14), He reveals Himself as "I will be what I will be," or "I am who I am." In His self-revelation, the revelation of His being, He never permits us to forget His freedom in choosing to reveal Himself to us. "So then, it is not of him that willeth, nor of him that runneth, but of God that showeth mercy,"(Rom. 9:16). The ground of being, the ultimate reality is, as a <u>Coincidentia-oppositorum</u>, a personal being.

The ambiguity between freedom and necessity is also evident in the practical aspects of personal community. For example, it provides the context for the possibility of Biblical love. When it exists, such love is a freely chosen act of self-enslavement, or self-determination, for the benefit of the beloved. Love is an example, in the practical sphere, of the sort of ambiguity that self-revelation is in the theoretical. In fact, it is not evident that love has an epistemic aspect. Does not the lover seek to know and to be known by his beloved? This affinity between loving and knowing is often alluded to by the Biblical writers, in conection with the love between men and women as well as that between God and mankind.

Finally, in understanding the person to be the point of union between the not-other and the radical other, I am of course in the center of the historical Christian tradition. What can be clearer than that the union of the two natures in the Person of Christ is precisely of this sort? From the perspective of the New Testament authors, the incarnation, the personal union of the divine (radically other) nature of Christ with His human (absolutely not-other) nature, is the central event in the history of the world. It is understood as a freely chosen act of self-enslavement in service of the self-revelation of God to mankind. "Although He existed in the form of God, He did not regard equality with God a thing to be grasped, but emptied Himself, taking on the form of a bond-servant, being made in the likeness of men. And being found in appearance as a man, He humbled Himself by becoming obedient to the point of death, even the death of the cross,"(Phil. 2:6-8). The self-revelation of God throughout the Scriptures is seen as being grounded in the incarnation of Jesus Christ. All His works, especially His death and resurrection, derive their significance from the fact of the incarnation. The distinction between the two natures is the distinction between created (not-other) and uncreated (other) being. In the Person of the Son of God these are united without confusion and without separation.

An epistemology and associated psychology which makes room for persons--for self-revelation and love-- is long overdue. Without such a positive foundation, the future of psychological investigation will be a continuation of the past--a series of retreats from a series of increasingly barbaric and sophisticated renderings of the thesis that man is a piece of meat. Clearly, we need another metaphor. The Bible gives us one. Man is the image of God--God who both hides and reveals Himself.

References

Barfield, O. What Coleridge thought. Middleton, Conn.: Wesleyan University Press, 1971.

Blanchard, B. The nature of thought. New York: Humanities Press, 1964.

Kant, I. The critique of pure reason. New York: St. Martin's, 1970.

Kleindorfer, G. B., & Martin, J. E. The iron cage, single vision, and Newton's sleep. Journal of Philosophy and Technology, 1983, in press.

Martin, J. E. Presentationalism: Toward a self-reflexive psychological theory. In W. B. Weimer & D. S. Palermo (eds.), Cognition and the symbolic processes (Vol. II). Hillsdale, NJ: Lawrence Erlbaum Associates, 1982.

Spencer-Brown, G. Laws of form. New York: Julian Press, 1972.

Urban, W. M. Beyond Realism and Idealism. London: Allen and Unwin, 1949.

Weimer, W. B. Psycholinguistics and Plato's paradoxes of the Meno. American Psychologist, 1973, 28, 15-33.

Weimer, W. B. Notes on the methodology of scientific research. Hillsdale, NJ: Lawrence Erlbaum Associates, 1979.

Weimer, W. B. Ambiguity and the future of psychology: Meditations Leibniziennes. In W. B. Weimer and D. S. Palermo (eds.), Cognition and the symbolic processes (Vol. II). Hillsdale, NJ: Lawrence Erlbaum Associates, 1982.

Footnotes

1 It might be argued that the computer could come to
specify its context if it were permitted access to
sensory information and the ability to interact with
its environment--in short, if the computer were
provided a body. This argument begs the question at
issue. Moreover, it naively assumes that the only
context at issue is the external environment. It does
not permit the computer to inquire concerning the
appropriate standards of validity (logical and
otherwise) in assessing theories it might develop.

2 It is interesting that Spencer-Brown himself has
interpreted the imaginary values of his logic in terms
of time. My proposal, in combination with his,
suggests an intriguing connection between value and
time. Time may be seen to proceed from the fact of
value. The dialectic constituted by a value (a good)
may determine temporal (and spatial) structure.

3 Beginning with God, the absolute good (or value),
the Biblical writers characterize a process of
development whose form corresponds exactly to the
developmental sequence described in the text. In the
Biblical account there are essentially three stages -
innocence, fall, and redemption. These correspond to
innocence, the tree of the knowledge of good and evil,
and the tree of life. They also correspond to
innocence, law, and grace. In his innocence, man takes
God for granted, there is no problem associated with
knowing and communing with Him. The radical nature of
the distinction between God and man has not yet been
acknowledged. Man then falls by partaking of that
knowledge in virtue of which his incompleteness and
radical difference from God is manifest. Finally, if
he is to recover communion with God, it must come to
him as a gift, a self-revelation, from God. It will be
shown how that self-revelation corresponds in form, to
the coincidentia-oppositorum described above.

4 The dilemma posed for epistemology by the radical
post-empiricists is irresolvable if we do not have
recourse to the category of revelation. I do not
suggest that we should avoid subjecting putative truth
(or, revelation) to criticism. My point is that it is
not possible to give the critical criteria in
advance. It is therefore impossible to show that an
alleged thruth will satisfy all the criteria which may

emerge. As we gradually come to understand it, the
truth must satisfy whatever reasonable criteria we may
have developed. And that responsibility is not
primarily our own. We must use the criteria we
possess. But tomorrow's questions require tomorrow's
answers. And tomorrow's answers depend on reality, not
on ourselves. Sufficient unto the day is the evil
thereof.

PART II

PRESCRIPTIONS

For

THEORY
BUILDING

117.

Chapter 8

Toward a Responsibilty Theory: Becoming Who We Are

Peter P. DeBoer
Professor of Education
Calvin College

Once again Americans seem taken up with the
question of excellence in education. Witness the
recommendation recently made by the National
Commission on Excellence in Education. According to a
news report (Grand Rapids Press, July, 1983),
Michigan's Superintendent of Public Instruction, for
example, reacted to the Commission's recommendations by
urging local school districts and colleges to study
such issues as these: (1) to review promotion and
graduation requirements and tighten them if necessary;
(2) to consider adding computer education to high
school courses; (3) to review evaluation procedures for
teachers and administrators; (4) to study the
possibility of stricter homework, attendance, and
discipline policies; and (5) to find ways to get more
community involvement with schools.
    The present flurry of attention to educational
excellence did not suddenly happen. Its recent roots
go back at least to the early to middle seventies when
we became aware of a discernible decline in Scholastic
Aptitude Test scores. Prominent educators and the
media have been playing a "back to the basics" theme in
variations ever since. Interest has been fueled by the
report of James Coleman (High School Achievement
New York: Basic Books, 1982) which contrasted the
achievement of private high school students to the
rather dismal record of public high school students.
Witness the attention given lately to Mortimer Adler's
(The Paideia Proposal New York: Macmillan, 1982)
prescription for improving American secondary
education. The frequent invidious contrasts of U.S.
education to that of the Japanese only serve to remind
some of us old enough to remember that in the 1950's it
was popular to draw similar contrasts between U.S.
education and that of the Russians. My fear is that if
the contemporary concern for excellence blossoms
similar to that of the late fifties and early sixties,

119.

we may have to endure another round of reactionism from the likes of John Holt, Paul Goodman, and all the other romantics. Spare us.

Christian education, at least that version that we who are Reformed Christians know so well, has not swung wildly from one extreme to another. Yet ideas about Christian education do not occur in a vacuum. We do respond to our environment. Though ideally rooted in the Word, our thinking about Christian education is often affected by the thought of our contemporaries. This is not only inevitable; it can be either healthy or dangerous.

In the pursuit of excellence in Christian education, I wish to lift up a theory that, of late, has been called a "responsibility theory" (see Nicholas Wolterstorff, Educating for Responsible Action [Grand Rapids, Michigan: Christian Schools International and Eerdmans, 1980]). I will attempt to show that in various formulations it has been about for a while. I will attempt to analyze it and extend or enlarge its scope. Finally, I hope to uncover certain emphases that I will recommend for Christian teacher education.

Some Origins

For Calvinists to speak of a responsibility theory for education ought to surprise no one. God's sovereignty and man's responsibility have long been central to a Calvinist or Reformed theology. When the Calvinist talked about responsibility he spoke about the heart. John Calvin's motto--"my heart I give to Thee, promptly and sincerely"--is fixed in the seal of Calvin College.

The first American Calvinist educator to attempt to deal with this matter with some system was Cornelius Jaarsma, who tried in the 1950's to weave the concept of "heart" into his learning theory. His attempt was met, in some quarters, with less than enthusiam. His critics thought they detected an anti-intellectual bias. Jaarsma insisted that the scriptural view of learning is this: that "nothing is really learned in school until a child comes to accept it in his heart" (Fundamentals of Christian Education: Theory and Practice, [Grand Rapids, Michigan: Eerdmans, 1953]). Jaarsma did not deny that certain learned behavior could be acquired by conditioning. Nor did he deny that "insight gives intellectual comprehension." But he maintained that learning is always more than modification of behavior and assimilation of knowledge. Real learning, said he, is "heart acceptance" (ibid.,

p. 253).

For that reason Jaarsma made "love" foundational to the education process. He remarked that before the Fall man loved perfectly. The Fall turned man's love in upon himself making him incapable of love. But by virtue of the grace of God becoming ours in the new life, all things become new, including man's capacity to love. Not first of all intelligence or analysis or feeling or volition or choice, he said, but love must now become the foundational principle for curriculum making as well as methodolgy. The basic unity of the education process, he said, is the "action of the heart" (ibid., pp. 248-249). Hence for Jaarsma, as I believe is true for all who lift up a responsibility theory, this question becomes central: "How can we," he asked, "get the child to accept in his heart what he ought?" (ibid., p. 253).

It was not a question raised in despair. Jaarsma confidently affirmed that if "gospel"--that is, that gracious action whereby God is in Christ reconciling man and the world to himself--means anything for Christian education, it means this: that man can again be made responsive to God and thereby responsive to the truth of God's world in all of man's resources. The Scriptures, then, tell us what is achievable. The essential question for the educator is: how do we get there? Or again, how can we help the child to be (and therefore know and feel and do) what he ought?

Some Anthropology

Asking the responsibility question--how can we help the child to be what he ought?--immediately raises a prior question: what is a child? or, what is man?

Without backing into a comprehensive discussion of the issue, let's say this: Calvinists, of late especially, are eager to locate man's uniqueness not first of all in some capacity--be it righteousness, or reason, or art, or language--but in this: that of all the created creatures, man is the only one given the task of developing the creation and directing all of it into the service of God and one's fellow man (Wolterstorff, Curriculum: By What Standard? [Grand Rapids, Michigan: CSI, 1966] p. 15; Henry Beversluis, Christian Philosophy of Education [Grand Rapids, Michigan: CSI, 1971] p. 23.). Of course, ultimately God needs the work of no man. But in his inscrutable wisdom he has chosen to make man the crown of his creation and endow him with duties and obligations; God made man uniquely responsible to Himself.

121.

Wolterstorff sums up man's responsibility this way: "We are responsible to God for how we act with respect to God. We are responsible to God for how we act with respect to ourselves and our fellow human beings. We are responsible to God for how we act with respect to nature." Or this: "Human responsibility... consists in God's holding us responsible to himself for acting in certain ways--that is, for obeying certain rules, certain normative rules." They are the rules of a loving God; consequently "our joy and fulfillment lie in carrying out our responsibilities" (Ibid., p. 9).

In summary, when Jacques Maritain (Education at the Crossroads Yale, 1943, p. 1) notes that the chief duty of man lies in "becoming who we are," we who are Calvinists nod approval provided we describe man in terms of the God-ordained task or calling to be a disciple. Ours is a discipleship of responsibility to God, self, neighbor, and nature.

Some Necessary Dispositions

Wolterstorff (in Educating for Responsible Action) calls attention to the difference that a responsibility theory ought to make in Christian education by his contrasting an older emphasis in the Calvinist tradition to the newer one. He claims that Reformed Christians used to emphasize the importance of understanding a "world and life view" or system of belief. He doesn't reject this largely cognitive emphasis, but he does call it an inadequate approach because Christian education ought now to aim at more than instilling a "view." Now it must aim at inducting students into or training them for a Christian way of life. Christian education must now point toward living the Christian life, in obedience, as agents of God's cause in the world (ibid., p. 14). Of course, to act responsibly one must know; hence those who hold a responsibility theory will include cognitive goals. To act responsibly one must have ability and skills; hence a responsibility theory includes ability learning. But to stop there, he argues, would short-circuit the fundamental intent of the theory. "One can have the knowledge and the abilities for acting responsibly and yet have no tendency to engage in such action." A responsibility theory must take the "further step of cultivating the appropriate tendencies in the child," tendencies ranging from unreflective habits to highly self-conscious commitments, acts, performances, (Ibid.). Christian education must now aim at producing fundamental alterations in how: students are inclined by their sinful natures to act toward God, self, neighbor, and nature. Cognitive goals and ability goals, for this, are not sufficient; Christian education must also aim at "tendency learning" if it holds to a responsibility theory (ibid., p. 15).

Wolterstorff's formulation of the matter clearly represents a restatement of a central concern of Cornelius Jaarsma. As we noted, that was: how can we get the child to accept in his heart what he ought?

It reflects, as well, Henry Beversluis' formulation (in Christian Philosophy of Education) of major learning goals. Beversluis, those of you who know his work will recall, urges Christian education to aim at inducing intellectual, moral, and creative growth (or, holistically, religious growth) in students so that they understand, accept, and respond to the religious vision or world and life view of the school, to the end that they live the Christian life knowledgeably, committedly, and productively.

Wolterstorff's formulation reflects the taxonomy of educational objectives adopted by Christian Schools International: that learning aims at intellectual, decisional, and creative growth (see Henry J. Triezenberg, "Up With Decisional Learning," Christian Educators Journal, November, 1976).

His case for a responsibility theory also harmonizes with the fundamental thrust of Geraldine Steensma and Harro Van Brumelen (see Shaping School Curriculum: A Biblical View, [Terre Haute, Ind.: Signal, 1977]). They, too, speak of discipleship, of "conforming oneself to the image of God." They, too, want learning to lead to a commitment displayed in deeds, to love that entails action, to obedient living as family member, friend, consumer, worker, citizen, and church member.

Others could be cited. My point is that against the common background of a Christian anthropology, Reformed Christians are now (with what I believe are minor differences) agreed on the fundamental dispositions to be cultivated in the learner including, most importantly, the notion of responsible or committed or discipled living of the Christian life.

An Anatomy of "Response"

Before we delineate some curriculum and methodological practices we should analyze what

Reformed Christian educators tend to mean by "response." The term is used in several different ways; to avoid misunderstanding we should be clear about its uses.

For example, Wolterstorff in a 1966 address urged, not response but what amounts to response when he called for "creativity" (_Curriculum: By What Standard?_ p. 16). He recommended that instead of merely lecturing to our students we engage them in discussion; instead of giving them pat answers we encourage them to think things through, to express their feelings, to speak and act for themselves. "Creativity," then, stood for active student involvement in learning rather than mere passive absorption.

But when one reads some of the other literature associated with Reformed Christian education, one discovers two other ways of using the term. One use is broad, the other narrow.

Broadly speaking, "response" refers to any action or reaction by the student, any sign of growth or learning. When one speaks of the student coming to know, to understand, to see, or sense, distinguish, name, symbolize, cut, shape, color, love, wonder, praise--or whatever--then we can say that he or she is responding.

More narrowly, "response" tends to lie at the tail-end of a process. For example (from the Curriculum Development Centre): "Our curriculum materials are organized around the student activity, which encourages students to explore, experience, reflect, and respond to what they learn in a variety of ways." (From Beversluis): Nothing is learned until it is "understood, appropriated, and responded to deep down where a person lives...." (From Steensma and Van Brummelen): "Analysis and critique ought to lead the student to action...."

This narrow use of the term, suggesting as it does perhaps some external observable sign of commitment, something coming after, some "fruit" by which we may "know them," some application of lessons learned is, up to a point, a legitimate use of the term. I have found that for instructing future teachers in devising lesson plans or unit outlines, the triad of consider--choose--commit or that of intellectual--moral--and creative dimensions helps alert the student to some elements in a total lesson or unit that may otherwise be overlooked. Yet such language is limited because it tends to suggest that the response signifying commitment is merely some final phase of a process of

124.

learning.

But in a responsibility theory, commitment ought not be mere final phase, but the condition of one's learning. It should not show up at the end; it should be there in the beginning. If becoming who we are means obedient discipleship, then no response lies outside the realm of responsibility. Though it is conceivable for a student to know something but not yet to have committed himself to acting on his knowledge, the weight of a responsibility theory ought not be understood as applying merely to his tendency to act, or to the "commit" phase of a consider/choose/commit sequence, but to the whole of his learning. In a responsibility theory, the student is responsible for knowing and doing, for seeing and believing. He is accountable for all his responses because his prior calling is to the <u>committed life</u>. Thus the broad meaning of the term "response" is the richer.

Student and Teacher Roles

But if the student is responsible for all that, what role in the classroom is left for the teacher? If the student is to be responsible, how ought he be educated to internalize such responsibilities?

The Curriculum Development Centre in Toronto has wrestled with these and other issues, and has provided, I believe, some insightful answers to questions about the freedom of the student and the authority of the teacher within a responsibility theory (see "Educating for Discipleship," <u>Joy in Learning</u> newsletter, Summer, 1978).

According to the Centre, learning is first of all a process of self-forming. The goal of learning is for the student to come to submit his "sensing, feeling, thinking, evaluating, appreciating, socializing, communicating--living--to Jesus Christ." In a sense no one can do this for the student; it must be the result of his own personal, willful choice. He must feel responsible for his own learning. His "office" or God-given calling is that of learner.

God created all of us with developmental abilities; by our nature we are capable of sensing, distinguishing, sharing, loving, wondering, and praising. Hence, according to the Centre, the first requirement in curricular planning is <u>not</u> to try to guarantee responses but to "confront" the pupil with meaningful experiences that challenge the pupil to respond. Such challenges must consider not only developmental level, but also the diverse interests and

special talents of each of the pupils. On the one hand
the pupil must be permitted freedom to find his own
best method and rate for learning. On the other,
curriculum content, however diverse, must "constantly
confront students with the common calling of learning
community": their talents must be cultivated for the
benefit of the community as a whole.

If learning is a process of self-forming then, for
the Centre, teaching is a process of forming.
"Education involves a conscious deliberate attempt to
lead people in a particular direction according to
certain norms." Children need guidance: teachers are
mandated to guide.

Such guidance, forming, or nurture should not (I
would add--not normally) be physical or emotional
manipulation, mental engineering, social pressuring, or
even persuading by logical argument. According to the
Centre, to do so would violate the religious nature of
the learner. Respect for that nature means that he is
never to become an object of the teacher's forming;
he must be guided in ways that help him remain a free
responsible subject in the learning process.

The basic task of the teacher is to lead the pupil
to the Truth-but not to "brainwash" him into accepting
it. Pupil responses must therefore not be prescribed;
students must be given the patience to "forge" a
response.

Ultimately, according to the Centre, learning and
teaching are not to be understood as mutually exclusive
or opposites. Learning-teaching is a confronting
relationship, but not between teacher and pupil.
Instead, together, teacher and pupil must confront
conflicting views and ways of life to the end that the
pupil freely and responsibly learns to live the
Christian life.

Some Illustrative Practices

A responsibility theory entails curricular as well
as methodological practices, though the reader,
especially the non-Reformed Christian reader, ought to
be cautioned that within Christian education as
practiced by Calvinists in North America there is not
consensus on all of the following.

Curricular Practices

Henry Beversluis reflected a solid respectable
tradition in Christian education when he conceived
curriculum as something to be encountered (Christian

Philosophy of Education, especially Chapter Three).
In an analogy to the theology of covenant wherein a
gracious God reveals himself to man and man is called
to respond to that revelation, so the response of the
student must be to an encounter with (or revelation
of) truth (ultimately an encounter with the God who is
Truth). Therefore for curriculum, Beversluis desires
that "the right things, the most educationally
rewarding things--the things that a school as school
must teach about the wholeness of life and truth as
given--must be studied" (ibid., p. 36).

The "encyclopedia" of things to be encountered
tends for Beversluis, and for other Reformed
Christians, to be limited almost exclusively to the
liberal arts and sciences. These liberal studies,
wrote Henry Zylstra, "are the main business of the
school as school" (Testament of Vision, [Grand
Rapids, Michigan: Eerdmans, 1958], p. 144), though by
"business" he meant not only knowing them, but judging
them, and referring them to a spiritual kingdom for
justification so that the student's choice for Christ
(made for him by his parents and by him as he continues
to grow) is reinforced and remade ever more consciously
and maturely (ibid., pp. 147-148).

There are signs among Reformed Christians of some
discontent with this rather singular devotion to the
liberal arts, without the discontented denying the
importance of the liberal arts. In the sixties
already, Wolterstorff commented that if Christian
education aims to prepare persons for living the
Christian life in the Christian community, then
Christians must recognize that in such a community
there are no inferior or superior occupations. Every
occupation is a calling. "The curriculum of the
Christian school must equip its students for their
future lives no matter what occupation they eventually
choose" (Curriculum: By What Standard? p. 13). The
context of his remark indicates the need not for a
common curriculum for diverse occupations but a fairly
diverse curriculum for varieties of Christian callings.

Of a different order is an interest in
"integrated" curriculum.

In the early 1950's Cornelius Jaarsma argued that
if Christian education intends to aim at "heart
acceptance" or the "acceptance of life in the heart,"
then curricular coherence demands "unified areas of
learning" (Fundamentals, p. 259). He wanted no mere
lumping together of the disciplines, no fused
"colorless mass." But he urged educators to help
students grasp the coherent relationships of life with

some sense of wholeness. So he recommended that the work in the primary grades be unified about the language arts, the intermediate grades about the natural sciences (and language arts), and the junior high years about social studies (including the other, in spiral curricular fashion) (ibid., pp. 260-63). Unfortunately very few Reformed Christian educators were listening.

Christian Schools International's recently published curriculum entitled "Man in Society" represents an integrated approach to Christian social studies at the secondary level. Much more could be done, however, with the schools by master teachers working alone or in groups instead of waiting for published materials from Grand Rapids or Toronto.

Two comments. First, while teaching skills and abilities "naturally" as part of multi-disciplinary or thematic units is an ideal way to teach skills, some learners much of the time and all learners some of the time may need concentrated practice at skill mastery. Second, though I have stressed that a responsibility theory seems to entail multi-disciplinary units, it also entails courses, units, or lessons that reflect single, discrete disciplines. By virtue of their being rooted in the scriptures, they too would be expressions of faith penetrating learning and are thereby "integrated."

Pedagogical Practices

In an article entitled "Effective Schools for the Urban Poor" (Educational Leadership, October, 1979, 15-24), Ron Edmonds after pressing the claims of a particular approach to education, one that stresses "school climate" in order to make learning effective for the urban poor, made this admission: "no one model explains school effectiveness for the poor or any other social class subset. Fortunately, children know how to learn in more ways than we know how to teach, thus permitting great latitude in choosing instructional strategy" (ibid., p. 22).

I think he is correct. Yet, if Christian education is to represent a genuine alternative to public education, and if a responsibility theory is a viable set of concepts about which one can organize thought, then it ought to result in a plan for deciding not only on curriculum but on methods of instruction, discipline, the social organization of classroom and school, and a host of other entailments. Hence, out of all the possible ways in which persons are capable of

learning and responding, we should be looking for those
ways most coherent with a responsibility theory aimed
at discipline.

Before we look at some examples, this first:
Henry Beversluis (Chapter Three in Christian
Philosophy of Education) speaks of two sides of
Christian education that ought never to be wrenched
apart. One can call the sides the "child" side, and
the "curriculum" side; John Dewey called them the
subjective side and the objective side. (Our present
national concern for excellence in education seems to
reassert the importance of the objective side; the
"romantics"--that is, John Holt and company--asserted
the importance of the subjective side.) Beversluis'
attempt to keep the two sides together led him to press
the equal importance of response (the child's side) and
encounter (the curriculum side).

The notion of "sides" can be understood in a
slightly different context. One side, the child's
side, would lift up the importance of insights from out
of developmental or maturational theories of learning,
the other side insights from socialization theories of
learning. In effect the commitment of the Centre at
Toronto to describing the role of the child in learning
as "self-forming" and that of the teacher as "forming"
reflects, I believe, an effort to profit from the
insights of both maturationst and socialization views.

I approve of such efforts. Fundamentally a
responsibility theory has to take both sides into
account. I think this biblical. Proverbs 22:6, for
example, is more often read: "Train up a child in the
way he should go," and when so read it tends to
reinforce the objective side or socialization side, the
side that sets up role-expectations, demands duties,
imposes obligations. But Proverbs 22:6 can just as
well read this way: "Bring up a child in the way of
his going..." (Jaarsma, Fundamentals, p. 405). Such
a rendering should remind us, Jaarsma insisted, of God-
ordained ways of child development (see his "Teaching
According to the Ways of Child Life" in Fundamentals,
pp. 280-350).

A responsibility theory, then, is one that pays
equal attention to who the person is--whether child,
or adolescent--as well as to what he is to become.
It grants equal importance to where the learner is
"coming from," as well as to where he is "going." This
delicate balancing also creates all sorts of potential
problems as well as challenges for the Christian
educator, since one can founder on either side.

Here are some pedagogical examples from the
literature of Reformed Christian education that, I
think, illustrate an attempt to respect both sides, in
the context of a responsibility theory.
1. Biblical Self-direction. A. Janse, a Dutch
schoolmaster ("Education for Self-Direction" in
Jaarsma, Fundamentals, pp. 367-369), criticized
Christian educational practice in child nurture
because, in disciplining children, the practice tended
to overemphasize the norm of obedience (see Col. 3:20;
Eph. 6:1) and disregarded the meaning of Col. 3:21:
"Fathers, do not fret and harass your children, or you
may make them sullen and morose." We may not break
children of their God-ordained independence, warned
Janse. We may not place burdens on our children too
heavy to bear. We must not frustrate self-control, nor
deprive children from reaching conclusions by
themselves. Instead, honoring both "sides" as it were,
Janse concluded: we must give children "the
independence appropriate to child life that they may
practice self-direction and thus grow up to act as
independent, self-directing people in the large areas
of life."
2. True Self-Acceptance. Beversluis seeks to
acknowledge both "sides" by juxtaposing encounter
(with curriculum) and response (to curriculum). But
his thought is more complex than that. Within response
itself, measured primarily by the child's ability to
grow intellectually, morally, and creatively,
Beversluis is playing delicately with the two sides in
at least this sense: that though intellectual and
moral growth can be understood as coming from the
objective side, that is, as expectations for the
learner to grow intellectually to know what is, and to
choose morally what ought to be, creative growth,
somewhat counteractively, involves his becoming aware,
says Beversluis, "that he has it in him to live a
personal life (Christian Philosophy of Education, p.
59).
     Beversluis' plea, not for individualism but for
uniqueness, reminds me of one of my favorite passages
from Jacques Maritain's Education at the Crossroads.
Maritain claims that to grow in self-perfection, or
better says he, to grow in the perfection of love, "is
not to copy an ideal. It is to let yourself be led by
Another where you did not want to go, and to let Divine
Love Who calls each being by his own name mold you and
make of you a person, a true original, not a copy"
(ibid., p. 36).
3. Tendency Learning. Wolterstorff concentrates on

what he calls "tendency learning," and then narrows the
discussion even more by analyzing tendency learning in
the context of our "moral responsibilities" (in
distinction from, say, our ecological, political,
aesthetic, or intellectual responsibilities)(cf. p.
33). Since writing the book, he has treated his
findings about tendency learning more broadly. He
raises this fundamental issue: if Christian education
is to teach the learner not just a way of thinking
about Christian life, not merely even thinking about
a genuinely alternative Christian way of living, but
instead aims at equipping the learner for living a
genuinely alternative mode of life in a
non-isolationist setting, then Christian schools must
be concerned with shaping how the learner tends to act.

For his answers he went to recent psychological
research and discovered that though nothing we do can
guarantee that learners will tend to act in certain
ways, yet certain strategies go far toward helping
learners internalize certain responsible tendencies
as well as cognitive structures for responsible
action. One is discipline, the granting of rewards
and punishments: praising students for acting
responsibly, chastizing them for not acting or acting
irresponsibly. But discipline, he notes, is far more
effective if combined with modeling, especially by
persons whom the student loves and respects, though
modeling is even more effective if practiced
consistently by the entire school community: "...to
teach the Christian way of life, the school must itself
exhibit that way of life. It must be a community of
peace [and] love" (Educating for Responsible Action,
p. 111). But given the non-isolationist setting of our
Christian schools, and assuming concordant modeling in
the home, church, and school, the learner still runs
the powerful risk of being exposed to discordant or
discrepant modeling from such sources as television,
radio, motion pictures, and print media. Therefore, to
be effective, a responsibility theory demands that we
give the learner reasons for acting in the right way.

This third strategy--reasons--will include the
step of teaching moral concepts, or enunciating certain
standards for acting in responsible ways, so that the
student has a cognitive structure with which to
operate. It will also include ability teaching so that
the student learns how to apply certain moral concepts
and norms; it will even include the teacher's
presenting biblically justified reasons why the teacher
himself (though preferably the school and the Christian
support community) thinks these reasons rather than

131.

some others justify certain morally responsible acts.

Wolterstorff argues that internalizing all this, so that the student will more than likely act responsibly, calls for combining all three strategies. In reverse order, a student will likely internalize, say, his ecological responsibilities if we combine the enunciation of ecological standards with appropriate discipline for their violation, reinforced by models "who enunciate these standards, who try to act on them, and who express their regret when they fail to live up to them and their satisfaction when they do" (ibid., p. 117.).

Implicit in this all too brief summary are subjective as well as objective conditions. For along with Wolterstorff's persuasive concern for inducting Christian youth into a Christian mode of living (objective) are his concerns for a mode of discipline (objective) that is not an affront to the dignity of the person (subjective), for models (objective) who are perceived by the student to be nurturing (subjective), and strategies for reasoning that give proper regard to the authoritative message of the Scriptures on the one hand (objective), while on the other respecting the fact that the learner is a free agent (subjective) capable of choosing to a great extent what he will act on.

4. Practicums for Nurturing Social Concern. There's an old adage that says: one learns to do by doing. John Dewey discovered the closest of ties between experience and education. In that light, Steensma and Van Brummelen speak of a multi-disciplinary core course for secondary education on the theme of the "Christian in Society": "In order that the student's knowledge will lead to loving action, he should have contact with the community during this course. Resource people from the community could be used effectively.... In his project work the student should go out into the community, perhaps interviewing people for written or oral presentations, perhaps spending one or two days in a community agency such as a home for the physically disabled. By the time the student is in grade 12, he should know how the press and radio may be used as a witness for the saving grace and Kingship of Christ; he should be able to analyze the significance of government policy and how such policy can be influenced; he should have experienced how groups of citizens can band together to provide services for the poor and destitute in our society; he should have had opportunities to exercise Christian love within our community. They add, "The curriculum must proclaim the

office God gave to man whereby he can respond in
righteous obedience within God's established
relationships. The implications...of this office need
to be understood, explored, and experienced in
school" (ibid, p. 17; italics added).
 Louis Voskuil ("Nurturing Social Concern,"
Christian Educators Journal, October, 1982, 12-14)
notes that the school must assume a responsibility to
educate the Christian community to its responsibilities
for social concern and action. He also claims that
unless we get students started on this early in life we
will never get them into the habit. Hence to promote a
"Christian social ministry" in the school, Voskuil
proposes, like Steensma and Van Brummelen, a practicum
that brings the student into contact with the world
outside the narrow Christian community.
 In a little piece called "What's Your Social
Quotient?" (Michigan School Board Journal, September,
1982, 27-28) I've indicated some examples and
possibilities: (1) children engaged in a bike-a-thon
to raise money for their own playground equipment; (2)
junior high students cleaning up a riverbank or city
park; (3) senior high students "adopting a grandparent"
at a senior citizen's center. I've even proposed to
middle school students that they learn, in school, in
enrichment classes held during the final period of the
day, basic skills like fixing a leaky faucet, or
repairing a screen door, replacing a broken window, or
painting a garage so that, thus equipped, the students
could organize an effort to perform such services for
the truly needy in their neighborhoods.
5. The classroom as Community. Leonard Sweetman
("Models of Man: Their Classroom Consequences,"
Christian Educators Journal, May, 1971, 7-9) argues
that if one's view of the child lifts up the doctrine
of total depravity above other factors in the
definition, then one's classroom is likely to be a
"battleground" of teacher vs. students, good vs. bad
students, student vs. teacher. If, however, one
subordinates that doctrine in one's view of the child
and lifts up instead the child's true statue as "holy
in the Lord," then there is the greater likelihood that
the classroom will be a community where teacher and
pupil share their most radical characteristic: they
are mutually in Christ; together, teacher and pupil are
new persons.
 In light of I Cor. 12, Sweetman draws the
conclusion that the true classroom community, like the
church of God, is a setting that respects
individuality, where each student is considered "custom

made," yet one where each uniquely made person responsibly shares his gifts and talents with the community.

6. Up with Cooperation. Gilbert Besselsen ("Competition or Cooperation," CEJ, May, 1976, 6-7) actually demonstrates Sweetman's sense of community in Besselsen's description of a personal experience with a remarkably responsible fifth grader. Eschewing competition in a game situation calling for arithmetic skill practice, Lynette asked Gil to structure the game they were playing together so that to win meant not--as usual--for one person to get a higher score faster than the other but to win meant both achieving the same score. Like Sweetman, Besselsen wonders whether the truly Christian classroom ought to play down competition, play up cooperation. In the end he observes poignantly, "A child taught me how to be productive without being competitive."

7. Multi-graded Classrooms: Maturity Demands and Assignments of Responsibility. A. Janse (op.cit., p. 368) argues that in order for the child to achieve true self-direction, Christian schools should get rid of their rigid "grade division."

Cornelius Jaarsma, too, lamented that teaching and learning continue in graded structures that group children merely by age. This, he claimed, was "not the fruit of Christian thinking" but the "product of the Enlightment" (in Fundamentals, p. 261).

I recently had a student from New Zealand who, some years earlier, had helped establish, and teach at, the Silverstream parent-controlled Christian school. Her one-room school consisted of approximately twenty-five children ranging in age from five to eleven. In a term paper, Nel van't Wout described her philosophy and some of its practices in this multi-graded classroom.

She recalls an eleven year old boy who could barely read when he came to the school, though he was, she notes, "good with children." He hated reading, and avoided it. So she set him to helping her instruct seven year olds with their reading. To do so he needed instruction; she gave it during her lunch hour. This instruction boosted his ego, she notes, and soon he was practicing with a friend in order to read stories to the five year olds.

Another lad was talented in science but socially insecure. She put him in charge of the science area; he used his talents to prepare science experiments for his classmates and soon became a respected member of the group. His abilities gave rise to a small science club, led by one the parents.

One of her students was a nervous, hyperactive boy who wasted much of his time. Each day, she notes, she sat down with him to draw up a "contract" in which he designated what he thought he could accomplish that day. Fascinating.

The classroom was a workshop--the children's workshop. So they had to know where materials were kept, and how to use them well. Every child had some special responsibility, from counting scissors to emptying the "resource" baskets, to being librarian, first-aider, film projectionist, or coffee-maker for teacher, visitors, and parent-helpers! The children helped plan and then built the school play yard, and joined their parents on Saturday mornings in "work-bees."

The children beautified the school grounds with shrubs and flowers. They grew plants in the school garden, hatched chickens, bottle-fed a pet lamb, cared for a rabbit and a stray duckling. There was even a local cat who made his home in the classroom during the day, not to speak of the white mice and the goldfish.

Nel's record only confirmed some of my own prejudices in favor of what I have called "informal" education (see "A Case for Informal Education in Christian Schools," CEJ, November, 1974, 24-30). I once concluded that we should transform at least the elementary classroom into "a workshop for learning:--a workshop carefully planned by the Christian teacher to reveal to the student his many-sided religious calling in life--a workshop where the child can learn how to learn, how to think, to speculate, to respond to beauty, to make choices--a workshop where he can nurture his analytical functioning in an atmosphere of responsible freedom--a workshop where he is free to do what he ought to do--a workshop where he can function independently and interdependently, privately and communally--a workshop where he can learn to love himself, and his neighbor in the same manner, because he has learned that he is, and all his classmates are (to use Sweetman's phrase), 'God's custom-made work.'"

Some Suggestions for Christian Teacher Education

1. At the least expose future teachers to a responsibility theory for Christian education, though I would prefer that the students accept it in their hearts!
2. Explore the fairly rich literature in psychology dealing with intrinsic motivation and with "pupil

135.

ownership" of problems.
3. Direct the students to much of the literature cited in this essay.
4. Have them explore the curricular implications of a suggestion from Wolterstorff (in Curriculum: By What Standard?) that teaching must address the life of the child: his present life as well as his future life, both in school and out.
5. Have them practice applying the consider, choose, commit sequence, or the intellectual, moral, and creative sequence in the construction of single-discipline and multi-disciplinary lessons (that could be extended into units).
6. Help them to understand that just as teacher aiding experiences in college and student teaching enhanced their education as teachers, so it is likely that practicums of various sorts may enhance the learning of their pupils.
7. Give them some exposure to multi-graded classrooms by at least reading and observation if not practice.
8. Give them some experience in committee- or group-construction of a unit so that when they join the teaching profession they can do likewise. God bless.

Chapter 9

Cybernetic Learning--A Christian Interpretation

by

Gerald D. Bouma
Associate Professor of Music
Dordt College

"Then God said, 'Let Us make man in our image,
according to our likeness; and let them rule over
the fish of the sea and over the birds of the sky
and over the cattle and over all the earth, and
over every creeping thing that creeps on the
earth.'
    And God created man in His own image, in the
image of God He created him, male and female He
created them" (Genesis 1: 26,27).

Christians of every age recognize man as the
crown of God's creation. We believe that man is
created in the image of God, yet seem to have only a
foggy notion of what that means.
    Man differs physically from the creation he rules
in many respects but his mind makes him unique: his is
a creative mind possessed of the ability to reason and
deal with abstractions. No one can deny that animals
can think and can be trained, but only man was created
with the power to be creative. Only man has an
imagination. Maltz (1960) described this difference
between man and animals and states that it makes man a
creator as well as a creature. This creative
imagination enables man to "subdue it (the earth); and
rule over...every living thing that moves on the earth"
(Genesis 1:28b). It allows man to react to his
environment, analyze it, and shape it.
    Being created in the image of God involves
tremendous power and carries with it great
responsibility. Man was not invited to subdue the
earth, he was commanded to do so; therefore, man must
assume responsibility not only for himself, but for the
care of the entire earth. Obviously, man lost much of
his creativeness and his power when he chose to disobey
God. No longer could man live in harmony with creation
and rule over it. Suddenly the world became a

137.

frightening place to live in, and man set up all kinds
of boundaries to protect himself (Wilber, 1979).

God, however, saw fit to redeem man and, through
man, all of creation. Romans 8 says that the whole
earth groans and waits to be delivered from the effects
of sin into the liberty of the sons of God. Through
the work of Christ, God has again made it possible for
man to live creatively and to subdue creation.

The Heidelberg Catechism (1563) teaches that the
three essentials for fruitful living are knowledge of
sin, of salvation, and of grateful service. In
response, we emphasize man's total depravity and
Christ's atonement for our sins, but we spend
relatively little time on what it means to live a life
of gratitude and service to God. We are taught that
humility is a desireable virtue. But there is a vast
difference between true humility and false humility
which allows and even encourages Christians to avoid
their responsibility to rule creation.

We are taught that in ourselves we can do nothing;
it is only through the work of Christ that man is
redeemed. Again, this is true; but to stop here is to
ignore the third part of the catechism and the reason
for God's redemption plan. Christ's work was not
simply for man's salvation; He suffered and died so
that man could once again live in obedience to God and
in harmony with creation. The redeemed man is called
to develop his creative imagination to its full
potential. This demands daring and faith far beyond
what the Christian community has been willing to commit
itself to in the past.

A Theory of Learning

Psychology is a relatively young field of study.
Unfortunately, many studies and, consequently, many
theories have been based on weak, if not false,
premises. For example, it has been assumed that, since
man is biologically similar to animals, he must also be
psychologically similar. The result has been countless
studies linking man's behavior to rats, mice, monkeys,
dogs, etc., ignoring the fact that man is unique,
created in God's image, and that perhaps he does not
function psychologically like any other creature.
Other theories, such as that of Freud, have been built
around one elemental need or response, ignoring the
fact that man functions as a total unit. Educators,
who should be leading the way, have often completely
ignored the question of how people learn.

Only recently have learning theorists concerned

138.

themselves with studies of "normal" people. Only recently have a few learning theorists had the courage to suggest that perhaps studies of a few subjects over a long period of time, such as those done by Piaget, are more valid than short term observations of a large number of subjects. It is significant to note that many of the leaders in the area of learning theory are neither psychologists nor educators.

Christian educators have a responsibility to try to understand how people learn and to articulate learning theories which are both Biblical and practical. We must realize that man has only <u>begun</u> to develop the vast potential with which he has been created and that redeemed man bears a special responsibility. Christian educators must be aware of advances in the area of learning theory and bold in trying new theories. If promising new theories call for radical changes in curriculum and/or methodology, Christian schools must be changed to meet the challenges.

<u>Learning Model</u>

The diagram on the following page is a learning model based in part on the theory of psycho-cybernetics as expressed by Maxwell Maltz (1960).

Learning Model

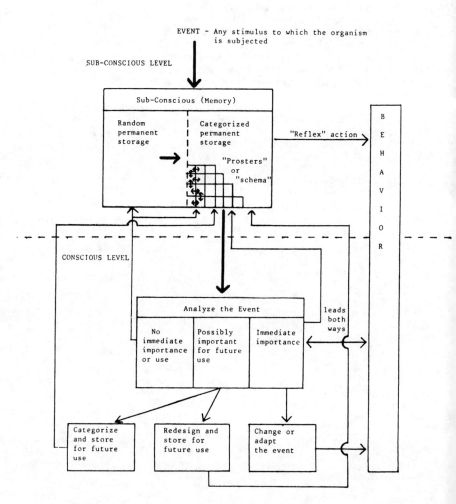

EVENT - Any stimulus to which the organism
is subjected

SUB-CONSCIOUS LEVEL

Sub-Conscious (Memory)

Random
permanent
storage

Categorized
permanent
storage

"Prosters"
or
"schema"

"Reflex" action

B
E
H
A
V
I
O
R

CONSCIOUS LEVEL

Analyze the Event

No
immediate
importance
or use

Possibly
important
for future
use

Immediate
importance

leads
both
ways

Categorize
and store
for future
use

Redesign and
store for
future use

Change or
adapt
the event

140.

The following definitions and/or descriptions are important to understanding the model:

Event: Any stimulus to which the human organism is subjected, including stimulii of which the person is not consciously aware.

Prosters: Borrowed from Leslie Hart (1975): a method of storing and processing information similar to Piaget's "schema." The word is formed from the words program structures.

Servo: Borrowed from Maxwell Maltz (1960): the internal guidance system which controls an individual.

Perhaps the best way to understand the model is to examine the two levels of the mind and the relationship between them.

Sub-conscious Level

The sub-conscious level is the more complex and difficult to understand. It is a vast domain which really embodies all human existence. Activity never ceases on the sub-conscious level, since all events to which a person is subjected are processed there. Most of these events never reach the conscious level, but information is constantly accepted, stored, and processed, and still affects the way a person acts and lives, even when the conscious level may be at rest. For example, the control and use of involuntary muscles and reflex actions seems to be located in the sub-conscious. Whether awake or asleep, a person continues to breathe and will respond to stimuli such as a pin prick.

The storage or memory of events is one of the keys to learning. The sub-conscious stores information in two ways. The first is random permanent storage. This can be compared to throwing articles in a room without organization. As the room fills up, the articles become more difficult to retrieve. Events stored in this manner are often, for practical purposes, not really a part of the conscious memory.

The sub-conscious is also capable of storing events in an organized fashion. People may categorize events in several different ways (e.g. alphabetically, chronologically, etc.). Piaget chose to call the units of organization "schema" while Hart refers to the units as "prosters." However a person categorizes events, the system or systems of organization are extremely complex. Not only are events categorized into separate prosters, but the prosters are also cross-referenced. Hart suggested that two measures of intelligence are how many prosters are formed and how many links are

established among prosters. Every event is either
stored in existing prosters or, if it does not fit in
any existing proster, in a new proster. Note that the
categorization of events does not guarantee recall, it
is merely an aid. Recall is dependent on the
communication link between the conscious and the
sub-conscious.

The sub-conscious level is the location of the
servo mechanism. Maltz described the servo as "An
automatic goal-seeking machine which 'steers' its way
to a target or goal by use of feedback data and stored
information, automatically correcting course when
necessary" (Maltz, pp. 40, 41). Maltz compared the
servo to complex computerized guidance systems in
missiles, though the human servo is infinitely more
complex than the most sophisticated computers.
Evidence suggests that the servo has a great deal to do
with learning, personality, physical well-being, and
spiritual well-being. When God, in His Word, speaks of
the "heart" of man, He may be referring to the servo.

The servo can be "programmed," either
automatically or deliberately. From birth, or earlier,
the servo is constantly affected by outside influence.
Part of the effect of original sin can be viewed as a
negative programming or pollution of the servo. When
God said, "I will never again curse the ground on
account of man, for the intent of man's heart is evil
from his youth;" He may have been referring to the
servo (Genesis 8:21). Regeneration may then be seen
as a reprogramming of the servo, possible only through
the redemptive work of Jesus Christ. Paul was giving
instructions for positive programming of the servo when
he admonished Christians to let our minds dwell on
whatever is pure and holy (Philippians 4:8).

Much of a child's personality and learning
capability is determined long before the child enters
school. A child who grows up in a home where love and
understanding are commonplace will be likely to exhibit
these characteristics as an adult. A child who is
encouraged to explore and ask questions will develop a
much greater capacity for learning than the child whose
questions are ignored or suppressed.

The school is another strong influence on the
servo, one which ought to be positive, encouraging and
enabling the child to explore new territories.
Unfortunately, the school often sets up boundaries or
limitations. Instead of developing an increasing sense
of wonder and appreciation for God's creation, the
child too often acquires a cynicism toward creation and
education. The school, with its typical constant
negative programming, bears much responsibility for the

142.

development of such an attitude. An example of negative programming found in the school is the grading system. From the time the child enters school, papers are returned to him with the mistakes checked. The child soon accepts the fact that the system is designed to call attention to his weaknesses rather than his strengths. Education becomes a game of avoiding mistakes rather than a discovery of potential.

The servo can also be self-programmed. However, the conscious will and and the sub-conscious servo often come into conflict; in such cases, the servo will always win the battle and ultimately rule over the will. People struggle constantly with such things as dieting, building self-confidence, and altering personality traits. While such a person may experience some short-term success, he will seldom experience lasting success until the servo is reprogrammed to accept and guide the change in lifestyle.

Maltz claimed that the servo cannot distinguish between a real and a simulated experience. Thus, while the servo cannot be commanded to behave a certain way, it can be "tricked" into assuming that certain data is real. One successful technique Maltz suggested for programming the servo is to spend a certain amount of time each day in total relaxation, imagining in great detail what life is like having already achieved a desired goal. For example, a person having difficulty understanding mathematics should spend time each day imagining that he is able to solve math problems. After a time, the servo will begin to act on that assumption and significant gains in the person's mathematical ability can be expected. Experiences with students have demonstrated that this kind of programming can produce dramatic positive results in educational achievement. The trumpet player who "thinks" he is third-rate will always be third rate. When that same trumpet player learns to "think" he is a first-rate trumpeter, his playing improves dramatically.

Conscious Level

Educators have typically been concerned primarily with the conscious level of the brain. Since it tends to be more analytical, the results of its activities are more behavioristic and more easily measured. A person's will, when seen as a conscious effort or resolve, is a part of the conscious level.

The conscious level may also be compared to a very sophisticated computer. Each bit of information which reaches the conscious level is evaluated, processed, and sent back to the sub-conscious for storage.

The first step, evaluation, is especially important in the conscious processing of information, for what happens to the information is almost totally dependent on that process. When faced with new information, the conscious level must choose one of three options: (1) the information is immediately important, (2) the information may have some importance, (3) or the information is not really important at all.

When the first choice is made, a number of things happen. First, the information is sent back to the sub-conscious for storage in a highly organized form. Information which is considered to be important is usually stored in the most accessible manner. Second, the information may be used as is or it may be adapted to suit the needs and existing prosters of the individual. Finally, the information usually results in some observable change in behavior and/or attitude. That change may be immediate or may occur over a period of time.

Similar, but not identical, events take place when the second choice is made. The information is categorized and sent back to the sub-conscious for permanent storage. Because it is not considered immediately important, the information may not be as readily accessible as if the first choice were made. It can either be adapted or used as is to suit the individual's needs, but is not as likely to produce a change in behavior or attitude.

The third choice is the least desireable from an educational point of view. The information is sent back to the sub-conscious for random storage, often making it completely inaccessible for all practical purposes. Furthermore, since it is considered unimportant, the information is not processed further. It would be easy to say that the third choice results in no change in behavior or attitude and, at times, this may be true. However, in many cases the third choice may actually produce or strengthen a negative behavior or attitude. For example, a person who considers poetry unimportant and dislikes it very much may only have those negative attitudes strengthened through another negative encounter with poetry.

The Conscious and Sub-Conscious

Recent research on types of brain activity shows evidence of two levels of activity: one analytical and

the other holistic. Advocates of this split-brain
theory have suggested that most analytical activity
takes place in the left brain while most holistic
thinking is done in the right brain. Research,
especially that done with epileptics, indicates that
this may be true (English, 1979). However, there is
conflicting research (Doman, 1964), particularly that
done with brain-damaged children, which seems to
indicate that any part of the brain can take over the
function of another damaged part. In fact, it is
possible for a person to lead a normal life with only
half a brain.

Whether or not the two types of mental activity
are actually seated in separate hemispheres of the
brain is really not important. What is important is
the fact that the two types do exist. Hart, however,
identified a third distinct type of brain activity.
The first he identified as instinct or reflex action,
which is almost completely sub-conscious. One does not
think about withdrawing from pain, nor does one think
about breathing, blinking, etc. Hart referred to this
essential function of the brain as the lowest form of
mental activity.

The second level Hart identified may be compared
to analytical thinking. In this mode, the person
consciously considers all possibilities and seeks to
arrive at a logical conclusion. It is this kind of
thinking which Western man has refined over the
centuries, and which has led to the scientific approach
to life. There are several problems involved with
relying too heavily on analytical thinking. First, all
of creation cannot be explained in terms of man's
logic. This is part of what God is teaching man by
saying that the wisdom of men is foolishness to God (I
Corinthians 3:18). Second, successful analytical
activity is dependent solely upon how much information
is stored in how many prosters. Analytical thinking
only encourages the formation and expanding of
prosters, not the formation of connecting links among
prosters. Analytical thinking is not really creative
thinking and does not lead to creative solutions to the
problems man faces. Hart stated that any time a person
finds himself in an uncomfortable or threatening
situation, he will "rut" into this type of thinking
because it is comfortable. Finally, serious
communication problems often occur between those who
rely primarily on analytical thinking and those who
think more holistically.

The third level of thinking is creative thinking
and involves active use of both the conscious and sub-

conscious levels as well as much communication between
the two. Creative thinking not only makes use of and
adds to existing prosters; it also requires and
encourages the formation of connecting links among
prosters. It is these connecting links which help to
make people unique creative individuals. Every new
idea, each new discovery, every invention involves a
unique connection among prosters in the originator's
mind. Creative thinking can then be encouraged by
programming the mind to ask as many questions as
possible about how things can be linked to or
associated with other things.

Creative thinking is usually the result of need,
occurring when analytical thinking fails to produce the
desired results. Creative thinking must be encouraged,
but cannot be forced. It is desireable, when facing a
difficult problem or situation, to consciously feed as
much relevant data as possible to the mind and then
push the problem out of the conscious level. The sub-
conscious will still be at work even when a person is
asleep. Almost everyone has experienced waking up with
a solution to a problem which could not consciously be
solved the day before.

Creative thinking can be encouraged by programming
the mind to view things from different angles and as
complete pictures. Western man is so accustomed to
taking things apart that he often fails to recognize
the holistic value and beauty of things. It is not
safe for the biologist to assume that by dissecting a
plant he will learn to better appreciate the plant as a
whole. The musician who can only analyze great music
is not really a musician.

To the extent that man is content to concentrate
on the development of only analytical thinking, he will
limit his potential as a complete human being and
create more problems than he solves. To the extent
that man seeks to develop the creative level of
thinking, he will learn to use rather than abuse the
resources he has been given and to have dominion over
the world as God intended.

Implications For Education

Education, once a sacred cow in the American way
of life, is presently suffering severe criticism. The
recent federal report merely echoes what persons like
Hart and Doman have been saying for some time; that
American public education is just not doing a credible
job of equipping students to deal with the world. It
is not safe to assume that only public education is in

146.

trouble. An honest evaluation of Christian education will reveal most of the same weaknesses.

President Reagan's proposal for merit pay, though a positive step, is not the solution to today's educational problems, neither is the National Education Association's cry for more money, nor is a nostalgic return to education of the past. Educators must realize that the system is about to fall apart and major surgery is needed, not a few bandaids. Painful though they may be, major reforms are needed, and the educational system must take on a whole new character if it is to survive.

The following selected recommendations are not intended to be a complete recipe for reforming education. They are intended to stimulate discussion and creative thinking leading towards positive and permanent reforms.

Purpose of Education

Educators must realize, in both philosophy and practice, that formal education exists for the students, not for the welfare of the education profession. Educators must finally admit that professional evaluation is not only a possibility but a necessity. Lack of commitment, poor teaching, and unwillingness to implement changes cannot be tolerated. Along with incentives for superior teachers must come better ways of screening out poor teachers.

Curriculum

A casual look at today's curriculum reveals a staggering array of courses ranging from sex education to driver education. In its attempt to provide everything for all people, American education has created hundreds of courses, many of which do not belong in the curriculum, with most designed only to teach secondary facts or skills.

Basic skills must be mastered, but students must also learn to use those skills in creative ways. A curriculum must be designed which has enough structure to insure skill and knowledge development and enough flexibility to meet the needs and interests of individuals. Rather than offering multitudes of frill courses, schools could better design a core curriculum, even for the lower grades, with enough time built in for remedial work and in-depth pursuit of individual interest areas.

Grade Levels

Some sort of organizational structure is necessary to maintain an orderly school system; however, American education has fallen into the trap of tying grade levels strictly to chronological age. It is assumed that a child is ready for school at age five and ready for the first grade as age six. It is further assumed that it will take one school year to master the material in grade one, or any other grade.

The fact is that children of any age level vary immensely in maturity and mental development and most are capable of learning far more than what is expected. As Doman (1964) points out, the biggest problem chldren face in school is boredom. It is not amazing for a three-year-old to learn to read; it is more amazing to make a child wait until first grade to learn to read.

It is possible to retain grade levels and still make provision for children to move through the levels at their own paces. If the teacher is viewed as a resource person rather than a dispenser of facts, personalized courses and techniques can be designed which will allow a child to take two years or two months to move through a given unit of instruction.

Teaching Techniques

Regenerated man is still suffering the effects of sin and is basically lazy; educators cannot assume that students will be naturally motivated. To do so is to invite the problems that many students experienced in open classrooms. In a few instances students will be highly motivated, but in most cases the teacher must create or, at least, stimulate the desire to learn. One of the teacher's primary tasks is to promote the first conscious choice mentioned earlier: the material at hand is immediately important and relevant.

Our educational system is built around negative programming: from the time he gets his first paper back, the student learns that his mistakes are emphasized, not his successes. A paper that is covered with a lot of red marks has a lot of errors. Grades are usually expressed in terms of percentage points deducted from a perfect score rather than points earned from a zero mark. Teaching techniques are often designed around detection and correction of errors rather than discovery and reinforcement of potential. Conductors, for example, usually stop an ensemble to point out and correct a mistake rather than to call attention to and reinforce aesthetic beauty. In its worst form, negative programming can take on the form of verbal and mental abuse to the point where the students not only don't <u>want</u> to learn, they don't <u>dare</u> to learn.

The teacher must be a constant source of encouragement to students. The student who is frustrated must be patiently encouraged to use his power of creative thinking to solve the problem at hand. Each small success must be enthusiastically called to the student's attention.

The student must be taught to set goals and, through exercises, to program his own servo to achieve those goals. He must be taught to think in terms of potential rather than limitations. The limitations will be discovered soon enough; the potential may never be discovered unless it is sought.

Students need help to strengthen the lines of communication between their conscious and sub-conscious levels. Daily recall exercises in the form of memory games and quizzes can help a great deal. Students must understand that this is the primary purpose of the exercises rather than student evaluation. They must be encouraged to spend a certain amount of time alone each day communicating with themselves, just as they spend devotional time communicating with their Savior.

The teacher must work to create an atmosphere of mutual respect and understanding, both in and out of the classroom, so that students will both want and dare to learn. There is no room for the element of fear, sarcasm, or disrespect in a teacher's dealing with students. There is no chance of creative thinking when students are afraid or uncomfortable. The teacher must realize that whether a class succeeds or fails is largely determined by the feelings generated already when the teacher enters the room.

Finally, student evaluation must be a positive experience. The teacher must create and use tools which the student recognizes as a cooperative endeavor to evaluate his progress. Evaluation is an essential part of the educational process but we must do everything possible to avoid the game playing that presently exists in so much of the evaluation process.

Conclusion

Despite all man's analytical achievements in technology, he has failed to solve the real problems that stem from a loss of creativity at the Fall. Old

educational systems and methods built on analytical
thinking will not help solve those problems. Man does
not need new gadgets, new tools, or new weapons; he
needs to develop his God-given creative powers to learn
to deal with his world, and with fellow human beings
also created in the image of God.

References

I Corinthians 3:18. (N.A.S.V.)

Doman, Glenn. How To Teach Your Baby to Read.
Garden City, New York: Doubleday and Company,
1964.

English, William S. Brain Research And Music.
Keynote address for the Canadian Music Educators
Association National Conference. Vancouver, B.C.,
March, 1979.

Genesis 1:26, 27. (N.A.S.V.)

Genesis 1:28b. (N.A.S.V.)

Genesis 8:21. (N.A.S.V.)

Hart, Leslie A. How The Brain Works. New York, New
York: Basic Books Incorporated, 1975.

Maltz, Maxwell. Psycho-cybernetics. Englewood
Cliffs, New Jersey: Prentice-Hall, Inc., 1960.

Matthew 17:20b. (N.A.S.V.)

Philippians 4:8. (N.A.S.V.)

Psalm 139:14. (N.A.S.V.)

Ursinus, Z. & Olevianus, C. The Heidelberg
Catechism. Philadelphia, Pennsylvania: United
Church Press, 1963.

Wilber, Ken. No Boundary. Los Angeles, California:
Center Publications, 1979.

Chapter 10

MOTIVATION FOR LEARNING FAITH-KNOWLEDGE

by

Marion Snapper
Professor of Church Education
Calvin Theological Seminary

"How can I motivate them?" is probably the most frequently asked question by teachers. We all want our students to learn, and motivation, most simply defined, is something that prompts a person to act in a certain way. It is an _inner_ urge that prompts a person to action. Inner is emphasized because it serves to distinguish motives from incentives or inducements which are _outer_. If a gold star is effective in getting students to do their work, then we have successfully used an inducement or incentive. But we do not know what their motives were for doing this work, although we can surmise.

There is something foolhardy about venturing into this area. It is probably the most troublesome one to the empirically minded psychologist. Edward J. Murray says that there are some psychologists who would eliminate motivation entirely as a topic for general psychology.

> They regard the subject as the last refuge
> of the humanists, the vitalists, and the
> teleologists. Perhaps they are right, in
> a way, because it is when we consider motives
> that the analogy between man and machine
> breaks down.[1]

Furthermore, the field is so unorganized that it is very tempting to embrace one of the competing systems--Instinct, Drive, Psychoanalytic, Cognitive, Learning, Hedonic, etc.--or to settle for considering only one set of human drives or social forces. Such oversimplication always leads to serious distortions of our understanding of human motivation.[2]

Therefore, as we narrow the discussion, the reader must be cautioned against thinking that the theory presented here is adequate to explain all of human behavior. It is not. What we must indicate here is how we went about narrowing the discussion.

First, it is not necessary to belabor the fact that some theories of motivation are philosophically unacceptable to Christians. This is not to say that there are no insights into human behavior to be obtained from them. Rather, when elevated to the level of explaining "What is man?" they violate, at least for Christians, our "control beliefs"[3] regarding man. Surely among them are those mechanistic theories which seek to explain all behavior in terms of stimulus-response (reinforcement, conditioning, etc.) connections. Such theories, when expanded to explain all human behavior posit, to use Gordon Allport's term, the "empty organism"[4] in which there are no intervening variables between stimulus and response. There is no room for such constructs as mind, heart, character, soul, personality. Such reductionistic theories are patently unacceptable to a Christian anthropology.

Secondly, in selecting a theory of motivation, we will be helped by selecting one which lends itself rather readily to analysis of Word teaching because that is most basically what a teacher does. Whatever else it may include, the teaching ministry in the church is a Word ministry. With all the valuable insight given us by dynamic theories of motivation (psychoanalysis), those approaches are so heavily intrapsychic and subjective that they allow little space for analysis of how words function. The most valuable help we get from them is in dealing with the problem of "the reason he gives" for behavior, which in many cases is not the real reason for the behavior. The real reason is hidden in the depths of the psyche, and the one given is called a "rationalization," not meaning good reasons, but to the contrary, wrong reasons. This most helpful insight, and the tools of psychoanalysis ought not to be lost on us, but the theory itself is inadequate both for philosophical and practical reasons.

Thirdly, a theory of motivation ought to flow easily out of the biblical concepts which surround any analysis of why people behave as they do--of what motivates people. The Bible does not provide us with a ready-made theory of motivation, though it has much to say about the roots of human behavior. There are evil hearts and there are good hearts. Out of the heart flow all the imaginations, thoughts, and plans of man; out of it are the issues of life (Gen. 8:21; Prov.

4:23; Rom. 1:18-32). The explanations are largely
theological; man does evil because his heart is evil
and therefore has wicked designs on his neighbor. Man
does good because he has a new heart; he is filled
with the Holy Spirit. It is within the framework of
such rather simple but profound assertions that we
should develop our thinking about motivation for
learning.

A Biblical Perspective on Man

Our beginning point, then, is with God's intention
for man whom He created in his own image. He created
man for shalom,[5] for wholeness. God's desire was
that the whole creation with one united voice would
glorify him. Man's chief end is to glorify God and to
enjoy him forever (Westminster Catechism). He was made
to live in love, peace, and harmony with God, himself,
and his neighbor. He was as vice-regent of creation,
to cultivate the earth so that it too would yield its
fruit in due season. He was to study, to plumb the
heights and depths, there to find new wonders of God's
laws which govern his creation. He was created to give
the creation a voice (Words) of praise to its maker.
Even though sin shattered that wholeness and
destroyed shalom, man's search for it continues.
Though God himself is the linchpin which holds
everything together, man even in unbelief, hides from
God and pretends that he can bring order and peace into
life. The story of redemption can, in considerable
part, be described as God's action in bringing shalom
back to his creation.
This theme which runs through the Scriptures is
powerfully pervasive. It is the final word in God's
benediction: "The Lord bless you and keep you: The
Lord make his face to shine upon you, and be gracious
to you: The Lord lift up his countenance upon you, and
give you shalom" (Num. 6:24-26). It describes his
covenant relationship: "For the mountains may depart
and the hills be removed, but my steadfast love shall
not depart from you, and my covenant of shalom shall
not be removed, says the Lord, who has compassion on
you" (Isa. 54:10).
The Septuagint translates shalom into the
Greek word eirene--peace in English. Again it is
pervasive in the New Testament. Paul, in his
salutations to the churches, invariably says, "Grace
and peace (shalom) be unto you..." It appears then
as the briefest way for Paul to say what his heart's

155.

desire is for God's people: "May you experience the
grace of God in Jesus Christ as it brings shalom unto
your lives." This biblical theme involves all areas of
life:

It is personal. "Have no anxiety about
anything, but in everything by prayer and supplication
with thanksgiving let your requests be made known to
God. And the peace (shalom) of God which passes
all understanding will keep your hearts and minds in
Christ Jesus (Philip. 4:6-7). Shalom here is that
personal sense of well-being which is the opposite of
gnawing anxiety, of feeling that one is coming
"unglued." It is that feeling which we experience with
intensity at times; that God is in heaven and all is
well with the world even though there are many
problems, perplexities, and bewildering events.

It is communal. Shalom is experienced in
our relations with others, especially those of the
household of faith. When Joseph's brothers got fed up
with what they saw as favoritism by father Jacob, they
could no longer speak shalom with Joseph; the
relationship between them was fractured. Shalom is
broken by lying and deceit: "Everyone deals falsely.
They have healed the wounds of my people lightly,
saying, 'Shalom, Shalom when there is no
Shalom'" (Jer. 8:10-11). The community which finds
its common life in Jesus Christ is admonished to be a
community of shalom: "Let us then pursue what makes
for peace and mutual upbuilding" (Rom. 14:19).

Shalom is pre-eminently a communal-covenant in
the Scriptures. Beginning with the narrow idea of the
shalom of the family and tribe, it expands into the
community chosen by a covenant-making God whose people
shall find great shalom in loving his law (Ps.
119:165). God makes eternal covenant with David,
promising that his love will never depart from his
house (II Sam. 7:11-16); that under his reign Israel
shall dwell secure, unmolested, in shalom (II Sam.
7:10). The vision is expanded by the prophets as God's
people are given the anticipation of the coming of the
"Prince of shalom" (Isa. 9:6-7).

The clear picture one gets from the Scriptures is
of the Christian community being a community of
shalom. Ethnic and racial walls are broken (Eph. 2).
There is a oneness, a wholeness. But it is not the
clannish, closed community. Rather, it stands in the
world as a kind of lighthouse, inviting all people to
join. The shalom community also seeks the shalom
of the city in which it is found (cf. Jer. 29:7).

It is with creation. Thorns and thistles are used in Scripture to point to the brokenness in creation (Gen. 3:18). Shalom points to a wholeness in which the wolf will lie down with the lamb (Isa. 65:17-25). The science of ecology today speaks of shalom when it seeks a wholeness and harmony in the environment. Plundering the earth's resources, devastating the environment are anti-shalom. Even the whole creation longs and groans, waiting complete redemption (Rom. 8:22). In summary, shalom speaks of whole persons, whole communities, and a whole world.

It is with God. Shalom is the good news of the gospel. No longer does man have to strive in order to placate the gods. No longer does he have to hide. The heart of the gospel is that "since we are justified by faith we have shalom with God through our Lord Jesus Christ" (Rom. 5:1). Paul L. Hammer says:

> This passage summarizes the major thrust of Romans, and lies at the heart of all Pauline theology. Challenged by a perspective that sought to make shalom a matter of achievement (i.e., keeping all the rules of cultic and ethical religious life), Paul emphasizes that shalom with God is not something to be achieved but to be received.[6]

"By his stripes we are made shalom" (Isa. 53:5b). Shalom is a gift of grace. It cannot be our goal any more than happiness can (as in hedonism). Rather, it is a gift which comes to those who live by faith and are obedient to the gospel and all that it entails. Observance of this order is important in our thinking about Christian ministry and the Christian life. Obedience to the gospel may, as a matter of fact, cause disruptions; one may have to leave father and mother in order to follow Christ. The Jesus who said, "My shalom I leave with you," also said, "Do not think that I have come to bring shalom on earth; I have not come to bring shalom, but a sword" (Matt. 10:34).

This contradictory aspect of shalom is important to note for two reasons. First, it distinguishes the quest for shalom from the search for happiness or quiescense. The metaphor for shalom is not the rockingchair. Instead it is a compelling vision which seeks in God's future-for-the-world a kingdom of Shalom rising above the plateaus and dark valleys of life. In a sinful world the Christian is sustained by the vision of what, finally, God will do. In the meantime the Christian seeks peace with all men, and is ordered to do so by the God who brings peace. The paradox may be stated as follows:

> The more one is a faithful disciple of Christ the more shalom is experienced.

> The more one is a faithful disciple of Christ the more clear the perception of need, brokenness, and lostness in the world around him.

This is to say that the experience of shalom leads to a deepened sensitivity to that which is anti-shalom.

Secondly, this contradictory aspect reminds us that all theorizing about motivation within this context must reckon with human perversity and sin--which is the breaking of God's law. We shall have occasion to return to this point when we deal with specific theories of motivation.

In conclusion, it is posited that the quest for shalom is the most deeply seated intrinsic motivation of man. Most basically man seeks to "get it together" so that he may achieve whatever goals or purposes he sets for himself.

Translating the Quest for Shalom into Motivation Theory

Because an adequate discussion of motivation theory is beyond the scope of this essay, we shall confine ourselves to a particular description and use of theory. We shall use a theory as a "Disclosure Model," a term used by Ian Ramsey.[7] He makes the distinction between disclosure and picture models. A picture model is like a model plane; the representation is taken as a rather literal representation of the thing itself. Much of science prior to the 20th century worked with picture models. Modern scientists no longer think in such terms. Ramsey points theology to the use of what he calls disclosure models, and finds a number of ways in which they can help us to articulate our theology. First, such models can be seen as "builders of discourse," as giving rise to large-scale interpretations of phenomena that so far lack a theological mapping. Secondly, such models enable us "to make sense of discourse whose logical structure is so perplexing as to inhibit literacy." Thirdly, such models enable us to talk of what eludes us.[8]

These suggested uses are most appealing for dealing with questions of motivation for learning. Our subject matter is baffling in its complexity, and it is hard to speak clearly about it. A disclosure model will turn us toward an effort to order our understanding of practice, of the experiences we have in teaching. It allows us, for better or worse, to lay aside the more abstract ontological, epistemological, and anthropological issues--at least for the time.

The test of validity of a disclosure model is not first of all its ability to produce verifiable deductions--although it may do so, but by its usefulness and stability over the widest possible range of phenomena.[9] We shall therefore be using motivation theory much like a road map, as a tool for plotting our understanding of what is going on, motivationally speaking, in the teaching-learning process. More specifically, then, we shall wherever it is possible and helpful utilize diagrams to indicate relationships.

We shall further limit ourselves to a brief description of one theory, that of Leon Festinger.[10] His theory of cognitive dissonance is attractive for a number of reasons. First, it represents a family of motivation theories which, among all the families, corresponds most closely to the concept of shalom. Deci names the family of theories of which Festinger's is a member with the term, "Uncertainty Reduction."[11] Other names given to members of the family include Dissonance Reduction, Discrepancy, Balance Theory, Principle of Congruence. All of these terms are, to some degree, antonyms of shalom. In other words each of the theories has as part of its basic premise the idea that people have an intrinsic motivation to "get things together," to get rid of inconsistency when it is present, in a word, to seek wholeness.

Second, it is a simple and clear theory, more devoid of metaphysical and ontological concerns than any other known to me.[12] It thus lends itself to being used within a Christian framework of thinking with little need to engage in the kind of foundational thinking required before one can use it in a theoretically consistent way. Thirdly, it is considered by some to be a learning theory, by others to be a theory of motivation, and by many psychologists to be both a theory of motivation and learning. It

159.

therefore is attractive to those interested in motivation for learning. Finally, the theory is formulated largely in the form of hypotheses which can readily be tested. Unlike so many theories, then, one can move with relative ease from theory to practice. This is important because educationists find most theory in psychology to be relatively useless to the practice of teaching.

Festinger's Theory of Cognitive Dissonance

Festinger makes the basic assumption that human beings try to develop a set of beliefs, attitudes, values, and behaviors which are consistent with each other. When we find someone who seems deliberately to hold to inconsistencies, upon closer examination we normally find that they are ready with explanations which, at least for that person, are adequate for them. Festinger cites the example of a person who wants good health and continues to smoke cigarettes. Most of us are familiar with the efforts of such persons to make their total behavior appear consistent. This kind of human effort is so common that we often fail to recognize it as an effort to gain consistency, to reduce dissonance. We must explain the sudden cure of a dying cancer patient, and one person invokes the miracle explanation while another asserts that there must have been some sudden biochemical shift in the organism. I personally devoted a few hours recently trying to explain to myself how a puzzle works; how did they get that wooden arrow through that hole in the wood block when both ends of the arrow are larger than the hole?

Because the word "consistency" has such heavy overtones of logical consistency, Festinger has chosen to use the word "dissonance" which is usually first associated with music, being quite opposite of harmony. Dissonant music is discordant. A close synonym is incongruous, that is, lack of congruence. It refers to a lack of fit. "In short," says Festinger, "I am proposing that dissonance is the existence of non-fitting relation among cognitions..."13 By the term cognition he means "any knowledge, opinion, or belief about the environment, about oneself, or about one's behavior."14

It is clear from this definition that Festinger is using the term cognition with a broader meaning than is often assigned to it. He calls cognitions "knowled-

160.

ges." And in knowledge he includes being <u>aware</u> of
and making judgements about oneself; what one does, how
one feels, what one wants or desires, and so on.15
Thus cognition is not something discrete from
attitudes, values, opinions, or feelings.

Any two elements in our knowledge--broadly
understood--can be related to each other in three ways.
First, they may be consonant. Mr. Smith was 90 years
old. Mr. Smith died. Those two items--age 90 and
death--are quite consonant; we are not much surprised,
perplexed, or bewildered when we juxtapose those two
items. Second, any two elements in our knowledge may
be dissonant. For example, if the preacher told his
catechism class that the church was an expression of
the communion of the saints, then a student might
experience some dissonance. "Mr. Jones is a member of
the church. Mr. Jones is a saint??" And finally, any
two elements in our knowledge may be irrelevant to each
other. "I weigh 161 pounds. Paul wrote the book of
<u>Romans</u>."

A number of hypotheses have been formulated on the
basis of these rather simple assertions, and they have
led to a considerable body of research. The
fruitfulness of Festinger's theory of cognitive
dissonance can be better understood by taking some of
his hypotheses or derivations from them, and
illustrating their applicability to the teaching
ministry of the church.

1. The magnitude of the dissonance increases as
   the importance or value of the elements
   increases.16

If, for example, the church is not seen as being
important in the life of the adolescent, he or she will
not be much bothered by the fact that there is
dissonance between the teachings about the church and
how the church is perceived. But it is rarely quite as
simple as this because elements tend to cluster.
The church is not a single element; rather it is a
cluster of elements--parents, peer group, pastor,
teacher, catechism class, and so on.

2. The presence of dissonance gives rise to
   pressures to reduce or eliminate the
   dissonance. The strength of the pressure
   to reduce the dissonance is directly related
   to the magnitude of the dissonance.17

The adolescents who find great magnitude in the
dissonance between what the church is supposed to be,
and how it appears to be, and how they feel about it,
and how they are supposed to feel about it, must do
something to reduce that dissonance. Festinger

suggests that there are three basic ways that this can be done. First, the person can change a "behavioral cognitive element." In the case of the church which causes the dissonance, the adolescent can try to bring his own feelings and actions into line with how he perceives the church to be. This would most obviously entail "giving in" and conforming one's own behavior and feelings to the situation--but this is not a very promising solution in this case. While it might succeed in eliminating some sources of dissonance, it tends to create new ones.

The second basic way to deal with dissonance is to change an "environmental cognitive element." In order to do this the person must have some control over the environment. The options for youth, for example, are quite limited. First, they might try to prevail on the council of the church to do something. Secondly, they might, if it is in their power, to find another church. Or thirdly, they might make a resolve to bide their time and when they get older and have more influence, to try to do something about it.

Thirdly, dissonance may be dealt with by adding "new cognitive elements."[18] This involves getting some new information and understanding. An unrealistic idealism about the church might be tempered by some study or observation of other churches. Or a hypercritical attitude might be affected by learning that all saints are yet sinners, including self.

Theological systems of thought contain many illustrations of this kind of effort. It requires some theological explanation, for example, to deal with the assertion that mankind is totally depraved and the observation of my non-Christian neighbor who is a marvelously kind, compassionate, caring, doer of good deeds for other people. As a matter of fact, this is what the science of apologetics spends most of its time doing.

No single item in Festinger's theory has caused so much discussion as his insistence on making a distinction between conflict and dissonance. Conflict, says Festinger, is a condition experienced when we are faced with a decision. For example, we have a choice of going to church or staying home and watching the Super Bowl football game. There is conflict; a decision must be made.

> After having made the decision he is no
> longer in conflict; he has made his choice;
> he has, so to speak, resolved the conflict.
> He is no longer being pushed to two or more

directions simultaneously. He is now
committed to the chosen course of action. It
is only here that dissonance exists, and the
pressure to reduce this dissonance is not
pushing the person in two directions
simultaneously.19

Festinger's distinction was not helpful to me
until I revised it and used my own definition of
decision. A biblical perspective suggests that man
has but one basic decision to make: "Choose you this
day whom you will serve..." (Joshua 24:15). Until that
one basic decision of the heart is made, man is in
conflict, torn between two allegiances, two commitments
of the heart. It is impossible to serve both God and
mammon; one must decide for one and reject the other.
But when that decision is made, then all that follow,
should be viewed as a working out of the dissonance
which rises in living out the consequences of that
basic choice.
    This is equally true for Christians and
non-Christians. Berelson and Steiner conclude their
summary of the best findings of social science research
with a description of twentieth century man which comes
out of that data:

        Perhaps the character of behavioral science
        man can best be grasped through his
        orientation to reality. He is a creature
        who adapts reality to his own ends, who
        transforms reality into a congenial form,
        who makes his own reality...In his quest
        for satisfaction, man is not just a seeker
        of truth, but of deception, of himself as
        well as others...He adjusts his social
        perception to fit not only the objective
        reality but also what suits his wishes and
        his needs.20

    The authors go on to point out that man's capacity
to manipulate reality depends heavily on his symbolic
capacity. Things can be named and manipulated without
touching them. They can be called by other than their
real names. Qualities can be assigned.

        This distinctively human quality--can it be
        called a form of manipulation?--is apparently
        what makes life tolerable, livable, bearable
        against all the burdens...In short, man lives

not only with the reality that confronts him
but with the reality he makes....*In the end
as well as in the beginning is the
word*.[21] (italics mine)

This distinction between conflict and dissonance
serves to legitimize the title of this paper,
"Motivation for Learning Faith-Knowledge." As I
understand and use the term, "faith-knowledge," it is
post-decisional, and in the case of Christian
education, it is post-decision-for-Christ.

Action, Dissonance, and Shalom

As developed so far, a dissonance theory of
motivation has a decidedly negative quality to it;
human behavior is seen as an effort to get rid of
something, namely, dissonance. In order to correct
this impression, it is necessary to put the activity of
dissonance reduction in a broader framework (Festinger
puts it in the context of decision-making).
Earlier we stated that the quest for shalom
(wholeness, concord, etc.) was indeed a quest, not for
a rockingchair existence, but for the Kingdom of God.
Man's purpose was to glorify God, to be the caretaker
and developer of the earth, and to seek shalom with
and for all people. Man was created and redeemed as
part of God's plan in Christ to "unite all things in
him, things in heaven and things on earth" (Eph. 1:10).
It is further indicated that the quest for shalom may
land one in jail.
Active obedience to God's revealed will is the
hallmark of the quest for shalom. Christians are
called to discipleship, to the "obedience of faith"
(Rom. 1:5, 16:26). Shalom comes as a gift to those
who live by faith in Jesus Christ. And, as Calvin
indicates, to live by faith, by faith-knowledge, "is
not so much to know who and what God is in himself" as
it is a "knowledge of the will of God respecting us"
(Institutes III.ii.6). The obedience of faith is
from the heart and not from the head, from the
affections rather than the understanding.
Shalom, then, must be understood as a goal which
is actively pursued but which is received as a gift of
grace by those who are obedient.
Shalom as a goal, then, does not function as do
immediate behavioral objectives in educational
thinking. Rather, it functions as a vision, as the

backdrop of the stage of life, as the eschatalogical horizon toward which our road winds. The obedient quest for shalom is for a city whose builder and maker is God.

A Paridigm for Analyzing the Quest for Shalom

The human quest for shalom does not lend itself readily or completely to patterning. But the effort must be made if bridges are to be built between a theory of human motivation and educational practice. The usefulness of a paradigm should be judged by its faithfulness in expressing the theory and its helpfulness in ordering our thinking about the teaching-learning process.

For purposes of illustrating and applying the theory I shall work with biblical studies and use the simplest paradigm--triangles.[22] The three corners represent major sources of information for the learner. One corner represents the learners; their memories, understandings, attitudes, values, hopes, etc. The second corner represents the Scriptures. The third corner represents the culture and tradition. By tradition I refer to the Christian tradition. By culture I refer to the broader context (as the Christian tradition in American culture).

Because our focus of application is the Bible, we may use two triangles; one for the original and the other for the contemporary setting. The Word of Scripture is the same for both. But in one the learners are the Jews and/or Christians of New Testament times. In the other the learners are eighth graders in the late twentieth century in the cultural and traditional context of today.

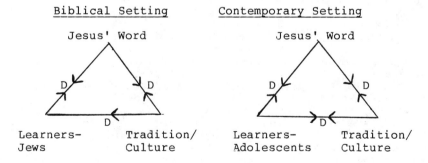

Biblical Setting	Contemporary Setting
Jesus' Word	Jesus' Word
Learners-	Tradition/	Learners-	Tradition/
Jews	Culture	Adolescents	Culture

165.

Our lesson has as its key concept, "Children of
Abraham." Our learners, working their way through
adolescence, may not care much about this concept
staring at them from the printed page. There is no
burning dissonance. Perhaps at most there is a touch
of perplexity. But who cares? Life is full of
metaphors. But we must motivate them. How? Create
dissonance! Or better, uncover it.

In this particular lesson one can look for
dissonance in at least six places, indicated by the
"D's" on the triangles. A cursory study indicates that
there was sharp dissonance in the biblical setting (cf.
Matt. 3:9; John 8:31-39; Gal. 3:6-9, 28-29). Jesus'
hearers picked up stones to throw at him, and Paul said
of those who were confusing the concept, "Let him be
accursed." The first thing, then, that the teacher
must do in order to identify dissonance is to carefully
study the biblical material and to identify as clearly
as possible what was going on in the minds of those who
heard the words of Jesus and Paul, especially what
their traditions were, and exactly what Jesus and Paul
meant by what they said.

In order to keep the lesson from becoming purely
theoretical, it is helpful to see our two triangles set
in two "story lines." The first is the "story line" of
those ancient people living out their lives in a faith
tradition formed largely by their understanding of the
Old Testament Scriptures. But then they run into
Jesus. The second is the "story line" of contemporary
adolescents nurtured in the Christian church who have
from birth been told that they are "children of the
covenant," having had the mark of the covenant put upon
them at baptism, identifying them as heirs to the
promises given to Abraham. But then they run into this
lesson.

Thus far we see that in both triangles we have a
common biblical Word, and learners who share something
in common---they have all been identified as "Children
of Abraham." So, we may ask, Why did Jesus' words
cause such violent dissonance? A study of the
Scriptures and the Jewish traditions provides the
answer. But can these same words cause dissonance in
the lives of contemporary adolsecents? It is right
here that the crunch comes. If we cannot identify any
dissonance between the words of Jesus and the learner's
understandings, then nothing of signficance can be
taught. They can be made to store some information
away. But it will probably soon be forgotten and will
not likely affect their hearts and minds. Or, to put it
in another way, if we find that their understandings

are in full conformity to the Word, then indeed there
is nothing to be learned. They already know it.
     What shall our strategy be? First, we might
consider getting these adolescents inside the "story
line" of the Bible. We could study the gospel material
(easier for these students than the Galatians
material) with a view to doing some kind of role
playing in which they would be asked to identify as
closely as possible with those ancient Jews. Let them
play out the dissonance that is in the original story.
Let them identify with people who saw their basic
identity being undermined. They were the priviledged
among all nations; chosen, and given status by virtue
of their blood line.
     Having done that, it is hard to know what might go
on in adolescent psyches. Perhaps they will see both
congruence and dissonance between their status/identity
as "covenant youth" and the status/identity of the Jews
of Jesus' day. Perhaps a simple invitation to talk
about it will result in their talking about their own
identity as "children of Abraham." If there is no
response one might select some material from the other
corner of the triangle---the tradition. Read a few
lines from the Form for Infant Baptism which talk about
Abraham, the promises, etc.
     Our second strategy, then, is to try to get into
the "story line" of these adolescents. The more we
know about them, their life situations, the way they
see themselves, the better we should be at sensing
where the dissonance might be found (It's there! We
must uncover it.). Regarding the concept we are
working with, we might reflect on how adolescents often
respond to their life histories. Erik Erikson suggests
that youth is "sensitive to any suggestion that it may
be hopelessly determined by what went before in life
histories,"[23] that their identity is really
predetermined. For example, this bit of strategy may
uncover dissonance:
     "My grandparents were Christians and members of
this denomination."
     "My parents were Christians and members of this
demonination."
     "I am a Christian and member of this
denomination?"
     Implicit in this is the thought that we are what
we are, not by choice but by a historical determinism.
I believe that, at one time or another, every
reflective adolescent is deeply troubled by this
possibility.

167.

I have not laid out a lesson plan. What I have
done is think about a concept to be taught, using a
paradigm which helps us apply our theory. I think
there are easier and harder lessons to which we could
apply our theory. But perhaps the discussion is
sufficient to warrant the following summary
conclusions.

First, neither this theory of motivation nor any
other is adequate to explain all of human behavior.
Another theory might serve better to explain the
student who simply can't stay in his chair. Secondly,
I would nevertheless assert that this theory of
motivation comes closer to dealing with what I think is
at the heart of teaching than does any other.
Teaching, as distinguished from counseling and other
forms of interpersonal influencing, is characterized
mainly by such questions as: Do you understand? Have
you got it straight in your thinking? Do you know what
it entails? Can your give me an example? How do you
relate it to...? And so on. It tries to get knowledge
and understanding together inside the learner in some
coherent, whole, meaningful way.

Thirdly, I think that this theory has wide
application. Piaget, for example, reminds us of its
central place in mathematical-scientific thinking as
well as in making moral judgments. Assimilation-
accommodation-equilibrium as theoretical constructs are
closely akin to a theory of cognitive dissonance. A
bit of reflection may call to mind sufficient
experience with literature, the arts, and history to
indicate that it is widely applicable. But what about
spelling? Perhaps we persist in the use of grades
because there are some things which must be learned but
will not yield to a theory of intrinsic motivation. So
we use an extrinsic form of dissonance theory by
saying, "I will flunk you and then you will not be
eligible for the basketball team!" That creates
dissonance, but it is extrinsic to the subject matter
at hand.

Finally, if properly understood and applied, it
keeps disciplining us as teachers to try to use our
subject matter to help students get their lives
together---which is a contemporary way of saying that
we want to touch them in their hearts.

FOOTNOTES

1. Edward J. Murray, <u>Motivation and Emotion</u>.
    Englewood Cliffs: Prentice-Hall, 1964.
    p. vi.

2. R. S. Peters, <u>The Concept of Motivation</u>.
    London: Routledge & Kegan Paul, 1960.

3. Nicholas Wolterstorff, <u>Reason within the
    Bounds of Religion</u>. Grand Rapids: Wm.
    B. Eerdmans, 1976, pp. 63-64.

4. Gordon W. Allport, <u>Personality and Social
    Encounter</u>. Boston: Beacon Press, 1964.
    p. 24-26.

5. In developing the concept of <u>Shalom</u> I made use
    of a number of sources. Most helpful was a
    trilogy of booklets:

    Paul L. Hammer, <u>Shalom in the New
    Testament</u>. Philadelphia: United Church
    Press, 1973. 30 p.

    Hugh C. White, <u>Shalom in the Old Testament</u>.
    Philadelphia: United Church Press, 1973. 30
    p.

    Edward A. Powers, <u>Signs of Shalom</u>.
    Philadelphia: United Church Press, 1973.
    160 p.

6. <u>Hammer</u>, p. 6.

7. Ian Ramsey, <u>Models and Mystery</u>. London: Oxford
    University Press, 1964.

8. <u>Ibid</u>., p. 15.

9. <u>Ibid</u>., p. 17.

10. Leon Festinger, <u>A Theory of Cognitive
    Dissonance</u>. Stanford, CA: Stanford
    University Press, 1957.
        This book contains the essential reading
        necessary to understanding the theory.
        Other books by Festinger are:

The Psychology of Insufficient Reward.
(Stanford, 1962).
Conflict, Decision and Dissonance.
(Stanford, 1964).

11. Edward L. Deci, Intrinsic Motivation. New
    York: Plenum Press, 1975. p. 58.

12. K. B. Madsen, Modern Theories of Motivation.
    New York: John Wiley and Sons, 1974.

13. Festinger, 1957, p. 3.

14. Ibid.

15. Ibid., p. 9.

16. Ibid., p. 16.

17. Ibid., p. 18.

18. Ibid., p. 21.

19. Ibid., p. 39.

20. Bernard Berelson and Gary A. Steiner, Human
    Behavior: an Inventory of Scientific
    Findings. New York: Harcourt, Brace and
    World, Inc. 1964, p. 664.

21. Ibid., p. 665.

22. James D. Whitehead and Evelyn Eaton Whitehead,
    Method in Ministry: Theological Reflection
    and Christian Ministry. New York: Seabury
    Press, 1980.
    I am indebted to the Whiteheads for some of
    my insights here.

23. Erik H. Erikson, Identity: Youth and Crisis.
    New York: W. W. Norton, 1969. P. 247.

Chapter 11

LEARNING AS INCARNATION:
A CONTEXTUALIST APPROACH TO LEARNING ABOUT LEARNING

by

Bert Hodges
Professor of Psychology
Gordon College

The problem of building a model or theory
that explains psychological understanding is
extremely different from problems faced by any
previous science. Einstein's theory is a tool
that sets the stage for understanding physics...
All scientific theories to date have presupposed
both a creator and a comprehender. Our basic
argument is that all extant theories of learning
and understanding tacitly presuppose a creator and
a comprehender as well... however, the
comprehender is the phenomenon being modeled.
(Bransford & Franks, 1976)

In his provocative article, "Psycholinguistics and
Plato's paradoxes of the Meno", Walter Weimer offers a
depressing assessment of what we have learned about
learning since Plato and Aristotle argued their cases
for anamnesis and associationism, respectively.

In 20-odd centuries we have managed to learn
nothing at all "new" about the nature of knowledge
and learning. And that does not augur well for
the future of psychology. Perhaps we are doomed
to have a (tolerably efficient) technology of
behavior modification, but no science of knowledge
and learning at all. (1973, p. 32; italics in
original)

I largely agree with Weimer's assessment, but am
reluctant to share his pessimism. Two sets of
prophetic voices have shaped my cautious optimism. One
set of "prophecies" are to be found in the
psychological literature, the other in the biblical
literature.

171.

The approaches from psychology that have helped me most in thinking about learning and the related issues of perception, memory, and action are the "contextualism" of James Jenkins (1974, 1979) and John Bransford and his colleagues (Bransford & Franks, 1976) and the "ecological realism" of James Gibson (1979), Robert Shaw and Michael Turvey (Shaw, Turvey & Mace, 1982).[1] A second theme I wish to explore is "learning as incarnation," a metaphor obviously adapted from the biblical literature. A third view rooted in both psychological and biblical studies has also influenced me, the "presentationalism" of James Martin (1982), a conference participant. I will not discuss systematically any of these other people's views, but will attempt to elucidate in a general way the character of learning. The value of the multiple perspectives is that they serve to discipline (constrain) each other and to free (open to further development) each other in exactly the same way these perspectives suggest learning in general constrains and frees the learner.[2]

LEARNING AS CONTEXTUAL

How is learning accomplished? What is learned? Who can learn? Psychological theory and research traditionally have focused on the first of these questions, but during the past 15 years have shifted their attention to the second question (Greeno, 1980). A few largely unheeded voices (e.g., Martin, 1982; Shaw & McIntyre, 1974) have suggested that the who question may be the most fundamental of the three. James Jenkins (1977, 1979) and his students (Bransford, 1979; Shaw & McIntyre, 1974) have argued persuasively that the who-what-how questions of learning mutually constrain one another, that learning is context dependent. This section will briefly explore the implications of the contextualist approach for learning. Critical revisions and extensions will be proposed.

Jenkins (1977,1979) has proposed a simple, but elegant tetrahedron model to help psychologists think clearly about learning. He presents a diagram of four sets of interacting (or mutually constraining) variables that are relevant to learning: characteristics of the learner, learning activities, nature of the materials to be learned, and criterial tasks by which learning will be assessed. Unless we have supplied a value or set of values for each of these classes of variables, Jenkins argues, we are in no position to make even approximately valid statements about learning. Usually investigators have naively held assumptions about these variable families (e.g., recall is an adequate index of learning) without examining them.

While Jenkins' argument may seem obvious in hindsight, traditional models of learning that focused on how and what questions have made very different assumptions. First, earlier models have assumed "equipotentiality": how learning occurs is neutral (or equipotential) with regard to what is being learned, by whom, and for what purpose (why). According to this assumption there are universal laws of learning that apply to any organism for any kind of task or material to be learned (Seligman & Hager, 1972). The second assumption is that a scientific explanation of learning is mechanistic. Mechanistic explanation in learning assumes (1) some basic level (irreducible, atomic) units of learning "material" that (2) may be combined into more complex but qualitatively similar units (cf., Jenkins, 1974, for a brief discussion). These units (e.g., words in language) and the conditions governing their occurrence and combination (e.g., reinforcement) are described. These basic units have no value or meaning until an organism organizes them into some larger whole that it associated with certain outcomes of structure (e.g., consistent cognitions) or process (e.g., reduction of hunger). Mechanistic accounts of learning imply: (a) the independence of the organism (who learns) and its environment (what is learned); (b) reductionism of complex to basic units; and (c) the independence of the objective world (the basic units) and value or meaning.

Research of the past 20 years indicates that the equipotentiality assumption is unjustified and the mechanistic assumption is seriously problematic. For example, the literature on biological constraints on classical and operant conditioning (e.g., Seligman & Hager, 1972) and the limitations of the "levels of processing" approach to memory (e.g., Bransford, Franks, Morris, & Stein, 1979) illustrate nicely the interactions outlined in Jenkin's model. Learning does not follow simple rules but varies across learners and materials and criterial tasks.

If the contextualist argument that the who-what-how questions of learning are mutually constraining is accepted, why have some contextualists argued the "who question" should be our first priority rather than our last? And why, if they are right, has psychology not

173.

focused on this question previously? In answer to the
first two questions, Shaw & McIntyre (1978) have
proposed:

> [T]he central question of cognitive psychology
> concerns the essential nature of the knowing-
> agent, rather than just what is known or even
> how what is known is known...If we can even
> roughly decide on the nature of the epistemic-
> who we will, at the same time, have to take
> a stand on the nature of the information
> processed from and about the environment, as
> well as on the nature of the psychological
> processes required to do so [p. 305; 307-
> 308; italics in original].

According to Shaw, the epistemological problem of
learning must be situated in the context of the
metaphysics of human identity. Similarly, Martin
(1982, p. 69) says, "The first psychological fact is
the fact of persons."
     One hint of Shaw's own rudimentary notion of the
who is his use of the term "knowing-agents." Knowing
and agency characterize beings that learn. Learning
presupposes perception and action. Perception is what
the environment means to the learner and action is what
the learner means to the environment. What is implicit
in this statement and explicitly asserted by the
contextualist and ecological approaches is (1) the
reciprocity of the learner and her environment and (2)
the centrality of meaning to that reciprocity, and
thus, psychology's task (cf. Shaw, Turvey, & Mace,
1982). What distinguishes contextualist-ecological
approaches to perception, learning, memory, and action
is that meaning is taken as the central psychological
problem and is treated as really there. "Percepts,
concepts, memories, ideas, and other contexts of mind
usually considered private and subjective, are in fact
as much 'out there' as particles, stones, tables, and
stars" (Shaw & McIntyre, 1974, p. 360).
     What is denied is that the traditional distinction
between subjective and objective is helpful or
necessary. It is a by-product of treating organisms as
independent of their environment (and vice versa).
Meaning is the specification of the animal-environment
relation and as such cannot be said to reside either in
the environment or in the organism. Meaning is neither
subjective nor objective, but both.

174.

> Contextualism holds that experience consists
> of _events_. Events have a _quality_ as a
> whole. By quality is meant the total meaning
> of the event. The quality of the event is the
> resultant of the interaction of the experiencer
> and the world...[Jenkins, 1974, p. 786; italics
> in original].

Shaw & McIntyre (1974) put it even more baldly: "The
challenge for cognitive theory is to grasp the full
implications of the statement that ideas are not in the
mind, nor objects in the world, but that both are in
the meeting of mind and matter" (p. 360).
      Thus, no level of scientific analysis (e.g.,
physical, biological, psychological) is more basic than
any other. All disciplines are on equal footing in
investigating events and their analyses are equally
real. Reductionism is precluded.[3] As Jenkins (1974)
puts it:

> [T]here is no one analysis, no final set of
> units, no one set of relations, no claim to
> reducibility, in short, no single and unified
> account of anything....a "complete" or "final"
> analysis is a myth....analyses mean something
> only in terms of their utilities for some
> purposes. [p. 787]

      What I find promising about the contextualist
thesis is that meaning is faced head on rather than
shunted aside as is typically done in the mechanistic
models common in the discipline. What I have found
appealing is precisely what traditional learning
theorists have found awkward. The assumptions of
equipotentiality and mechanistic explanation in
psychology have made it difficult to treat issues such
as meaning, value, and selfhood in a rigorous fashion.
The most thoughtful theorists in this tradition (e.g.,
Hebb, 1974) have relegated such issues to the
humanities, realizing their importance but unable to
make them accessible to a discipline that presumably
studies organisms that are self-conscious, meaning-
seeking, and valuing.[4]
      To summarize, a contextualist approach to learning
and knowing can be characterized by the following
themes. (1) There are multiple equally real levels of
analysis that mutually constrain each other. (2)
Knowing is contextually embedded (or ecologically
situated) and cannot be understood apart from that
context. (3) An organism (O) and her environment (E)
form an ecosystem (a community of learning that is

reciprocal). (4) Meaning is the specification of the organism-environment relationship and is the central concern of psychology. (5) The O-E ecosystem is a set of events and the organism and environment can be understood only in terms of their roles in those events. (6) Event meaning is both person-relevant and environment-relevant and thus both subjective and objective.

The contextualist approach indicates the who question can be answered only by examining the O-E relationship, the various roles the organism can play in her world. Shaw & McIntyre (1974) stated the who-what-how triad of questions is a "closed set." I suggest that this is incorrect. A fourth question is implicit in the other three: why do we learn? Why we learn affects what we learn, how we learn it, and what prior ability and experience are necessary for us to learn it. Conversely, criteria for properly evaluating whether something has been learned depends on the nature of the learner and of the material learned.[5] Recently, it dawned on me that the why question is "sitting there" in Jenkin's tetrahedron in the criterial task. What is the purpose of learning? By what criteria are we to judge learning?

The usual answer I have gotten from colleagues in psychology when I have asked the "why" question is "survival." In the face of this question they make a faith appeal to evolutionary theory. On both contextualist and biblical grounds this seems inadequate to me. However, there are some helpful hints in evolutionary theory that may be elaborated into a more useful theory.

Biological adaptation to the physical environment is necessary for survival. If we think of perception as short term adaptation and evolution as long term adaptation, learning may be thought of as medium range adaptation (cf. Turvey & Johnston, 1980). But there is more to survival than biological adaptation. "Life" is not defined by the biologists alone. We may live or die (by ignoring real world structure) psychologically, historically, aesthetically, or theologically, just as certainly as we may die biologically. Failure to "learn the fear of the Lord" (Deut. 17:19) leads to (theological) death as certainly as failure to learn the fear of cliffs leads to (biological) death. The environments to which we must adapt are multiple. Roughly they might be partitioned into the physical, social, and theological environments.[6] The biblical data indicate that biological survival alone is inadequate to ground human knowing and doing: mankind shall not live by bread alone, but by all the words of

God (Matt. 4:4). When contextualists give the biological answer to the why question, they become reductionists. So do Christians who speak of life only in theological terms.

If the criteria by which learning are judged are living biologically, socially, aesthetically, theologically, etc., the identity of the learner begins to take shape. A learner is (1) a creature of and for the biological-physical environment; (2) a creature of and for the social-cultural environment; and (3) a creature of and for the theological environment. The biblical literature suggests the fundamental identity of humans is to be caretakers of the environment, neighbors of other humans, and servants to God. The question is: Why is learning necessary to actualize that identity?

The answer is not so obvious as we might expect. I think it is because creation is fundamentally "event." If I were a literature professor, I would probably say that the creation is to be understood as "story." The point is the same: (1) creation is history; and (2) creation is novel. The literary puns of the last sentence should be noted: (1) creation is God's (His)story; and (2) creation is new- dramatic-like a novel. Creation is both old and new. If humans are to adapt to creation, they must embody history and novelty. "What is learned and comprehended is both (a) related to what was already known and (b) novel with respect to what was already known" (Bransford & Franks, 1976, p. 94). The burden of the Bransford & Franks article is that current theories of learning focus almost exclusively on (a) and are inadequate for (b). We will return to the problem of novelty later.

The epistemological problem of learning must be situated, as we have seen, in the metaphysical context of the identity of the learner. But it must also be situated in the ethical context of action. C. I. Lewis elegantly makes the case for the ethical character of knowing and doing if the world is taken as meaningful.

> "The primary and pervasive significance of knowledge lies in its guidance of action: knowing is for the sake of doing. And action, obviously, is rooted in evaluation. For a being which did not assign comparative values, deliberate action would be pointless..."
> [1946, p. 1]

Because organisms are finite, they must choose. Perception, learning, and action are selective, and what an organism selects instantiates its "value

177.

commitments."

The letter to the Hebrews sharpens the centrality
of ethics to the epistemological task, implying that
learning is always moral development:

>"...you need milk instead of solid food...but
>grown men can take solid food; their
>perceptions are trained by long use to
>discriminate between good and evil."
>(Heb. 5:12,14 NEB)

As Eleanor and James Gibson have argued (Gibson &
Gibson, 1955) learning is always discrimination
(differentiation) of what is good (life affirming) and
evil (life denying). To live biologically,
psychologically, sociologically, aesthetically,
theologically, etc. is to differentiate what is
biologically good or evil, etc. What the passage from
Hebrews suggests is that this ability requires
commitment, discipline, and perserverence.

Other biblical passages such as the parable of the
wheat and weeds and Jesus' warnings about the "leaven
of the Pharisees" illustrate the difficulty of
discriminating between good and evil. "Training by
long use" seems to be necessary, or what the Gibsons
refer to as "the education of attention." Our
educational efforts should be focused toward refining
the abilities of us and our students to discriminate
between good and evil "affordances" (Gibson's term for
possible actions) in agriculture, art, science,
government, and worship.[7] The weight of moral
responsibility rests as heavily on the scientist or
farmer as it does on the priest or prophet. We are all
priests; many are prophets.

The reason moral responsibility is a weight is
because of the Fall. Choosing after the fall is a
scary, sweaty, painful business (Genesis 3). To be
adapted to the current social or physical environment
may hinder or prevent adaptation to the Divine
environment. Ecological rupture resulted from
humanity's rejection of their identity as servants-
caretakers-neighbors. Ecological theorists often seem
to ignore the problem of multiple environments and the
ecological tension resulting from human evil.

Since humans rejected their God-given identity at
the Fall, they are now in the precarious position of
not knowing what it is that they must learn to survive
(never mind, live abundantly). Even when we seem to
know what needs to be learned, we are unsure of how it
is to be learned. (For example, many people want to
"learn war no more," Isaiah 2:4, Micah 4:3, but is this

learned by building up or reducing armaments?)
Recovering our identity requires "learning Christ"
(Gal. 4:20) who identified with his creation in the
Incarnation. To that we turn next.

LEARNING AS INCARNATION

What is the nature of the incarnation that it
might clarify and complicate our view of learning?
What does God's becoming a body in our world have to do
with learning? Phillipians 2:5-8, Hebrews 5:8-14, and
I John 4:9-12 suggest a number of incarnational themes
that are provacative. I will list some I have noticed
with brief comment, then indicate how they might shape
our view of learning.[8]   (1) In the incarnation God
the Son was sent (I John 4:9). Christ is God's
communication to creation. To borrow a term from
Martin (1982), Christ was a "presentation" of God's
love. As presented and present, Christ is gift. (2)
Christ was sent into the world (I John 4:9),
becoming contextually embedded in a particular place
and time. Since the world is event, Jesus became a
historical event himself. The one "in whom all things
cohere" (Col. 1:17) became localized. Jesus was also
historical in the sense that he was not God's first
"sending." God had gifted us creation and then the
prophets and priests. Like the unfaithful vineyard
keepers (Matt. 21:33-39), we had rejected the
presentations. In the fullness of historical time, God
sent his perfect, unique re-presentation (Heb. 1:1-3).
God risks His only Son, His heir, to bring his story to
shalom.
(3) To be sent into the world is to be embodied
(John 1:14; Phil. 2:7). Jesus, born of Mary, was a
finite body constrained by the very physical,
biological, and psychological processes which were
created through Him as God's first-born of all
creation" (Col. 1:15). (4) As the "image of the
invisible God" (Col. 1:15) Christ's coming into the
world was sacramental. The invisible,
incomprehensible God became the visible means of grace
for the world. As John puts it: "And the Logos became
flesh and dwelt among us, full of grace and truth; and
we beheld his glory...and from his fulness have we all
received, grace upon grace" (1:14,16). The not-to-be-
imaged (unimaginable) God (Exodus 20:4) was directly
and concretely imaged in the Son. (5) Humility was
the prerequisite to Christ's being sent to embody grace
for the world (Phil. 2:6-8). The ordinariness of the

sacraments of water, bread, and wine mirror the
humility of the Water, Bread, and Vine of Life.
     (6) The incarnation was <u>passionate</u>. God made
love to the world in Christ (I John 4:7-9). We are
born of that love and carry His name. God's
commitment to His creation carried His only son to the
Passion. (7) Christ's commitment required
<u>discipline</u>. "He learned obedience through what he
suffered" (Heb. 5:8). "He became obedient unto death"
(Phil. 2:8). (8) The great paradox of the incarnation
is that through discipline and death Christ brought
<u>freedom and life</u> (John 10:10; Gal. 5:1; I John 4:9).
"In him was life, and the life was the light of men:
(John 1:4). The light of Christ opens God's word in
creation and scripture to reveal grace and truth (Luke
24:45). (9) The other great paradox of the incarnation
is that it is utterly new--the Good News, in fact--and
yet in the historical sense described in (2) above, it
is the oldest story--God is love. God <u>risks</u> His
(only begotten) Son to <u>conserve</u> (save) His (adopted)
children. God's new creation in Christ becomes
incarnate in the old creation. (10) God in sending
His Son, Christ, in his learning obedience and
passionate loving of the world, and we in receiving
grace, truth, and life are <u>active</u>. Grace, truth, and
life are not "cheap," but require the giver, gift, and
gifted to embody these ideals in action.

     REVELATION AND COMMUNION EMBODIED IN ACTION. What
is to be learned is always to be taken as revelation.
We know God and the physical and social worlds because
they reveal themselves to us. We are used to realizing
that unless God acted first (in sending Christ or
giving the law) we would not know Him. We are less
accustomed to understanding that unless other persons
or species or non-organic physical entities act (or react) we will never know them. Learning (knowing) is
inseparable from doing.
     Not only must the physical, social, or divine
environment present itself in action for learning to
occur, but the learner must actively notice and explore
the presentation. The learner must engage in the
"education of attention, the tuning of his or her
perceptual systems to the appropriate "wavelength" to
pick up the environment's presentation. This requires
action. Learning to catch a ball, to speak a language,
to draw a picture, to do a science, requires its doing.
Only in the activity of doing the skill we wish to
learn, however unskilled our first attempts at it are,
will we be able to discover the information that will

make possible our competent performance of the skill.

Learning is the embodiment (incarnation) of environmental information in the learner. As such it is tacit (Polanyi, 1966). Consciousness and language are not prerequisites for learning and knowing (Jaynes, 1977, p. 31-36). Knowledge is also dispersed. Learning is a skilled interaction with the world and is dispersed throughout the body of the learner. Thus, learning involves a restructuring (a constraining) of a body, its muscles, nervous system, etc., not just a change in conscious ideas. When someone learns, the new information restructures the learner so that he/she is a new person. "The consequence of personal experience is not that the old animal has new knowledge, but that it is a new animal that knows better" (Michaels & Carello, 1981, p. 78). Similarly, to "learn Christ" is to become a "new creation" (II Cor. 5:17).

Since learning in embodied, tacit, and action-orientated, verbalization is only a modest help in the education of attention. Reading about riding a bicycle, doing a scientific experiment, or writing a sonnet will never substitute for the doing of those activities. Bicycle riders, scientists, and poets know more than they can tell the novice. Knowledge cannot be directly communicated to another body simply by words. Only as the other body actively interacts with the world will it be tacitly constrained and restructured in ways similar to those bodies already "in the know."

The behaviorists were right in assuming the central importance of behavior and learning, but wrong in assuming the community of learners they studied were more passive and mechanistic than they themselves. The irony of much behaviorist research (and much of what passes for cognitive psychology) is that subjects merely adapt to their (simplistic) learning environment so that their presentation is compatible with the expectations of those who receive it. Simple environments reveal simple learning. I suspect that if we thought of learning as revelation and ourselves as part of the communities we wish to know, we might proceed differently than we usually do in our methodological and explanatory theorizing (cf. Martin, 1982; Van Leeuwen, 1983).

The learner and what is learned form a communion of action, a community of meaning.

THE PARADOX OF LEARNING. Learning partakes of the paradoxes of the incarnation. Jesus Christ was both

something already known (human) and yet completely
"other" and unknown (God). Similarly, what we learn
must be related to what we already know (old) and yet
different from what we already know (new). Learning
embodies its past; it memorially re-enacts its history.
But it anticipates its future; it approximates some
ideal of competence toward which it is moving.
Learning realizes its past, just as Christ completed
(fulfills) the old covenant. At the same moment
learning takes the next new step toward an as yet
unrealized (unfulfilled) level of competency, just as
Christ instituted a new covenant that is not yet
realized completely. (See Bransford & Franks, 1976;
Martin, this volume; and Weimer, 1973 for more
elaborate discussions of this paradox. The problem
they all point to is the inability of traditional
learning theories to account for the forward looking
nature of learning.)
    A second way of expressing this paradox is to say
that learning is sacramental: it embodies an abstract
and unrealized ideal and also re-enacts concrete
historical events. The Christian sacrament of
communion re-enacts (re-presents) explicit historical
events (Passover, Jesus' death) and presents to us a
foretaste of the Supper of the Lamb. Jesus, a
particular body at a specific time and place, revealed
the universal God who is transhistorical.
    Learning is both concrete and abstract, realized
and unrealized. Initial learning is always
contextually embedded, and what is learned is often not
recognized out of the original context in which it was
learned. But as Bransford (1979, p. 230-233) points
out, if learning is to be truly successful, it must be
applicable to new contexts. What is concretely
understood must become abstract. Our knowing must
become "decontextualized." Paradoxically, concrete,
contextualized learning interactions may reveal a
decontextualized abstraction that allows for our
knowing and doing the novel. As in the sacraments,
there is a "primacy of the abstract" (Hayek, 1968) in
our coming to know the world, but those abstract rules
or values are learned directly through the contextually
embedded action of the learned and the learner.
    Leaving the theoretical problem of how to account
for these paradoxes (cf. Bransford & Franks, 1976;
Weimer, 1973), what practical problems do the paradoxes
pose? Let me suggest three.
    Each winter to get my cognitive psychology class
thinking along contextualist lines, I ask them what
they want to get out of the course, why, and how

they think it might best be accomplished. (Of course, in doing this they tell me a good deal about who they are.) Their answers are usually vague and not very revealing, so I press them. Will it be important in 10 years for them to remember what texts they read? What about the particular studies, methods, and theories they describe? Will it matter whether they can remember (even in an abstract way) any specific lecture I give, or even my name? Etc. Should I lecture to them or should we discuss the readings or design, run, and analyze research projects? Should specific recall be tested or their ability to apply their knowledge to novel situations? Etc. Quite simply, what I do is make them take themselves seriously as learners by facing what they expect teachers to decide for them.[9]

One difficulty of education is that we are not sure what it is we are to learn. When we know what it is we want to learn, to be a scientist or to be like Christ, for example, we are not sure how we are to do it. As a consequence of this uncertainty, learning is always a faith-commitment in which the learner tacitly embodies in action values that instantiate some unrealized ideal of himself and his environment.

Another practical problem is the relationship of examples to the abstract concepts they illustrate. The mystery or paradox is that the abstract is best communicated through concrete exemplars. Examples are the sacraments of concepts. But it is not so simple. A friend once told me about a "great" Peter Marshall sermon he heard and proceeded to describe with relish an illustrative story Marshall had used. When he finished Marshall's story I asked what the idea was that it had illustrated. The reply was, "Oh, I don't remember that, but it was a great sermon!" Maybe. Maybe not. Perhaps truly great sermons are not remembered at all, only embodied in the changed behavior of the listeners. What promotes specific recall may not always be correlated with conceptual memory. Even the specific/conceptual memory distinction seems inadequate to describe the "embodied memory" of changed action without awareness (even conceptually) of the means of change. Considerable theory and research development is necessary before we will be able to say when and how examples become the means of grace for abstracted skills.

A third problem involves our research practice. Before we make much headway on either theory or application in learning, we will need to take more seriously the historical nature of learning. Publish or perish pressure, and many other social psychological

183.

factors, have restricted many learning studies to narrow temporal confines. We like our studies to be quick and easy, but learning often is neither. I will give an example from my own area of research. Virtually, none of the hundreds of studies on "impression formation" in which one person learns about (forms an impression of) another has examined the formation process over substantial periods of time. For example, primacy or recency effects of serially ordered information are measured over minutes, not days or weeks. Fortunately, there are examples of learning research where the temporal character of learning has been honored; for example, the research on children's acquisition of language. Such research needs to become the rule, not the exception.

DEVELOPMENT: THE PARADOX OF CONSCIOUSNESS.
Having argued that learning is primarily tacit, dispersed, and action-oriented, what is the role of consciousness? What does explicit awareness have to do with knowing and doing the truth?

A clue for the usefulness of consciousness comes from social psychology. Research on "objective self-awareness" has revealed that when persons are self-conscious (e.g., they see themselves in a mirror as they carry out some task), they act more in line with their "internal" value systems and are less influenced by situational pressures. For example, persons are more likely to be honest when they are objectively self-aware than when they are not (e.g., Beaman, Klentz, Diener, & Svanum, 1979). What this research suggests is that consciousness might function as conscience.

But there are problems. Self-consciousness often seems to get in the way of knowing and doing the truth. Being conscious of my fingers moving while I am typing is counterproductive. If I am self-conscious about how I look and sound while I am lecturing, I will not look and sound very good. A related problem is that since we can consciously control very little of our knowing and doing, choosing good over evil needs to be tacit and automatic. Events are too numerous and occur too quickly to allow conscious deliberation of every (or even most) behavior. Research from attention (Kahneman, 19973), language (Slobin, 1979), and learning and memory (Zechmeister & Nybers, 1982) suggest that voluntary conscious control plays a very small role in the use of these skills. For example, conscious intent to learn is not necessary to learn; incidental learning can be as good or better than

184.

intentional learning.

Following a fairly obvious biblical lead, I want to suggest that humans became self-conscious at the Fall. The first consequence of the Fall noted in Genesis (3:7) is that Adam and Eve became selfconscious of their nakedness. Pre-Fall knowing and learning was tacit and unselfconscious, but when they rejected their identity as finite learners, they became conscious of good and evil. Consciousness came to function like the Law which was given later to provide a communal consciousness. It made explicit covenantal obligations; it pointed to the values which knowing and doing should embody. Since there is always a discrepancy between norm and knowledge, law and consciousness reveal us as unworthy of esteem, as sinners. But that same law-consciousness tutors us as a governess might (Gal. 3:23-24). The law helps us learn to discriminate good and evil by raising our consciousness (conscience). Thus, the Law raised our consciousness so we could learn to become less self-conscious and focus on our task of loving God and neighbor and taking care of the world.

When grace came in its fulness in Christ's incarnation, the law was fulfilled and self-consciousness and unself-consciousness became fused. As the pledge (or first fruit) of what is to come for us, Christ was completely self aware of his own identity as God and yet in the incarnation "loses" that identity to become what we were supposed to be, servant. Just as Christ learned obedience, consciousness now disciplines our knowing and doing so that it becomes more graceful.

Consciousness is both curse and blessing in the same way discipline is. Discipline is painful and reminds us how short of our norm we are. But discipline rehabilitates and frees us athletically, academically, or spiritually. Without explicit discipline we will never be free to be an Olympian, scholar, or saint. Consciousness gives us both hope and humility.

What is the role of the explicit relative to the tacit? I venture that the explicit serves a "pointing out" function; it tutors attention. It calls attention to some relationship, a critical detail or a global pattern, as important for the purposes of the person. The role of explicit teaching, preaching, and theorizing in physics, psychology, or theology is to "point to" relationships, to "educate attention." Like art, verbalization and theory cause us to notice such-and-such from a particular perspective. The explicit

knowledge gained may lead to changed perceptual
activity so that the skill (e.g., of running a good
physics experiment; of loving our neighbor as ourself)
develops and becomes "automatic," out of conscious
awareness.

HUMILITY AS A PREREQUISITE OF LEARNING. Knowledge
that is tacitly embodied in action is unselfconscious.
And when we are self-conscious of our actions we
understand that our actions incompletely realize
competence. True knowledge produces humility, the
awareness that no matter how far we have come we have
not yet arrived. Two of the activities that are
crucial to learning are asking questions and listening.
Bransford (1979) suggests that the humility necessary
to ask a question is a necessary prerequisite to
learning.

> Effecting learning therefore seems to involve
> a critical attitude regarding our current level
> of knowing, which prompts us to ask questions,
> test ourselves, seek alternate opinions...
> [However] it is frequently less threatening to
> hold to one's current ideas than to explore
> alternatives and hence face being wrong...If
> people are too defensive, they may fail to
> evaluate their current level of understanding
> and thereby lose many opportunities to learn...
> The development of general learning skills
> seems more closely related to the ability to
> ask relevant questions (or ourselves and
> others) than to the ability to state factual
> content [pp. 201-202].

Learning truth is more a matter of asking the right
questions than devising clever answers to the questions
handed to us by tradition (e.g., parents, religious or
scientific mentors).
    If the education of attention requires the
humility of asking questions, it also requires the
humility of listening to answers. Often the activity
necessary to knowing is quiet listening. A pride which
has nothing to learn is quick to speak, while humility
patiently awaits new information revealed by another's
perspective. One value of community (e.g., religious,
scientific) is that occasionally one is forced to shut
up and listen to someone else (e.g., a sermon, a review
of an article submitted for publication). But
listening as a learning skill has a broader meaning
than hearing verbal utterances: listening is attending
to the environment and not ourselves. Listening in

186.

this sense is being open to the data, receptive (tuned) to environmental information. Instead of deciding in advance what a person will say, what the environment will look like, or what the research data will show, listening is patient and expectant (rather than expecting) (cf. Halwes, 1974).

LEARNING AS RISKY AND CONSERVATIVE. Since learning involves doing, it must be passionate. The knowledge God requires of humans is a knowledge that is physically embodied in the way Adam knew Eve and the way Christ knew the world. Knowing requires loving. The Jewish passion for learning (Wilson, 1976) is based on the Old Testament conception of knowing as intimate and moral. "To 'know' God was to walk faithfully in His ways and to 'act out'the terms of His covenant...In short, for the Hebrew, to 'know' was to 'do'" (Wilson, 1976, p. 361). Learning to play tennis, or to love our children, or to research learning requires passionate action. As I have noted elsewhere, loving/knowing is often a humble, tedious business.

> scientific and Christian faith both demand activity, sweaty seeking of truth. Both require getting our hands dirty in the data of existence; neither vocation allows theorizing unsullied by "messy" data. Christians and scientists often forget that knowing is a humble, physical business that demands patience. [in press]

Learning as an activity involves choices; it is intrinsically value-laden and demands responsible commitment to what is already known. This commitment serves as the "conservative" element in truth-seeking, the attempt to "conserve" ("remember") over time the truths of the organism-environment relation. Knowing requires the humility to learn from the past. But as we have seen, committed action also involves the humility of openness to "new" information that emerges with time and activity. The "education of attention" to this previously unnoticed information inevitably means "comprehensive criticism" (Weimer, 1979), being willing to change even our most cherished notions about God, the world, others, or ourselves. This is the "risk" element in truth-seeking. Knowing risks the humility of asking a question that reveals ignorance, of taking another look; by "listening" to another observer's "point of view." If the learner is willing to be both critical and committed, learning can occur.

187.

The comprehensive criticism that Weimer (1979)
urges does not preclude commitment to a scientific
paradigm, or a person, or a way of life. In fact,
Weimer argues that sometimes the most effective way of
being critical is to work to articulate and extend a
paradigmatic commitment. It increases the chances of
"anomalies" being recognized that will lead to a
"crisis" and a "revolutionary" advance. Being
committed may lead to novelty, to a revision in the
nature of the commitment. Any commitment that is true
must change and grow; else it is a dead faith.
Learning is a risky business. Certainty is not
required for the commitment of learning, but the
humility of a perservering faith is.

CONCLUSION. If we have the humility to
perservere, if we are disciplined by a passionate
continuing dialogue with God, the world, and other
persons, we can learn the truth about our environments,
the truth that makes us free (John 8:32).
Paradoxically, being constrained by our environment
through active interaction frees us by opening us to
new competencies of thought and action. We discover
our true selves, our true freedom, not by asserting our
autonomy, but by acknowledging our dependence on God,
each other, and the physical environment.

Endnotes

1. I will not differentiate these views for purposes of this paper. Contextual and ecological will function as synonyms.

2. Incidentally this is what "faith-learning integration" (as it is usually called) is properly about. Actually, it involves multiple faiths mutually constraining and enhancing each other so that we can live rich, diverse lives with "singleness of heart" (BCP).

3. In rejecting mechanistic, reductionistic approaches contextualism does not opt for a phenomenological approach. As valuable as such approaches may be, they seem to take a "territorialist" (Evans, 1977) approach to protect against the loss of meaning in the traditional physical science model.

4. The ecological-contextualist thesis espoused in this paper is a version of faith-learning integration that would roughly fit Evan's (1977) radical humanist category. It argues the multiple perspectives are co-implicative and thus mutually constraining, not independent as in perspectivalism. Since the contextualist thesis asserts that psychological, sociological, theological, etc. perspectives constrain physical, biological, etc. perspectives, even the "natural" sciences are not different in kind from social sciences. All are strands of a single cloth.

5. I think Shaw believes the question of purpose or intent can be subsumed under the "who" question. Perhaps this is so, but it seems clearer to me to pose it separately.

6. God as creator is the "ultimate" or "universal environment."

7. No clearer vision of the value of liberal Christian education can be given than this, I think, regardless of whether the training is in the practical or theoretical arts.

8. Concerning the genesis of the incarnation metaphor for learning, it was the points given as 3-5 in the list below that first occurred to me and that set me thinking and reading. That learning involves

189.

embodiment of environmental information is the centerpiece of the metaphor. The list is not presented as a theology of incarnation, although I hope what I say is theologically sound. Some of the psychological implications I discovered in looking at the Biblical references to Christ's incarnation I expected to find; others I did not expect to find. The contextual approach certainly influenced my biblical "literature review," but biblical assumptions have always shaped my understanding of contextualism as well. A contextualist view of knowing says that one cannot easily pull apart what is primarily Christian, or middle-class, or masculine, etc. in what I or anyone says. This poses underappreciated problems with picking out the good we discern in other theoretical approaches (e.g., behaviorism, psychoanalysis), while avoiding the evil we discern. Mary Vander Goot (1980) has the right idea with her notion of recontextualization.

9. I do much less than I should to encourage them to decontextualize their knowledge. They do not complain since such an evaluation procedure would require their knowing the material much more thoroughly.

Bibliography

Beaman, A., Klentz, B., Diener, E., & Svanum, S.
"Self awareness and trangression in children:
two studies." Journal of Personality and Social
Psychology, 1979, 37, 1835-1846.

Bransford, John. Human Cognition: Learning, Understanding, and Remembering. Belmont, CA:
Wadsworth, 1979.

Bransford, John & Franks, Jeffrey. "Toward a framework
for understanding learning." In G. Bower (Ed.)
The Psychology of Learning and Motivation, Vol.
10. New York: Academic, 1976.

Bransford, J., J. Franks, C. Morris, & B. Stein. "Some
general constraints on learning and memory
research." In L. Cermak & F. Craik (Eds.)
Levels of Processing in Human Memory.
Hillsdale, NJ: Erlbaum, 1979.

Bransford, John & McCarrell, Nancy. "A sketch of a
cognitive approach to comprehension." In W.
Weimer & D. Palermo (Eds.) Cognition and the
Symbolic Processes. Hillsdale, NJ: Erlbaum,
1974.

Bransford, John, N. McCarrell, J. Franks, & K. Nitsch.
"Toward unexplaining memory." In R. Shaw & J.
Bransford (Eds.) Perceiving, Acting, and
Knowing. Hillsdale, NJ: Erlbaum, 1977.

Evans, Stephen. Preserving the Person. Downers
Grove, IL: Intervarsity, 1977.

Gibson, Eleanor. Invited address to the Eastern
Psychological Association, 1983.

Gibson, James. The Ecological Approach to Visual
Perception. Boston: Houghton Mifflin, 1979.

Gibson, J. & Gibson, E. "Perceptual learning:
Differentiation versus enrichment."
Psychological Review, 1955, 62, 32-41.

Greeno, James. "Psychology of learning, 1960-1980:
one participant's observations." Technical
Report No. 5, Feb. 25, 1980, Univ. of

Pittsburgh.

Halwes, T. "Structural realism, coalitions and the relationship of Gibsonians, constructivist, and Buddhist theories of perception." In W. Weimer & D. Palermo (Eds.) Cognition and the Symbolic Processes. Hillsdale, NJ: Erlbaum, 1974.

Hastie, Reid. "Memory for behavioral information that confirms or contradicts a personality impression." In R. Hastie et al. (Eds.) Person Memory: The Cognitive Basis of Social Perception. Hillsdale, NJ: Erlbaum, 1980.

Hayek, F.A. "The Primacy of the abstract." In A. Koestler & J. Smythies (Eds.) Beyond Reductionism. Boston: Beacon Press, 1969.

Hebb, Donald. "What psychology is about." Psychological Review, 1974, 29, 71-79.

Hodges, Bert. "Love is more than a feeling." His, 1983, 43, 13-15.

Hodges, Bert. "Perception is relative and veridical: ecological and biblical perspectives on knowing and doing the truth." H. Heie & D. Wolfe (Eds.), in press.

Jaynes, Julian. The Origin of Consciousness in the Breakdown of the Bicameral Mind. Boston: Houghton-Mifflin, 1977.

Jenkins, James. "Remember that old theory of memory? Well, forget it!" American Psychologist, 1974, 29, 785-795.

Jenkins, James. "Why it is hard to move from the laboratory to the classroom: a four pointed problem." Unpublished paper, Univ. of Minnesota, 1977.

Jenkins, James. "Four points to remember: a tetrahedral model of memory experiments." In Cermak, L. & Craik, F. (Eds.) Levels of Processing in Human Memory. Hillsdale, NJ: Erlbaum, 1979.

Kahneman, Daniel. Attention and Effort. Englewood Cliffs, NJ: Prentice-Hall, 1973.

Kuhn, Thomas. The Structure of Scientific Revolutions. Chicago: Univ. of Chicago, 1970.

Lewis, C.I. An Analysis of Knowledge and Valuation. LaSalle, IL: Open Court, 1946.

Martin, James. "Presentationalism: Toward a self-reflexive psychological theory." In W. Weimer D. Palermo (Eds.) Cognition and the Symbolic Processes, Vol. 2. Hillsdale, NJ: Erlbaum, 1982.

Martin, James. "Learning as revelation: a paradigm clash." [this volume]

Michaels, Claire & Carello, Claudia. Direct Perception. Englewood Cliffs, NJ: Prentice-Hall, 1981.

Neisser, Ulric. Cognition and Reality. San Francisco: Freeman, 1976.

Polanyi, Michael. The Tacit Dimension. Garden City, NY: Doubleday, 1966.

Seligman, M. & Hager, J. (Eds.). Biological Boundaries of Learning. New York: Appleton-Century-Crofts, 1972. Review, 1970, 77, 406-418.

Shaw, R., Turvey, M., & Mace W. "Ecological psychology: the consequence of a commitment to realism." In W. Weimer & D. Palermo (Eds.), Cognition and the Symbolic Processes, Vol. 2. Hillsdale, NJ: Erlbaum, 1982.

Shaw, Robert & McIntyre, Michael. "Algoristic foundations of cognitive psychology." In W. Weimer & D. Palermo (Eds.) Cognition and the Symbolic Processes. Hillsdale, NJ: Erlbaum, 1974.

Slobin, D. Psycholinguistics. Second Ed. Homewood, IL: Scott-Foresman, 1979.

Spelke, E., Hirst, W., & Neisser, U. "Skills of divided attention." Cognition, 1976, 4, 215-230.

Tulving, Endel. "Relation between encoding specificity and levels of processing." In L. Cermak & F. Craik (Eds.) Levels of Processing in Human Memory. Hilldale, NJ: Erlbaum, 1979.

Turvey, Michael & Johnston, Timothy. "A sketch of an ecological metatheory for theories of learning." In G. Bower (Ed.) The Psychology of Learning and Motivation, Vol. 14. New York: Academic, 1980.

Vander Goot, Mary. "Perspectives on psychology." Reformed Journal, 1980, 30, 24-26.

Van Leeuwan, M. S. The Sorcerer's Apprentice: A Christian Looks at the Changing Face of Psychology. Downers Grove, IL: Intervarsity, 1983.

Weimer, Walter. "Psycholinguistics and Plato's paradoxes of the Meno." American Psychologist, 1973, 28, 15-33.

Weimer, Walter. Notes on the Methodology of Scientific Research. Hillsdale, NJ: Erlbaum, 1979.

Wilson, Marvin. "The Jewish concept of learning: A Christian appreciation." Christian Scholar's Review, 1976, 5, 350-363.

Zechmeister, Eugene & Nybers, Stanley. Human Memory: An Introduction to Research and Theory. Monterey, CA: Brooks-Cole, 1982.

Chapter 12

PAST, PRESENT, AND FUTURE DIRECTIONS
IN LEARNING RESEARCH

by

Paul Moes
Assistant Professor of Psychology
Dordt College

This presentation seeks to apply the Biblical
principle of the wholeness and unity of man's nature to
a reinterpretation of past and current psychological
learning theories. The hope is that a more unified and
scriptural interpretation of research results can be
established and applied to instruction.
The fundamental question to be addressed will be,
how does learning occur? I would like to propose that
there is one unified process common to all learning
situations. I feel this unified approach is not only
Biblically reliable but is also supported by much of
the current research. The key word in this approach
will be that of principles. While a more complete
description will follow, for the present time a
principle can be described as a summary or abstraction
of two or more bits of information into one bit of
information. The notion of abstraction is not a new
one, but in the past abstraction was thought to occur
apart from man's emotional and spiritual nature.

Biblical Directives

To work toward the establishment of a truly
Christian understanding of learning theory and research
certain Biblical assumptions must first be confirmed.
Duane Kaufman has in his article, "Toward a Christian
Theory/Model of Learning" (1978), skillfully
articulated several Biblical assumptions which he says
should serve as "control beliefs" for a Christian
learning theory. Therefore, I restate three of his
nine assumptions here, appended with two assumptions of
my own. Note that not all of these control beliefs are
as directly defensible from Scripture as are others;

some require a more indirect argument of proof and are subject to debate.

1. God has communicated and is communicating His desire to His people. Christians thus believe in the authority of the Bible as the guide for life, and that God continues to work in His people through the ministry of His Spirit.

2. Man, created in God's image, is a responsible being, engages in purposeful activity, makes choices between alternatives, demonstrates a life of wholeness before God and his fellow men (i.e. growth in wisdom, stature, and favor with God and man). As such, man is discontinous from the animal world in the higher levels of his functioning.

3. The Christian emphasis on the whole person makes learning more than a cognitive activity. Knowledge and skill demand the involvement of the complete person, especially affective and interpersonal responses to cognitive learning.

I add the following assumptions:

4. True "spiritual" wisdom should be the ultimate goal of learning for any person. All learning should bring the person closer to a fuller knowledge of God's unfolding of creation, and man's responsibility.

5. All learning operates according to certain created principles in two respects, (a) different situations, although they may result in different outward behavior, always reflect a fundamental change in the total understanding of God's creation, (b) certain basic principles of learning are common to man and animals because of the order in creation and "common design" found in all living beings.

Some of these assumptions need clarification or comment. Assumption one suggests that God is active in the learning process. Through the mysterious working of the Holy Spirit and through Christ's upholding hand learning is guided according to the Father's will and is not haphazard.

The idea in the third assumption is that the whole person, mind, body, soul, emotion and behavior all

interact in the learning process. Kaufman also seems
to be suggesting here that responses (behaviors) are
not completely separable from the rest of the person.
Assumption number four is self-evident from
Scripture (See Proverbs 2). However, one fundamental
truth can be gleaned from this assumption: if learning
can be divided at all, it should be divided between
true learning (i.e. gaining wisdom and knowledge of
God's working) or false learning (i.e. learning which
perverts man's thoughts and actions away from a true
understanding of God's working).
Finally, the last assumption is a working
assumption which will receive support later in the
chapter. It is stated here since I feel there are some
basic Biblical concepts which lend support to the idea.
First of all, no distinction is made in scripture
between any type of learning. All types of learning
seem to reflect gaining new insights in the context of
our total spiritual condition. In other words,
learning does not occur in a vacuum. For example, the
writer of Proverbs, after observing the slothful man's
vineyard and the growth of thorns that results, states,
"I applied my heart to what I observed and learned a
lesson from what I saw" (Prov. 24:32; NIV).
This pattern of gaining understanding is a common
one throughout the Old Testament; "instruction" is
gained in a similar way from nature (Eccl. 1:13), from
the study of human behavior (Eccl. 16:3-12), by object
lessons (Exodus 16:32), and by parables. In each
situation raw information is taken in and a new insight
or principle is gained based on the application of the
heart. This application of the heart occurs whether or
not the person is aware of it. Ruth Beechick in her
book A Biblical Psychology of Learning (1982)
suggests that this Biblical reference to heart implies
the sum total of spiritual, moral, emotional,
motivational, and thought patterns. Although this
consistent pattern does not prove that there is only
one type of learning, it does suggest at least from a
scriptural standpoint that there is no basis for making
a distinction between spiritual learning and secular
learning.
The second part of the last assumption may seem
contradictory in some respects since animals do not
respond to God as humans do. Indeed there is a
difference in the way humans and animals should learn;
both qualitatively and quantitatively (See Psalm 32:9).
Certainly, animals cannot apply the heartfelt aspects
of their being in the same way that humans do.
However, I believe animals do apply emotional and

197.

motivational aspects to learning situations. In
addition, we share a common design with animals.
Therefore an understanding of some basic learning
principles can be gleaned from animals. At the same
time we must not overgeneralize findings from animal
studies since they are not created in God's image.
Rather, the study of animal learning should serve as a
springboard for establishing an understanding of the
learning process in humans.

Research and Theory in Learning

With several Biblical directives to guide our
thinking, past and current research on learning can now
be evaluated in a "brighter light." The history of
learning theory begins with the familiar experiments of
the Russian physiologist, Pavlov, and with the American
psychologist, Thorndike (Schultz, 1981). These two men
have so shaped the thinking and research in learning
psychology that their work deserves a brief overview.

Being a physiologist, Pavlov was not originally
interested in learning at all but in the functioning of
neurological reflexes (Mackintosh, 1974). For example,
he studied how food placed in a dog's mouth resulted in
saliva being produced. (I will contend that this
predisposition of Pavlov toward studying reflexes is of
great significance since it is one of the contributing
factors in the development of the notion of a reflexive
type of learning in behavioristic thought.) Pavlov
noted that not only would the animal salivate when
food was placed in its mouth, but it would salivate
shortly before the feeding if regular cues that the
food was coming were provided. Pavlov astutely
followed through with a series of experiments in which
he presented a stimulus, such as a tone, which was
followed closely by the presentation of food causing
the salivation. When the tone and the food were
presented in close pairings on several occasions, the
animal began to salivate in response to the tone,
before the food was presented. The food and the
original salivating response were called the
unconditional stimulus (US) and unconditional response
(UR), respectively, because they were part of a natural
or "unconditioned" reflex. The tone and the salivation
in response to the tone were called the conditioned
stimulus (CS) and the conditioned response (CR),
respectively, since these represented the two
components of a learned or "conditioned" reflex.

The establishment of new reflex responses was for
Pavlov the basic element of all types of learning. The

apparently complex behavior of animals and humans, if broken up into component parts, would reveal simple connections and "chains" of connections between stimuli and responses. Pavlov even hypothesized that the brain was a sort of switching center that received stimuli and after enough training would cause an output of the appropriate response (Mackintosh, 1974). Therefore, some reflexes were learned and were found in "higher" centers.

Thorndike, unlike Pavlov, was trained as a psychologist and more deliberately set out to understand the basic components of the learning process. By monitoring simple responses of animals and then giving the animal a reward following the response, Thorndike noted that the animal was likely to repeat the response in the future. Therefore, in this type of learning situation there is no reflex at the onset; rather, a new reflex is established between some stimulus and some previously random behavior. This finding led Thorndike to formulate the law of effect. Stated simply, the law of effect says that when a response is followed by a something pleasant, the response is more likely to occur in the future; when a response is followed by something unpleasant, the response is less likely to occur (Hilgard & Bower, 1975).

The research generated by Pavlov and Thorndike, as well as many of their predecessors, seemed to lend a great deal of credence to their views. Indeed, animals appeared to learn a variety of responses with certain carefully prescribed situations and reinforcements. In America, Watson demonstrated that Pavlov's type of learning could be accomplished in humans by demonstrating that a child could develop a phobia to an animal by Pavlovian type conditioning. Although a split existed in America for quite some time between Pavlovian (or classical) conditioning and Thorndike's approach (also known as operant conditioning), the distinction between classical and operant conditioning has diminished over the years (Rescorla & Wagner, 1972). Thus, despite their false guiding principles and their mechanistic approach, behavioristic researchers were at first, on an operational level, quite successful in producing their predicted results. The desire to make psychology a respectable science pushed many psychologists to accept behaviorism with its scientific rigor without question.

By the 1930's and 1940's, behaviorism was thoroughly embedded in psychological thought. Theoretical model building continued to grow and reached a pinnacle with Hull. Hull (1943, 1952) developed an elaborate and thoroughly mechanistic model of learning which was called a "drive-reduction" theory of learning because of its reliance on motivation as a major component in the learning process. Motivation for Hull was a very integral part of the learning process. Without a basic drive such as hunger or thirst to motivate the animal, learning simply did not occur.

B. F. Skinner in his work Science and Human Behavior (1953) felt that there was no need to complicate the picture with elaborate hypothesizing. Rather, Skinner sought a descriptive and "technological" approach which sought to describe all possible conditions and their necessary behavioral outcomes. Skinner was simply pushing behaviorism to its logical mechanistic conclusion. At this point Skinner also took behaviorism out of the academic animal laboratory and applied it to a variety of situations including education and the control of abnormal behavior. The techniques that Skinner used in the classroom and in clinical settings showed phenomenal success in certain situations. Indeed, behaviorism seemed to be riding the crest of its successes. As P. Lichtenstein states,

> By the 1930's behaviorism was dominant and solidly entrenched in American psychology. Of course there were the competing views of Tolman, Hull, Guthrie, and Skinner, but the belief was widely held that eventually one would emerge as superior. In the 40's it seemed that Hull might be a clear winner with his hypothetico-deductive approach which seemed to bring to psychology needed rigor and precision. Hullian papers abounded at professional meetings and in the journals so that young and older psychologists alike felt that in order to be abreast of the times they must master the somewhat esoteric Hullian symbols. (1980; p. 450)

How should Christians respond at this point? Is the behavioristic approach one that we should adopt? Many Christians have adopted behaviorism at varying levels of acceptance (Kaufman, 1977). Some have embraced the theories in their entirety, while others reject the mechanistic and deterministic "beliefs" but have accepted the "technology" and have painstakingly contorted behavioristic and theological concepts in order to bring the two into an uneasy juxtaposition.

The fundamental problem with this marriage of thought
is that not only do the presuppositions of behaviorism
run contrary to Scripture, but the "technique" of
behaviorism falls far short in describing the true
process of learning as pointed out in the Bible and as
shown in much of the research. We can be thankful,
however, that behavioristic notions have not gone
unchallenged; a challenge not only of its
presuppositions but of it research predictions and
techniques as well.

The death rattle for behaviorism actually came
very early on from the "neobehaviorist" Tolman. Tolman
felt that rats and humans alike possessed a more
purposive behavioral ability than was assumed by the
strict behaviorist and conducted a number of
experiments to demonstrate this capability. One of
Tolman's classic experiments serves to illustrate his
findings best. The experiment involved a 3 way maze
(see Figure 1) in which the rat is allowed on several
occasions to leave the start box and to explore the
maze by random choices to find the food in the goal
box. The rat was shown as having established a
preference for alley one over alley two over alley
three. This result was accountable by behavioristic
theory since it predicted that the sooner a response is
followed by a reward, the more likely the response is
to be performed. Therefore alley one is preferred
because the reward is obtained the quickest.

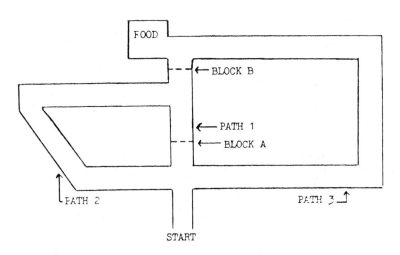

Figure 1. Maze used in Tolman's "cognitive map" experiment.

201.

But what should have happened if a block was put in alley one at point A? Behavioristic theory predicted that alley two would be chosen, which is in fact what did occur. What should have happened if a block was put at point B? Again, behavioristic theory predicted that the animal would choose alley two, despite being a dead end solution, because it was still the second strongest "reflex" for the animal. However, the animal consistently chose alley three when faced with the block at point B, contrary to the behaviorists' prediction, but much more intuitively logical.

What these findings imply is that even animals are capable of selecting responses from an integration of information rather than responding automatically and mechanically to sensory input. Tolman further explained these results by suggesting that the rat doesn't learn "because of the reinforcer but rather he learns about the reinforcer" (Rescorla, 1978; p. 39). In this particular situation the rat made the correct choice because, as Tolman suggested, the animal made sense of all the relevant information including the reward and organized it according to a logical pattern. Stated another way, it made a "cognitive (mental) map" of its environment.

Of course this one experiment did not completely preclude the existence of stimulus-response type associations or reflexes; it only suggested that other possibilities do exist. In fact, Tolman provided evidence to support, at least with a casual analysis, the potential for reflexive stimulus-response associations being made under some conditions. If in the same maze a rat was forced to traverse each alley separately to obtain a reward, a somewhat different result was obtained. At first all alleys were blocked, except alley one, with the animal going through 100 trials to this procedure. This procedure was repeated 50 times for alley two and 10 times for alley three. When a block was then placed at point B (with the other two alleys open) the animal did choose the ultimately futile alley two. Thus when the animal was not able to form an integration of the available information, it appeared that a stimulus-response type of reflex was created.

Therefore, some psychologists as a result of this and subsequent studies suggested that there were two types of learning, one being response oriented, the other being concept oriented. However, Tolman's finding went relatively unnoticed during the heyday of behavioristic research. Therefore, the notion of two types of learning did not develop in strength until Tolman was rediscovered in the 60's and 70's.

Further decline in the behavioristic monopoly came with a devastating critique of Hull and others by Koch (1954). Koch criticized not only the philosophical and theoretical aspects, but the research predictions as well. The simple truth was that many behavioristic theories simply could not make accurate predictions of animal responses. Since that time several researchers and writers have slowly undone many behavioristic ideas. Even Thorndike's law of effect, which is one of the hallmarks of behavioristic theories, has been called into question. As N. J. Mackintosh states in his review of the data, "There is a considerable body of evidence inconsistent with the analysis provided by the law of effect" (1974, p. 268). Thus, one of the cornerstones of behavioristic theory which has been applied to all types of human endeavors is slowly crumbling, not because of human studies but because of the very type of animal studies which were originally thought to support such theories.

Before turning to some of the new directions in learning, an examination of one more aspect of animal learning must be made. Early behavioristic approaches assumed that any stimulus could be associated with any response provided the correct reinforcements were given. More recent research findings (Seligman, 1970; Kalat & Rozin, 1977) suggest that some associations are made much more easily than others. For example, rats associate sweetened water with an induced illness much more easily than they associated a light stimulus to illness. This finding is not unreasonable since it seems to suggest that an organism's learning system is ready to associate logically related information. In other words, an organism's brain is organized in such a way that it is complimentary to the organization inherent in creation.

New Directions

Cognitive Theory.

As we have seen, behavioristic notions have been found to be lacking in their ability to explain how learning occurs. New cognitive or mentalistic theories of learning have gained popularity in explaining much of the animal research. The usual explanation now given for the process of learning in classical or operant conditioning situations is that the animal or

203.

person gathers information relevant to any learning task, organizes that information into some meaningful scheme or rule, and then acts on that scheme when motivated to do so. Therefore, the definition of learning is no longer based solely on performance, but is thought to reflect a change in the person's cognitive structure. From this starting point, cognitive psychology has attempted to determine how this organizing occurs and how information is processed by examining such internal mental processes as memory, consciousness, and concept formation.

However, cognitive psychology is a long way from being able to tie together all aspects of the learning process. We as Christians need to respond to the challenge and help to shape the ongoing development of cognitive learning theory.

One of the fundamental precepts of cognitive psychology is that new incoming information alters old, previously stored information, and old information affects the way in which new information is received, organized and stored. A simple example of how an older memory structure affects incoming information is the way in which people memorize a list of words. If a group of subjects in an experiment are given a list of words to memorize, and then ten minutes later are asked to recall the list, they tend to recall the list according to categories rather than in the order presented. For example, if the list had been: "apple, tree, horse, bush, orange, cow" the subjects would tend to recall in a manner such as: "apple, orange, horse, cow, tree, bush." Most people do this type of mental organization without being aware of it. This type of recall suggests that we tend to organize new information according to existing patterns.

New information can also affect old memories. In one experiment (Loftus & Palmer, 1973) subjects were shown a film about a traffic accident and were then asked questions about what they had witnessed. Those who were asked, "How fast were the cars going when they smashed into each other?" gave much higher estimates of speed than those subjects who were asked "How fast were the cars going when they hit each other." A week later when asked if they had seen any broken glass, the people who had been asked the question "smashed into" were twice as likely to say yes, even though no glass had actually been broken.

What these and many other experiments suggest is that we are constantly organizing and reorganizing new and old information into coherent schemes. This process has been termed bottom-up and top-down

204.

processing. Both of these ideas are similar to Piaget's notions of assimilation and accomodation. Top-down processing refers to applying a certain principle, already formed, to the processing of new information. The organizing principle in any set of information is imposed onto it by a preexisting scheme. Bottom-up processing refers to abstracting a new principle or discovering a common element inherent in the pieces of information without the aid of preexisting schemes. In other words, bottom-up processing is data-driven. Thus learning involves the constant interplay between new abstractions and existing principles. As Palmer (1975) notes, it is impossible to determine which type of processing comes first or is most important,

> ...which happens first: interpreting the whole
> or interpreting the parts? How can someone
> recognize a face until he has first recognized
> the eyes, nose, mouth, and ears? Then again,
> how can someone recognize the eyes, nose,
> mouth, and ears until he knows that they are
> part of a face? This is often called the
> parsing paradox. It concerns the difficulties
> encountered with either a pure "bottom-up"
> (part-to-whole) or a pure "top-down"
> (whole-to-part) strategy in interpretive
> processing (p. 295).

One solution to the dilemma is to assume that organisms possess a preexisting structure of knowledge when they enter the world. As stated previously, organisms appear to have a learning structure which contains an inherent organization.

A final issue related to cognitive theory which must be resolved is whether or not we are still capable of a reflexive type of learning in addition to concept learning. As we have seen, animals appear to respond automatically or reflexively at times. We may also recognize that learning principles alone will not help us in playing basketball; we must also practice so that certain actions become automatic. Indeed principles, abstractions, and rules seem to have little relevance when executing a "slam-dunk." Although cognitive psychology has been weak in explaining this type of learning, an understanding of brain function may help us here.

When a ballet dancer first executes a new move, a portion of the brain responsible for voluntary movement is at work. However, with practice the movements become almost programmed and are increasingly

controlled by a different area of the brain, the
cerebellum, which is responsible for controlling finely
tuned movements. Thus learning still occurs by a
constant modification of a principle or rule, but when
the task becomes well learned it is put on "automatic-
pilot."
We experience this phenomenon sometimes when
driving our cars. When going to the bread store we may
make a turn toward our place of employment rather than
toward the bread store if we are not paying close
attention. We do this because we tend to set in motion
a whole set of prerecorded behaviors (often called
scripts) whenever we begin a familiar task. However,
we can at any time override these habits or alter the
habit with new practice. Therefore practice with
constant feedback is important for translating concepts
into behavior.
We have now arrived at a totally different view of
what learning is: the abstraction of information into
principles and then, with informational feedback, being
able to put that principle into practice. Under this
approach rote memorization is not a form of learning.
This should not be too surprising since our everyday
language already reflects this idea. For example, when
discussing the progress of human society we often say,
"Humankind is learning more all the time." This
statement does not imply the acquisition of more facts
as a society but suggests that humankind has discovered
principles, which already exist in the created order.

Toward a Christian Theory of Learning.

Cognitive approaches should not be considered to
be synonymous with a Christian theory of learning.
Cognitive theories still reduce learning to specific
mechanical events which are sterile, and lack any
notion of personhood. However, we can see that the
cognitive approach comes much closer to the Biblical
principle that man makes responsible choices. In
addition, the notion that we organize incoming
information according to existing principles has close
parallels to the idea of applying the heart to what we
see.
When we learn, we first of all learn from the
"laws written on our hearts," as well as from the Holy
Spirit. We are not blank slates when we enter this
world as the behaviorists propose, but come endowed
with a cognitive structure which is shaped by genetic,
physical, emotional, and spiritual characteristics (all
of which are established by our creator). Our

cognitive structure is ordered in such a way that relationships in the created order coincide with the way in which we learn. We do not acquire new information in a vacuum, but we come with a set of presuppositions about the world. When we see the world for the first time we already know that God is in control and this should shape how information is organized.

Top-down and bottom-up processing, if they are occurring, are constantly being shaped by God's guiding hand. We not only apply our cognitive structure to new learning, but we apply the sum total of our emotional, cognitive and spiritual nature to new information. In this way we are truly discontinuous from the animals because God has not established a special relationship with animals as with mankind. An animal enters the world with a cognitive structure established only by its genetic inheritance and is not endowed with the ability to apply spiritual principles to new learning.

Of course there is a dark side to man's learning. Sin has perverted man's nature, his relationship to God, and his "heart." Therefore in an apostate condition, a person can organize new information but often times that organization is perverted and does not match the original order created by God. True wisdom comes only when, through redemption, regeneration and sanctification, our whole being is restored.

REFERENCES

Beechick, R. A biblical psychology of learning.
Denver, CO: Accent Publications, Inc., 1982.

Hilgard, E. R., & Bower, G. H. Theories of learning,
4ed. Engelwood Cliffs, New Jersey: Prentice-
Hall, Inc., 1975.

Hull, C. L. Principles of behavior. New York:
Appleton, 1943.

Hull, C. L. A behavior system. New Haven, CT: Yale
University Press, 1952.

Kalat, S., & Rozin, P. "You can lead a rat to poison
but you can't make him think." In M.E.P. Seligman
& J. Hager. The biological boundaries of
learning. New York: Appleton-Century-Crofts,
1977.

Kauffman, D. "Behaviorism, psychology, and Christian
education." Christian Association for
Psychological Studies Bulletin, 1978, 3,
17-21.

Kauffman, D. "Toward a Christian theory/model of
learning." Christian Association for
Pychological Studies Bulletin, 1978, 4, 27-31.

Koch, S. "Clark L. Hull." In W. K. Estes, et al.,
Modern learning theory. New York: Appleton-
Century-Crofts, 1954.

Lichtenstein, P. "Theoretical psychology: Where is it
headed?" The Psychological Record, 1980, 30,
447-458.

Loftus, E. F., & Palmer, J. C. "Reconstruction of
automobile destruction: An example of
the interaction between language & memory."
Journal of Verbal Learning and Verbal Memory,
1973, 13, 585-589.

Matlin, M. Cognition. New York: Holt, Rinehart,
and Winston, 1983.

Mackintosh, N. J. The psychology of animal
learning. London: Academic Press, Inc.,
1974.

Palmer, S. E. "Visual perception and world knowledge:
Notes on a model of sensory-cognitive
interaction." In D.A. Norman & D.E. Rumelhart
(Eds.), Explorations in cognition. San
Fransisco: Freeman, 1975.

Rescorla, R. A. "Some implications of a cognitive
perspective on Pavlovian conditioning." In S. H.
Hulse, et al., Cognitive processes in animal
behavior. Hillsdale, New Jersey: Erlbaum,
1978.

Rescorla, R. A., & Wagner, A. R. "A theory of
Pavlovian conditioning: Variations in the
effectiveness of reinforcement and
nonreinforcement." In A. Black & W.F. Prokasy
(Eds.), Classical conditioning: II. Current
research and theory. New York: Appleton, 1972.

Seligman, M. F. P. "On the generality of the laws of
learning." Psychological Review, 1970, 77, 406-
418.

Schultz, D. A history of modern psychology, 3ed.
New York: Academic Press, Inc., 1981.

Skinner, B. F. Science and human behavior. New
York: Macmillan, 1953.

Conclusion: The Challenges
That Confront Us

by

Norman De Jong
Professor of Education
Trinity Christian College

The scholars and teachers who gathered in Palos
Heights on November 11 and 12 came, not because they
wished to enjoy a respite from their classes and
responsibilities, but because they collectively chose
to face the challenge of an unfinished and not
sufficiently addressed task. They came because they
corporately sensed the need to unravel the mysteries of
knowledge and to formulate for themselves and for
future generations the outlines of distinctively
Christian perspectives on learning theory.
What transpired at that conference and what has
now found its way into the foregoing pages is a
significant step in a novel direction. The issues and
concepts that were discussed and debated represent a
fresh new approach to the theoretical and psychological
bases of educational psychology. What is contained in
these pages represents a radical departure from the
somewhat standardized textbooks currently being
published for use in educational psychology courses.
It is obvious from a survey of the extant
literature that a Christian approach to learning theory
is not the most burning topic on the educational
horizon. The vast majority of classroom teachers, I
suspect, have never seriously posed the question as to
how we learn. They have all taken at least one course
in educational psychology, have done that which was
necessary to get a satisfactory grade, and have
operated with relatively unexamined assumptions ever
since. Some educators might even argue that the task
has long since been completed and that we are merely
exercising our theoretical cogitations on unnecessary
endeavors. Some educational leaders might also now be
chiding us for trying to re-invent the wheel.
In spite of such possible reactions, I am
convinced that there is still necessary and important
work to be done. If it is true, as Pestalozzi once so
cogently asserted, that "As the child learns, so must
one teach," then it should be obvious that we have a

long way to go in establishing a valid, workable, and widely accepted explanation of the learning process. Certainly amongst secular research scholars there is no uniformity of opinion concerning the theories currently extant. Although the names of such theorists as Pavlov, Thorndike, Hull, Spence, Skinner, Miller, Piaget, and Mowrer are well known to most of us, there is not concensus of opinion that any or all of them have produced a theory worthy of acceptance. On the contrary, even a cursory review of the literature will indicate that the secularists are stridently attacking and condemning each other's inadequate answers. Winfred F. Hill, for example, concludes his survey of psychological interpretations with a chapter entitled "The Hope for a Better Theory of Learning" in which he asserts that "the goal of building a general theory of learning---remains an ultimate aspiration." Additional analyses of research studies will indicate, furthermore, that the most frequent conclusion in research studies is a call for more research. To conclude that the secular theorists have reached satisfactory answers to the questions about learning would be naive, even though some of them promote their partial and tentative findings with unabated missionary zeal.

If the secularists have not solved the riddles of learning, what of the Christians? Are there those amongst the body of Christ who have discovered the magic formulae that will unlock the mysteries of the learning process? Do we have the answers which can be published and promoted for all the world to study and implement? I think not yet, although my ignorance of such should not preclude their existence. What we have in this volume is a beginning, however; a primer, as we stated in the introduction.

We gathered, then, to work on the problem and to share with each other, as fellow Christians, the insights and understanding that God has given to us. Some of us have groped with newly formed ideas, tentative in our conclusions, and reticent on the matter of putting our views in the spotlight of public scrutiny. Others of us were bold and confident at this stage of our endeavors, but left with the sense of having our conceptual efforts so thoroughly chewed over that they were not worthy of regurgitation. When we put together a smorgasbord of papers such as we have here, we also realized that no one might savor our dish. To be ignored, I have often felt, is the greatest insult of all, although such treatment can also be rightfully construed as the highest compliment.

212.

Christianity itself has been studiously ignored by vast
numbers of secularists who see in it a formidable
challange to their basic assumptions and their way of
life.
At the conclusion of the conference, Nicholas
Wolterstorff reminded all of us that we had just begun
a major and necessary undertaking. He calculated that
it might take a decade of communal, scholarly effort to
complete the task. He reminded us, too, that the next
major assignment would be the formal articulation of a
Biblical, psychological model of the learner. From
that base, he argued, we could continue to develop a
distinctively Christian approach to learning that was
long overdue. What has been accomplished thus far and
is represented in these pages is a clearing of the
lot, a surveying of the property, and a digging of the
holes in which the foundations could be laid. All
necessary and important work, but preliminary
nonetheless.
With all those concerns now in focus, we all are
challenged to the highest level of excellence as we
embark on this task of formulating and refining a
Christian approach to learning. If we are going to
produce any single theory or multiplicity of theories
that will be of lasting value, there are a number of
criteria that must be met.
First, if we are to construct a theory worthy of
acceptance, we will need to be students of philosophy.
By that I do not mean to imply that we have the
prerequisite of a degree in philosophy or that we be a
professor in a philosophy department. I don't mean to
suggest either that we must have read all of Plato's
Dialogues, Augustine, Aquinas, Locke, Kant, or Piaget.
What I do wish to recommend is that all of us be
"lovers of wisdom" and realize in a meaningful way that
interest in learning theory did not originate with us.
If there is any one criticism which must be leveled at
the twentieth century psychologists who have dominated
the field, it is the charge that they have ignored
almost every idea which has been espoused prior to the
20th century. Psychological studies, which, they
claim, are the only legitimate area for such
theorizing, had their origins somewhere around the turn
of the century. Everything before that is classified
as the dark ages dominated by ignorance. Such an anti-
historical stance will do none of us any good.
As responsible educators we need to familiarize
ourselves with the significant questions which have
been raised by scholars before us. We need to have a
working acquaintance with Plato's theory of the eternal

213.

soul, with Augustine's perspective on innate resistance
to learning, with Aquinas' dualistic explanation of
nature and grace, and with John Locke's empiricist
arguments for a tabula rasa. We should not ignore the
wisdom of the ages or the thought of the sages. We
don't enter the dialogue at the source, but find
ourselves floating thousands of miles downstream, swept
along by centuries of accumulated flood waters.

Secondly, I want to assert that mere knowledge of
where we are in the current will not suffice. We also
need to "test the spirits to see whether they are from
God; because many false prophets have gone out into the
world" (I John 4:1). Because we are Christians, we
need to be critical of existing theories. We need to
examine and analyze not only their surface
pronouncements and explanations, but also the
assumptions and presuppositions which undergird them.
Many of the connectionist or S-R theories which are
popular today rest on the assumption that the learning
process originates in material objects, which emit the
stimuli that bombard our senses. They simply start the
whole learning theorem with a large capital S and
consider it unnecessary to get beyond that declaration.
Others build their theories solidly on Darwinian
assumptions, implying with all of their research
laboratories that man is merely an animal advanced
beyond the levels of rats, pidgeons, and orangutan.
They assume an unbroken line of development between
animal and man, and infer that there is not qualitative
difference between human and animal learning. Such
blatantly false presuppositions cannot be productive of
true conclusions.

Ever since the Age of Enlightenment, the modern
mind has been progressively cast into a materialistic
and scientistic mold, rejecting or ignoring the whole
concept of Revelation. The third challenge with which
I want to present you is that of re-establishing the
basic belief in Revelation. The history of
Christianity and the pages of Holy Writ are filled with
the language of revelation. Rejected as a wholly
unscientific notion by our age, we need to reassert its
authenticity. God, as the omniscient source of all
knowledge, reveals Himself and gives to us
understanding in two fundamental ways. First, He
reveals Himself through all of creation, "which is
before our eyes as a most elegant book", and, second,
"He makes Himself more clearly and fully known to us by
His holy and divine Word." Once we catch the full
import of that, we will realize that Revelation is
neither unscientific nor irrational, but a beautiful

explanation which answers more questions than a secularist even cares to ask. In the light of Revelation, a flower or a bird is not the origin of stimuli, but another means or medium through which God transmits wisdom to us. Some of the chapters in this book have caught the vision of that marvelously complex and mysterious concept of revelation, but much remains to be done. We know its significance but still seem woefully ignorant of its mechanics.

Reasserting the primacy of Revelation will not be a simple or easy task, for the world of ideas is not a neutral place or a children's garden. In the spirit and admonition of Martin Luther, whose 500th birthday we have recently celebrated, we need to remember that Satan is alive and operative, also in academia. Therein lies the fourth challenge with which I want to present you. As Christians, we may not ignore the antithesis as we go about our theorizing. We may rejoice in the fact that God is operative in our learning processes, but we also better shudder and remember that the father of lies constantly seeks to distort and pervert the truth. Already in Genesis 3:15 God warns us that life is a bruising, crushing battle which will not finally be consumated until the great day of judgment. As long as we walk through the thistles and thorns of this sin-scarred, imperfect world, we will have to acknowledge the power and presence of Satan. Any theory which ignores that great antithetical character of man's existence will have diminished the two most powerful forces in our daily lives.

As part of our educational task, we need to re-awaken our students also to the significance of the antithesis. One of the themes that runs throughout all of Scripture is the conflict that comes to earliest expression in the Garden of Eden - the struggle between God and Satan for the allegiance of men. In various terms, this antithesis is between good and evil, between Truth and falsehood, between light and darkness, between discernment and distortion. We need to be reminded that the father of lies is still constantly at work, trying to delude people into following him by subtly distorting the truth. Satan is too smart to come into our Christian colleges like a bull in a china shop. No, he comes as an angel of light in the most popular textbooks on the market today. Subtly preaching the theory of complete human autonomy, he likes nothing better than to ignore quietly the whole question of divine involvement in the learning process.

In the Sept. 2, 1983 issue of <u>Christianity</u> <u>Today</u>, CBN University ran a full page ad which headlined their and our perspective: "We're Preparing For War On the East Coast." Unabashedly announcing that they want their students to "fight the good fight of faith," they put everything into Biblical perspective by saying, "it isn't physical war we're prepping for - it's spiritual warfare."

Some of us may take umbrage at such a boldly polemical stance, while others may cheer only softly. Satan, I suspect, though, quivers at such courage.

In the fifth place, we need to reassert the sovereignty of God over all of life and to work diligently to bridge the gap between divine omniscience and human intelligence. This conference has moved all of us at least one step forward in that necessary and difficult process. As we listen and ponder, question and critique, I trust that all of us will proceed with a prayer for God's guidance and direction. In doing so, we need to re-examine our own educational experiences, and take a hard look at the manner in which our own thought processes were formed.

Most of us, I would conjecture, may have been at least partially schooled at our prestigious and thoroughly secular universities. We sat at the feet of brilliant and famous professors who mesmerized us with their profundity and wisdom. We also have pored over volumes of coldly analytical studies and research reports which seemed to be so close to the truth that we felt foolish when we even entertained thoughts of rejecting them. We consoled ourselves, I suspect, with rationalized capitulations built around the concept of common grace. In spite of these professors' denial of Christianity, we argued, they are still instruments of advancing wisdom and recipients of God's bountiful knowledge, which He showers generously on all men. When those same professors' lectures found their way into print, we cheered their success and boasted to our friends that "I know the author."

To counteract that kind of subtle influence on our thought processes and theory making, we need to enlist our best efforts and our most committed and capable Christian scholars. We need to do our homework carefully and then take our message to the world. We need to plow into our work with the confidence and assurance that Christianity contains the best answers to life's most pressing problems and most basic questions. Our job is to find those answers and to stop paying homage to the learning laboratories in our

prestigious universities. In doing so, we need to be
reminded of what G. K. Chesterton once said:
"Christianity has not been tried and found wanting. It
has been found difficult and never sufficently tried."
    The sixth challenge on which I want to focus is
for all of us to Biblical scholars. I need to be
reminded frequently to go back to God's Word and to
search there for basic answers to fundamental
questions. God doesn't operate in mystical, unreal
ways, although His divine intervention in our lives is
often beyond our comprehension. In the language of the
confession quoted earlier, He reveals Himself "more
clearly and fully" through the Scriptures. In spite of
criticisms which may be levelled against us, we need to
dig through His gold mine of eternal wisdom to find the
foundational principles on which truthful and permanent
learning theories can be constructed.
    There is, in conclusion, one final challenge with
which I want to present you. I make this point first
of all as a reminder to myself, for I know my own
weaknesses and tendencies rather well for having lived
with them longer than any one else. I suspect,
however, that all of you are essentially not much
different than I. The challenge to all of us, then, is
that we learn through and from this symposium. If
you assume from that statement an implied definition of
learning, you are, of course, correct. Without
elaborating on that implied definition, let me assert
that each of us has an innate capacity to resist
learning. We come to each new situation with our
concepts fairly well articulated, our minds neatly
ordered, and answers sometimes locked in place. Along
comes a new idea, a different perspective, or some
strange new terminology. Of course, I resist. But to
the degree that I resist I also prevent learning from
happening. Learning implies, of necessity, that some
kind of change occur in the learner. If there is no
change, there is no learning.
    If all of us finish these chapters with all of our
opinions, ideas, and theories wholly intact, we will
have learned little or nothing. We need to be open to
change, to admitting new ideas, new approaches. In
some respects that is threatening, but it is also
exilerating. The process of learning is always
painful, but the results of true learning are
enjoyable and uplifting.
    As we learn together and from each other, I trust
that we will do so in a spirit of mutual dependence on
God and genuine love for each other. If we really
believe that God is involved in the learning process,

217.

then we need to pray for a special measure of His presence as we dialogue on these issues.

To the extent that we understand how all of us learn, to that extent we will be more capable and effective servants of Christ in the classroom. That is our challenge as we continue the task of developing Christian approaches to learning and teaching.